For MCL and the kids.

Acknowledgments

I couldn't have written this book without the help of many talented and creative people.

I would like to thank Neil Edde, associate publisher, and Maureen Adams, acquisitions editor, for recognizing the need for an introductory Oracle DBA text. Many thanks to production editor Susan Berge and copyeditor Linda Recktenwald for their valuable advice. Thanks also to technical editor Betty MacEwen for her attention to detail and helpful suggestions throughout the book.

The nature of this book required a great deal of artwork. Jeff Wilson and the rest of Happenstance Type-O-Rama did an excellent job of creating artwork that was appropriate for the book. They say a picture is worth a thousand words, and their art is an essential part of this book. Somehow they were able to decipher my Microsoft Word cave drawings and turn them into real graphics.

Many of my professional colleagues at both Lands' End and Greenbrier & Russel were a source of both inspiration and guidance. Also, regards to my long-lost friend from fourth grade, Janice, who I'm sure is a DBA out there somewhere.

Finally, I want to thank my family for all of their support and patience. I was still able to give the kids a bath, play some cards, and read books at bedtime, even with the short deadlines. The journey wouldn't have been half the fun without them.

Oracle Database Foundations

Bob Bryla

SYBEX

San Francisco ◆ London

Associate Publisher: Neil Edde
Acquisitions and Developmental Editor: Maureen Adams
Production Editor: Susan Berge
Copyeditor: Linda S. Recktenwald
Compositor: Craig Woods, Happenstance Type-O-Rama
Graphic Illustrator: Jeff Wilson, Happenstance Type-O-Rama
Proofreaders: Amy J. Rasmussen, Nancy Riddiough
Indexer: Ted Laux
Book Designer: Judy Fung
Cover Designer: Ingalls + Associates
Cover Photo: Jerry Driendl, Taxi

Copyright © 2004 SYBEX Inc., 1151 Marina Village Parkway, Alameda, CA 94501. World rights reserved. No part of this publication may be stored in a retrieval system, transmitted, or reproduced in any way, including but not limited to photocopy, photograph, magnetic, or other record, without the prior agreement and written permission of the publisher.

An earlier version of this book was published under the title Oracle9i DBA JumpStart © 2003 SYBEX Inc.

Library of Congress Card Number: 2004109313

ISBN: 0-7821-4372-5

SYBEX and the SYBEX logo are either registered trademarks or trademarks of SYBEX Inc. in the United States and/or other countries.

Screen reproductions produced with FullShot 99. FullShot 99 © 1991-1999 Inbit Incorporated. All rights reserved.

FullShot is a trademark of Inbit Incorporated.

Internet screen shot(s) using Microsoft Internet Explorer 6 reprinted by permission from Microsoft Corporation.

TRADEMARKS: SYBEX has attempted throughout this book to distinguish proprietary trademarks from descriptive terms by following the capitalization style used by the manufacturer.

The author and publisher have made their best efforts to prepare this book, and the content is based upon final release software whenever possible. Portions of the manuscript may be based upon pre-release versions supplied by software manufacturer(s). The author and the publisher make no representation or warranties of any kind with regard to the completeness or accuracy of the contents herein and accept no liability of any kind including but not limited to performance, merchantability, fitness for any particular purpose, or any losses or damages of any kind caused or alleged to be caused directly or indirectly from this book.

Manufactured in the United States of America

10 9 8 7 6 5 4 3 2 1

Contents

Introduction

When you're learning any new topic or technology, it's important to have all of the basics at your disposal. The Sybex Foundations series provides the building blocks of specific technologies that help you establish yourself in IT.

So, you want to be an Oracle database administrator (DBA), but you're not sure what the job might be like? Well, this is a good place to start! This book is intended to bridge the gap for people who are technically oriented and need something to bridge the gap to Oracle database administration. If you don't have a lot of direct experience with databases, this book can get you up to speed on enough of the basics to feel comfortable going into more advanced topics and other introductory coursework.

What You Need

Oracle Database Foundations assumes some minimal level of expertise in using an operating system such as Windows or Unix in a graphical user interface (GUI) environment. Any experience with a personal database, such as Microsoft Access, is helpful but not required.

To follow along with the examples in the book, you will need an installation of the Oracle database software version 9.2 or preferably 10*g*, Standard or Enterprise Edition, including the sample schemas provided by Oracle in the installation package, preferably on a Microsoft Windows platform. However, if you're adept with Linux, then RedHat, SuSE, or other distributions of Linux will work fine, too, as the operating system platform.

What This Book Covers

This book provides all the information you need to understand the job of an Oracle DBA. It is organized as follows:

Chapter 1, "Relational Database Concepts" Covers the basics of relational database technology. It defines terms such as tables, rows, and columns, and it provides an introduction to database design.

Chapter 2, "SQL*Plus and iSQL*Plus Basics" Introduces the various ways to send SQL commands to the database. It explains the tools available for issuing SQL commands and how to interact with the database.

Chapter 3, "Oracle Database Functions" Focuses on Oracle functions, both built-in and user-defined, and how they can make an application developer's or DBA's job easier.

Chapter 4, "Restricting, Sorting, and Grouping Data" Describes how to manage queries by restricting and sorting their results.

Chapter 5, "Using Multiple Tables"   Moves from accessing single tables to joining multiple tables in a multitude of ways, with both the old and new join syntax.

Chapter 6, "Advanced SQL Queries"   Covers some of the more advanced functions and explains how to nest a query within another query to retrieve the results you want.

Chapter 7, "Logical Consistency"   Describes how to make sure that the rows entered into the database tables are accurate and consistent with data in other tables in the database. This chapter discusses how you can validate the data before it is inserted into a row of a table.

Chapter 8, "Installing Oracle and Creating a Database"   Shows you how to install the database software on the server and create a database using Oracle's GUI-based tools.

Chapter 9, "Reporting Techniques"   Investigates techniques for making reports easier to understand and manage.

Chapter 10, "Creating and Maintaining Database Objects"   Explores the different ways to create tables, indexes, views, sequences, and synonyms. It also describes how to use data dictionary views and dynamic performance views.

Chapter 11, "Users and Security"   Focuses on how to prevent unauthorized or unintentional actions in the database. It covers how to create user accounts, grant and revoke privileges, and keep tabs on who is accessing what kind of object and when.

Chapter 12, "Making Things Run Fast (Enough)"   Explores techniques for tuning the database so it will respond to queries as quickly as possible. This chapter covers how the Oracle optimizer works and how you can use indexes judiciously to make queries run in a reasonable amount of time.

Chapter 13, "Saving Your Stuff (Backups)"   Describes how, by using the right combination of backup and recovery techniques, the DBA can minimize or even eliminate the possibility of losing any committed data in the database.

Chapter 14, "Troubleshooting"   Reviews some of the places to look for error messages, along with some general troubleshooting techniques.

Making the Most of This Book

At the beginning of each chapter of *Oracle Database Foundations*, you'll find a list of topics that you can expect to learn about within that chapter.

To help you absorb new material easily, I've highlighted *important terms* and defined them in the margins of the pages. You'll also find three kinds of notes with supplementary material:

Notes provide extra information and references to related information.

NOTE

Tips are insights that help you perform tasks more easily and effectively.

TIP

Warnings let you know about things you should do—or shouldn't do—as you learn more about what an Oracle DBA's job is like.

WARNING

At the end of each chapter, you can test your knowledge of the topics covered by answering the chapter's review questions. At the end of the book is a glossary of all the terms that have been introduced throughout the book. You'll find the answers to the review questions in Appendix A. Appendix B contains a brief overview of other database platforms and how they might fit into an enterprise's database infrastructure.

About the Author

Bob Bryla is an Oracle8*i*, Oracle9*i*, and Oracle 10*g* certified professional (OCP) with more than 15 years of database design, database application development, and database administration experience in a variety of fields. He is currently an Internet database analyst and DBA at Lands' End, Inc., in Dodgeville, Wisconsin. You can contact Bob by e-mail at `rjbryla@centurytel.net`.

Chapter 1

Relational Database Concepts

In This Chapter

- How spreadsheets compare with databases
- Relational database concepts
- Data modeling concepts
- Object-relational database concepts

Every organization has data that needs to be collected, managed, and analyzed. A relational database fulfills these needs. Along with the powerful features of a relational database come requirements for developing and maintaining the database. Data analysts, database designers, and database administrators (DBAs) need to be able to translate the data in a database into useful information for both day-to-day operations and long-term planning.

Relational databases can be a bit intimidating at first, even if you're a specialist in some other informational technology area, such as networking, web development, or programming. This chapter will give you a good overview of current relational and object-relational database concepts. It begins by comparing a database with another tool that most everyone has used—a spreadsheet (also known as the "poor man's" database). Then you'll learn about the basic components of a relational database, the data modeling process, and object-relational database features.

Are Spreadsheets Like Databases?

Most people are familiar with some kind of spreadsheet, such as Microsoft Excel. Spreadsheets are easy and convenient to use, and they may be employed by an individual much like a database is used in the enterprise. Let's look at the features of spreadsheets to see how good of a database tool they actually are.

Similar to databases, spreadsheets are commonly used to store information in a tabular format. A spreadsheet can store data in rows and columns, it can link cells on one sheet to those on another sheet, and it can force data to be entered in a specific cell in a specific format. It's easy to calculate formulas from groups of cells on the spreadsheet, create charts, and work with data in other ways. But there are many ways in which a spreadsheet is not like a traditional database table:

Spreadsheet	Database
More than one datatype can be stored in a spreadsheet column.	Usually, only one datatype can be stored in a database table column.
Cells in a spreadsheet can be defined as a formula, making the contents variable depending on other cells.	Columns in a database table have a fixed value.
A spreadsheet has only the physical row number to make it unique and no built-in way to enforce uniqueness of a given spreadsheet row.	Single rows of a database table are uniquely identified by a unique value (typically a primary key, as described later in this chapter).
Usually, only one user can have write access to the spreadsheet at any given time; anyone else is locked out, even if the second user is on a different part of the spreadsheet.	Multiple users can access a database table at the same time, with various combinations of read and write capabilities in different parts of the database.
A spreadsheet does not have any built-in transaction-control capabilities, such as ensuring that a group of changes to the sheet is completely applied or not applied at all. The Save button is about the best a spreadsheet can do to simulate transaction control.	A database usually has transaction-control capabilities, making it possible to "roll back" a change if something happened to prevent it from completing successfully (such as a power failure).
A corrupt spreadsheet cannot usually be repaired; the entire spreadsheet must be restored from a backup, which may have occurred yesterday, last week, or never!	There are many tools for repairing and recovering databases.

This is not to say that a spreadsheet isn't a valuable tool in the enterprise for ad hoc and "what-if" analyses. Furthermore, most spreadsheet products have some way to connect to an external database as the data source for analysis.

Relational Databases

The relational model is the basis for any relational database management system (RDBMS). A relational model has three core components: a collection of objects or relations, operators that act on the objects or relations, and data integrity methods. In other words, it has a place to store the data, a way to create and retrieve the data, and a way to make sure that the data is logically consistent.

Hierarchical and Network Databases

Dr. E. F. Codd first proposed the relational model in 1970. At that time, databases were primarily either of the hierarchical or network type.

A hierarchical database is similar in nature to a filesystem, with a root or parent node and one or more children referencing the parent. This makes for a very fast data-access path, but it has the disadvantages of low flexibility, lack of an ad hoc query capability, and high application maintenance.

A network database has some advantages over the hierarchical model, including a data definition language, a data manipulation language, association records to support multiple parents per node, and data integrity. However, like hierarchical databases, network databases suffer from rigidity in database structure and high application maintenance costs.

Hierarchical and network-based databases are still used for extremely high-volume transaction-processing systems. IBM claims that 95 percent of the Fortune 1000 companies in the world still use IMS, a hierarchical database management system that is also web-enabled.

A *relational database* uses relations, or two-dimensional tables, to store the information needed to support a business. Let's go over the basic components of a traditional relational database system and look at how a relational database is designed. Once you have a solid understanding of what rows, columns, tables, and relationships are, you'll be well on your way to leveraging the power of a relational database.

relational database
A collection of tables that stores data without any assumptions as to how the data is related within the tables or between the tables.

While this book focuses on the Oracle RDBMS for all of its examples and techniques, it's good to know how Oracle fits in with other database vendors and platforms. Appendix B, "Common Database Platforms," has an overview of the major RDBMS vendors and their products.

NOTE

Tables, Rows, and Columns

A *table* in a relational database, alternatively known as a *relation*, is a two-dimensional structure used to hold related information. A database consists of one or more related tables.

——— *NOTE* ———

Don't confuse a relation with relationships. A relation is essentially a table, and a relationship is a way to correlate, join, or associate two tables.

table
The basic construct of a relational database that contains rows and columns of related data.

A *row* in a table is a collection or instance of one thing, such as one employee or one line item on an invoice. A *column* contains all the information of a single type, and the piece of data at the intersection of a row and a column, a *field*, is the smallest piece of information that can be retrieved with the database's query language. (Oracle's query language, SQL, is the topic of Chapter 2, "SQL*Plus and iSQL*Plus Basics.") For example, a table with information about employees might have a column called LAST_NAME that contains all of the employees' last names. Data is retrieved from a table by filtering on both the row and the column.

——— *NOTE* ———

SQL, which stands for Structured Query Language, supports the database components in virtually every modern relational database system. SQL has been refined and improved by the American National Standards Institute (ANSI) for more than 20 years. As of Oracle9i, Oracle's SQL engine conforms to the ANSI SQL:1999 (also known as SQL3) standard, as well as its own proprietary SQL syntax that existed in previous versions of Oracle. Until Oracle9i, only SQL:1992 (SQL2) syntax was fully supported. As of Oracle 10g, the Core SQL:2003 features are fully supported with a couple minor exceptions.

Primary Keys, Datatypes, and Foreign Keys

The examples throughout this book will focus on the hypothetical work of Scott Smith, database developer and entrepreneur. He just started a new widget company and wants to implement a few of the basic business functions using the Oracle relational database to manage his Human Resources (HR) department.

relation
A two-dimensional structure used to hold related information, also known as a table.

——— *NOTE* ———

Most of Scott's employees were hired away from one of his previous employers, some of whom have over 20 years of experience in the field. As a hiring incentive, Scott has agreed to keep the new employees' original hire date in the new database.

row
A group of one or more data elements in a database table that describes a person, place, or thing.

You'll learn about database design in the following sections, but let's assume for the moment that the majority of the database design is completed and some tables need to be implemented. Scott creates the EMP table to hold the basic employee information, and it looks something like this:

EMPNO	ENAME	JOB	MGR	HIREDATE	SAL	COMM	DEPTNO
7369	SMITH	CLERK	7902	17-DEC-80	800		20
7499	ALLEN	SALESMAN	7698	20-FEB-81	1600	300	30
7521	WARD	SALESMAN	7698	22-FEB-81	1250	500	30
7566	JONES	MANAGER	7839	02-APR-81	2975		20
7654	MARTIN	SALESMAN	7698	28-SEP-81	1250	1400	30
7698	BLAKE	MANAGER	7839	01-MAY-81	2850		30
7782	CLARK	MANAGER	7839	09-JUN-81	2450		10
7788	SCOTT	ANALYST	7566	19-APR-87	3000		20
7839	KING	PRESIDENT		17-NOV-81	5000		10
7844	TURNER	SALESMAN	7698	08-SEP-81	1500	0	30
7876	ADAMS	CLERK	7788	23-MAY-87	1100		20
7900	JAMES	CLERK	7698	03-DEC-81	950		30
7902	FORD	ANALYST	7566	03-DEC-81	3000		20
7934	MILLER	CLERK	7782	23-JAN-82	1300		10

Notice that some fields in the Commission (COMM) and Manager (MGR) columns do not contain a value; they are blank. A relational database can enforce the rule that fields in a column may or may not be empty. (Chapter 3, "Oracle Database Functions," covers the concept of empty, or NULL, values.) In this case, it makes sense for an employee who is not in the Sales department to have a blank Commission field. It also makes sense for the president of the company to have a blank Manager field, since that employee doesn't report to anyone.

On the other hand, none of the fields in the Employee Number (EMPNO) column are blank. The company always wants to assign an employee number to an employee, and that number must be different for each employee. One of the features of a relational database is that it can ensure that a value is entered into this column and that it is unique. The EMPNO column, in this case, is the *primary key* of the table.

Notice the different datatypes that are stored in the EMP table: numeric values, character or alphabetic values, and date values. The Oracle database also supports other variants of these types, plus new types created from these base types. Datatypes are discussed in more detail throughout the book.

As you might suspect, the DEPTNO column contains the department number for the employee. But how do you know what department name is associated with what number? Scott created the DEPT table to hold the descriptions for the department codes in the EMP table.

DEPTNO	DNAME	LOC
10	ACCOUNTING	NEW YORK
20	RESEARCH	DALLAS
30	SALES	CHICAGO
40	OPERATIONS	BOSTON

column
The component of a database table that contains all of the data of the same name and type across all rows.

field
The smallest piece of information that can be retrieved by the database query language. A field is found at the intersection of a row and a column in a database table.

primary key
A column (or columns) in a table that makes the row in the table distinguishable from every other row in the same table.

foreign key
A column (or columns) in a table that draws its values from a primary or unique key column in another table. A foreign key assists in ensuring the data integrity of a table.

referential integrity
A method employed by a relational database system that enforces one-to-many relationships between tables.

The DEPTNO column in the EMP table contains the same values as the DEPTNO column in the DEPT table. In this case, the DEPTNO column in the EMP table is considered a *foreign key* to the same column in the DEPT table. With this association, Oracle can enforce the restriction that a DEPTNO value cannot be entered in the EMP table unless it already exists in the DEPT table. A foreign key enforces the concept of *referential integrity* in a relational database. The concept of referential integrity not only prevents an invalid department number from being inserted into the EMP table, but it also prevents a row in the DEPT table from being deleted if there are employees still assigned to that department.

Data Modeling

data modeling
A process of defining the entities, attributes, and relationships between the entities in preparation for creating the physical database.

Before Scott created the actual tables in the database, he went through a design process known as *data modeling*. In this process, the developer conceptualizes and documents all the tables for the database. One of the common methods for modeling a database is called ERA, which stands for entities, relationships, and attributes. The database designer uses an application that can maintain entities, their attributes, and their relationships. In general, an entity corresponds to a table in the database, and the attributes of the entity correspond to columns of the table.

NOTE

Various data-modeling tools are available for database design. Examples include Microsoft Visio (www.microsoft.com/office/visio) and more robust tools such as Computer Associates' AllFusion ERwin Data Modeler (www3.ca.com/Solutions/Product.asp?ID=260) and Embarcadero's ER/Studio (www.embarcadero.com/products/erstudio/index.html).

The data-modeling process involves defining the entities, defining the relationships between those entities, and then defining the attributes for each of the entities. Once a cycle is complete, it is repeated as many times as necessary to ensure that the designer is capturing what is important enough to go into the database. Let's take a closer look at each step in the data-modeling process.

Defining the Entities

associative table
A database table that stores the valid combinations of rows from two other tables and usually enforces a business rule. An associative table resolves a many-to-many relationship.

First, the designer identifies all of the entities within the scope of the database application. The entities are the persons, places, or things that are important to the organization and need to be tracked in the database. Entities will most likely translate neatly to database tables. For example, for the first version of Scott's widget company database, he identifies four entities: employees, departments, salary grades, and bonuses. These will become the EMP, DEPT, SALGRADE, and BONUS tables.

Defining the Relationships between Entities

Once the entities are defined, the designer can proceed with defining how each of the entities is related. Often, the designer will pair each entity with every other entity and ask, "Is there a relationship between these two entities?" Some relationships are obvious; some are not.

In the widget company database, there is most likely a relationship between EMP and DEPT, but depending on the business rules, it is unlikely that the DEPT and SALGRADE entities are related. If the business rules were to restrict certain salary grades to certain departments, there would most likely be a new entity that defines the relationship between salary grades and departments. This entity would be known as an *associative* or *intersection table* and would contain the valid combinations of salary grades and departments.

In general, there are three types of relationships in a relational database:

One-to-many   The most common type of relationship is *one-to-many*. This means that for each occurrence in a given entity, the parent entity, there may be one or more occurrences in a second entity, the child entity, to which it is related. For example, in the widget company database, the DEPT entity is a parent entity, and for each department, there could be one or more employees associated with that department. The relationship between DEPT and EMP is one-to-many.

One-to-one   In a *one-to-one* relationship, a row in a table is related to only one or none of the rows in a second table. This relationship type is often used for subtyping. For example, an EMPLOYEE table may hold the information common to all employees, while the FULLTIME, PARTTIME, and CONTRACTOR tables hold information unique to full-time employees, part-time employees, and contractors, respectively. These entities would be considered subtypes of an EMPLOYEE and maintain a one-to-one relationship with the EMPLOYEE table. These relationships are not as common as one-to-many relationships, because if one entity has an occurrence for a corresponding row in another entity, in most cases, the attributes from both entities should be in a single entity.

Many-to-many   In a *many-to-many* relationship, one row of a table may be related to many rows of another table, and vice versa. Usually, when this relationship is implemented in the database, a third entity is defined as an intersection table to contain the associations between the two entities in the relationship. For example, in a database used for school class enrollment, the STUDENT table has a many-to-many relationship with the CLASS table—one student may take one or more classes, and a given class may have one or more students. The intersection table STUDENT_CLASS would contain the combinations of STUDENT and CLASS to track which students are in which classes.

intersection table
See *associative table.*

one-to-many relationship
A relationship type between tables where one row in a given table is related to many other rows in a child table. The reverse condition, however, is not true. A given row in a child table is related to only one row in the parent table.

one-to-one relationship
A relationship type between tables where one row in a given table is related to only one or zero rows in a second table. This relationship type is often used for subtyping.

many-to-many relationship
A relationship type between tables in a relational database where one row of a given table may be related to many rows of another table, and vice versa. Many-to-many relationships are often resolved with an intermediate *associative table.*

Assigning Attributes to Entities

Once the designer has defined the entity relationships, the next step is to assign the attributes to each entity. This is physically implemented using columns, as shown here for the SALGRADE table as derived from the salary grade entity.

GRADE	LOSAL	HISAL
1	700	1200
2	1201	1400
3	1401	2000
4	2001	3000
5	3001	9999
6	10000	12500

Iterate the Process: Are We There Yet?

After the entities, relationships, and attributes have been defined, the designer may iterate the data modeling many more times. When reviewing relationships, new entities may be discovered. For example, when discussing the widget inventory table and its relationship to a customer order, the need for a shipping restrictions table may arise.

Once the design process is complete, the physical database tables may be created. This is where the DBA usually steps in, although the DBA probably has attended some of the design meetings already! It's important for the DBA to be involved at some level in the design process to make sure that any concerns about processor speed, disk space, network traffic, and administration effort can be addressed promptly when it comes time to create the database.

Logical database design sessions should not involve physical implementation issues, but once the design has gone through an iteration or two, it's the DBA's job to bring the designers "down to earth." As a result, the design may need to be revisited to balance the ideal database implementation versus the realities of budgets and schedules.

Object-Relational Databases

object-relational database
A relational database that includes additional operations and components to support object-oriented data structures and methods.

An *object-relational database* system supports everything a relational database system supports, as well as constructs for object-oriented development and design techniques. Object-oriented constructs are found in modern programming languages such as Java and C++. Both Oracle9i and Oracle 10g fully support all of the traditional object-oriented constructs and methods.

While the full range of object-oriented techniques is beyond the scope of this book, you will get a good idea of some of the object-oriented capabilities of Oracle, including abstraction, methods, encapsulation, and inheritance. Let's define those terms now.

Abstraction

One of the ways in which Oracle supports the object-relational model is by using abstraction. As noted earlier, Oracle has many built-in datatypes, such as numeric, string, date, and others. In addition, you can define user-defined objects as an aggregate of several other datatypes. These new user-defined types are called *abstract datatypes*.

    For example, when Scott's widget company grows, there may be other systems where he needs to represent an employee or a customer, or in more general terms, a person. Scott can define a datatype called PERSON that stores a first name, last name, middle initial, and gender. When the new customer tables are being built, Scott just needs to use the new PERSON type in the table definition. This brings to the table two immediate benefits: reusability and standards. Creating the new table is faster, since the datatype has already been defined, and it's less error prone than creating four individual fields. In addition, any developer who moves from an employee-oriented project to a customer-oriented project at Scott's company will find familiarity in common objects and naming conventions.

abstract datatypes
New datatypes, usually user-created, that are based on one or more built-in datatypes and can be treated as a unit.

Methods and Encapsulation

Another way in which object-oriented techniques are reflected in the Oracle object-relational database is through the use of methods and encapsulation. *Methods* define which operations can be performed on an object. *Encapsulation* restricts access to the object other than via the defined methods.

    Take a simple example of an employee object: It contains characteristics such as the employee name, address, and salary. A method against an employee object might be to get the name or change the name. Another method might be to increase the salary but never to decrease the salary. The encapsulation of the employee object prevents the direct manipulation of the characteristics of an employee object other than what the methods, driven by business rules, dictate.

methods
Operations on an object that are exposed for use by other objects or applications.

encapsulation
An object-oriented technique that may hide, or abstract, the inner workings of an object and expose only the relevant characteristics and operations on the object to other objects.

Inheritance

Inheritance allows objects that are derived from other objects to use the methods available in the parent object. If a new object is created with an existing object as a base, all of the methods available with the existing object will also be available with the new object.

    For example, if Scott were to implement a new EMPLOYEE type and a new CUSTOMER type using the PERSON type as the base, then any methods that already exist for PERSON would be available when using one of the two new types. The method ChangeLastName, defined with the PERSON type only once, can be used with objects defined with the CUSTOMER or EMPLOYEE type.

inheritance
Acquiring the properties of the parent, or base object, in a new object.

Object-Relational Support

object view
A database construct that overlays an object-oriented structure over an existing relational database table. As a result, the table can be accessed as a relational table or as an object table and make the transition to a fully object-oriented environment easier.

Oracle Database 10g provides additional features to ease the transition to an object-oriented database application. *Object views* allow the developer to define an object-oriented structure over an existing relational database table. In this way, existing applications do not need to change immediately, and any new development can use the object-oriented definitions of the table. This makes the transition from a relational to an object-relational database relatively painless, because object definitions can reference existing relational components.

Terms to Know

abstract datatypes	object view
associative table	object-relational database
column	one-to-many relationship
data modeling	one-to-one relationship
encapsulation	primary key
field	referential integrity
foreign key	relation
inheritance	relational database
intersection table	row
many-to-many relationship	table
methods	

Review Questions

1. Name the most important element of a relational database and its components.

2. Which type of table relationship associates more than one record in a given table with more than one record in another table?

3. What type of key can be used to enforce referential integrity between two tables in a database?

4. What are some reasons why using a spreadsheet is not a good alternative to using a large-scale database?

5. What are some of the benefits of abstraction in an object-relational database management system?

6. What object-relational feature of Oracle eases the transition between relational and object-relational applications?

7. What are the three steps in the ERA process for database design?

8. Name the three Oracle-compliant ANSI SQL standards.

9. What is the difference between a relation and a relationship?

10. Which type of relationship associates one row in a given table with one or no rows in another table?

Chapter 2

SQL*Plus and iSQL*Plus Basics

This chapter begins with a few formalities and definitions and then dives right into a discussion of the different ways to run SQL commands. Then it introduces the basics of SELECT statements and how we can retrieve and display either all columns or only certain columns of a table.

You will also find out about how to make changes to the rows in a table by using INSERT, UPDATE, MERGE, and DELETE statements. In the remainder of the chapter, you will explore various ways to change the structure of tables in the database as well as control the permissions on tables.

Some SQL Formalities

SQL (Structured Query Language)
The industry-standard database language used to query and manipulate the data, structures, and permissions in a relational database.

A database engine is the part of an RDBMS that actually stores and retrieves data to and from the data files. The database engine is not very useful unless you can send *SQL (Structured Query Language)* commands to it and receive the results from those SQL commands (if any).

NOTE

"SQL" is usually pronounced "sequel," but if you refer to "S-Q-L" in a conversation with other database developers and DBAs, they will certainly know what you're talking about!

It is also important to separate the SQL commands from the command processor itself. For example, Oracle's SQL*Plus client tool (available on virtually any platform that the Oracle server itself runs on) has a number of other "built-in" commands that look like SQL commands but operate only within the SQL*Plus environment; these are called SQL*Plus commands. A SQL*Plus command may actually send many SQL commands to the Oracle server.

Tools for Running SQL

tiers
Locations where different components of an enterprise application system reside. In a typical three-tier environment, the client tier runs a thin application such as a web browser, which connects to a middleware server that is running a web server. The web server and its related components typically manage the business rules of the application. The third-tier database platform controls access to the data and manages the data itself. This approach partitions the application so that it is easier to maintain and segregates the tasks into tiers that are best equipped to handle a particular function.

Most Oracle database environments consist of two, three, or more *tiers*. In the simplest two-tier scenario, a database developer might be using SQL*Plus on a Windows PC connecting to an Oracle database on a Linux server. More complex environments may include a web server, application server, or authentication server on a number of other servers in between the client and the database server.

Here, we will explore the various client-based tools that can be used to run SQL, including SQL*Plus, iSQL*Plus, SQL*Plus Worksheet, third-party tools, Open Database Connectivity (ODBC), Java Database Connectivity (JDBC), and Oracle Call Interface (OCI).

SQL*Plus

SQL*Plus has been around as long as the Oracle RDBMS itself. It is the most basic tool available for connecting to the database and executing queries against the tables in a database. On Unix systems, it can be run in character-based mode, even on a dumb terminal connected to the Unix system via a serial port.

The "Plus" part of SQL*Plus defines some of the extra functionality available above and beyond executing SQL statements and returning the results. Some of this functionality is proprietary to SQL*Plus and may not be available in non-Oracle database environments. Here are some of the things you can do using SQL*Plus:

- ◆ Define headers and footers for reports.
- ◆ Rename columns in the report output.

◆ Prompt users for values to be substituted into the query.

◆ Retrieve the structure of a table.

◆ Save the results of the query to a file.

◆ Copy entire tables between databases using only one command.

While many other tools surpass SQL*Plus in functionality as well as in look and feel, those other tools don't help much when the database is down and all you have is a character-based terminal emulator connection to your Unix server! No matter which environment you're in—Unix, Windows, minicomputer, or mainframe—SQL*Plus will always be there and have the same look and feel across all of those environments.

Under the various versions of Microsoft Windows, SQL*Plus runs as a Windows application and as a command-line application. The Windows functionality available in the Windows SQL*Plus session includes those features normally available in a Windows text-based editor: cutting and pasting text strings, searching for text in the session window, and saving or loading the last command executed. The Windows version also allows you to change the SQL*Plus environment settings using a GUI dialog box or through the command line. The GUI dialog box is accessible from SQL*Plus by selecting Options ➢ Environment.

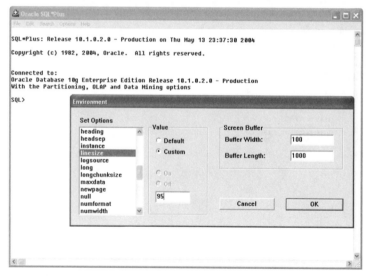

You'll need to log on with a valid username and password to initiate a SQL*Plus session, as shown below. You'll also need to enter a host string value. The *host string* is an alias to a set of parameters, such as the name, address, protocol type, and port number of the Oracle database to which you want to connect. The database may be on the same machine that is running the SQL*Plus client tool, or it may be on a different host machine on the network. For the purposes of this book, all database connections will use the rac0 host string.

host string

A text string that represents a shortcut or reference to a set of parameters that provide the information needed to connect to a database host from the client application.

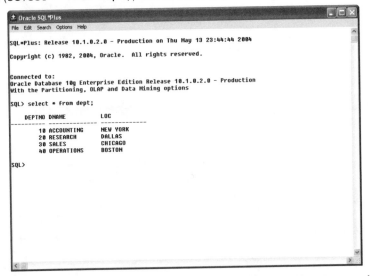

NOTE **Your default Oracle installation may not have the user** SCOTT **enabled, or the password may have been changed from the default** TIGER. **Check with your local DBA to see if this is the case.**

The user SCOTT owns a number of database tables, including the DEPT table, which contains a list of all the department numbers, department names, and department locations. As you'll learn a little later in this chapter, the SQL SELECT statement allows you to extract information from a database. The example below shows a SELECT statement that retrieves all of the rows in the DEPT table (select * from dept;) and its results.

Notice that the case of the keywords and column names is important only for readability. In practice, you can enter them in any case. To enhance this sample query, let's do the following:

- ◆ Add a report title of "Department Report" using the TTITLE SQL*Plus command.
- ◆ Change the headers for each of the columns to make them more readable using the COLUMN SQL*Plus command.
- ◆ Save the output from the query to a file using the SQL*Plus SPOOL command.

The sequence of SQL*Plus commands, the SQL statement, and the results from the command are as follows:

```
SQL> ttitle "Department Report"
SQL> column deptno heading "Department|Number"
SQL> column dname heading "Department|Name"
SQL> column loc heading "City|Location"
SQL> spool c:\temp\deptrept.txt
SQL> /

Tue Aug 13                                      page     1
                    Department Report

Department Department      City
    Number Name            Location
---------- --------------- -------------
        10 ACCOUNTING      NEW YORK
        20 RESEARCH        DALLAS
        30 SALES           CHICAGO
        40 OPERATIONS      BOSTON

SQL> spool off
SQL>
```

Notice that we didn't type in the entire SELECT statement again. Instead, we used the / SQL*Plus command, which reruns the last complete SQL statement executed.

SQL*Plus commands differ from SQL statements in that they don't need a semicolon at the end (although SQL*Plus commands can be terminated with a semicolon without SQL*Plus complaining about it). SQL statements can be written across many lines without any type of continuation character; they are complete whenever you type a semicolon or use the SQL*Plus / command. SQL*Plus commands must be contained entirely on one line, unless the - continuation character is used at the end of each line. The example below shows how the SQL*Plus continuation character is used:

```
SQL> column deptno heading -
> "Department|Number"
SQL>
```

iSQL*Plus

With iSQL*Plus, you connect to the database indirectly via a very "lightweight" middle tier. The iSQL*Plus tool is essentially the web-enabled version of

SQL*Plus, with a few restrictions, which we will cover shortly. It is implemented as part of a three-tier Oracle environment, although iSQL*Plus could very well run on the same machine as either the client or the Oracle server itself.

iSQL*Plus offers a 100 percent web-enabled, *thin client* solution. From a DBA's or network administrator's point of view, the more clients that need only a web browser to get their work done, the better. No Oracle client software installation is required for iSQL*Plus!

To start iSQL*Plus, use your favorite web browser (preferably any version of Mozilla, Microsoft Internet Explorer 5.0 or later, or Netscape Navigator 4.7 or later) and navigate to the URL http://<your_server_name>/isqlplus. The string <your_server_name> is the name of the middleware server that is running the iSQL*Plus web application.

thin client
A workstation or CPU with relatively low-powered components that can use a web interface (or other application with a small footprint) to connect to a middle-ware or a back-end database server where most of the processing occurs. iSQL*Plus is an example of a web application that runs on a thin client.

NOTE

Depending on the configuration of the server, you may need to add a port number to the server name, for example, http://www.internal.esweb.com:7779/isqlplus. **Check with your local system administrator for the URL that supports iSQL*Plus.**

connection identifier
See *host string.*

SQL*Plus and iSQL*Plus are similar. In fact, iSQL*Plus requires that the SQL*Plus executable be accessible on the middleware server that is running the iSQL*Plus service. The iSQL*Plus login screen below shows the user SCOTT logging into the same server as he did with SQL*Plus earlier in this chapter. In this case, rac0 is specified as the *connection identifier*, rather than the host string as it is with SQL*Plus; they have different names but mean the same thing.

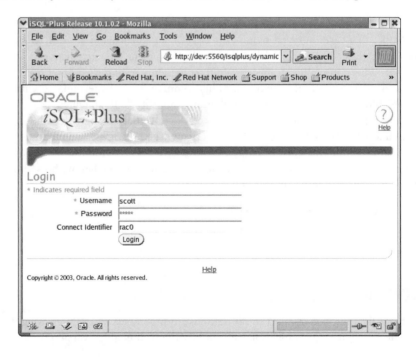

Here is an example of running the same query in iSQL*Plus that you saw earlier under SQL*Plus.

Notice that with iSQL*Plus, if only one SQL statement is being run at a time, no semicolon is required. This would be the equivalent of typing / in a SQL*Plus session after entering a SQL statement without a terminating semicolon. Also notice that the area where commands are entered is a fixed size, regardless of how many commands you are entering. Rest assured, as in SQL*Plus, this is easily configurable. Just click the Preferences link in the upper-right corner of the browser to change the command area size and other iSQL*Plus environment settings.

The Apache HTTP web server is used to host iSQL*Plus, as well as any other Oracle web-enabled services on Microsoft Windows Oracle installations. Apache isn't just for Unix anymore!

NOTE

All of the examples later in this chapter and throughout the book will use iSQL*Plus as the tool for executing SQL commands and reports.

SQL*Plus Worksheet

Oracle Enterprise Manager (OEM)
A GUI tool that allows access, maintenance, and monitoring of multiple databases or services within a single
application.

If *Oracle Enterprise Manager (OEM)* is installed, another variation of
SQL*Plus, called SQL*Plus Worksheet, is available to the DBA. Here's the
OEM Login dialog box:

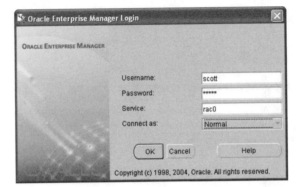

SQL*Plus Worksheet supports all the commands that standard SQL*Plus
supports, in a two-pane query/result format, as shown below. It's a slightly more
graphical application; in other words, it needs an operating system such as
Microsoft Windows or a similar GUI client to run. Beyond that, it's really just
SQL*Plus with a slightly better front end!

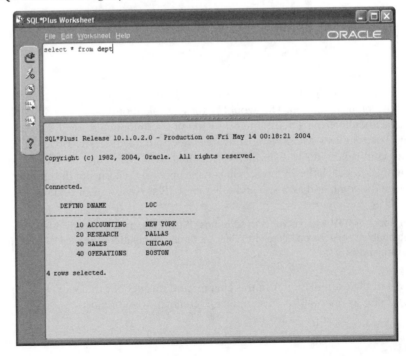

Third-Party Tools

Basic network client connectivity is provided during an Oracle client installation. Starting with release 9, Oracle's network connectivity package is known as Oracle Net Services. Third-party developers can leverage this functionality in their own applications to provide tools customized for a more specific audience and to provide an additional layer of functionality that may not be available in Oracle's offerings.

An example of a third-party tool is TOAD, which stands for Tool for Oracle Application Developers. TOAD is not just for developers; it has a lot of functionality that DBAs can use also. There are both a freeware version (that can even be used as freeware in a corporate environment) and a licensed version. The licensed version has many more DBA-friendly features and SQL debugging tools available. (Visit `www.toadsoft.com` or `www.quest.com/toad` for more information.) Shown below is the DEPT table query executed using the freeware version of the TOAD browser. Notice the other database navigational capabilities in this pane.

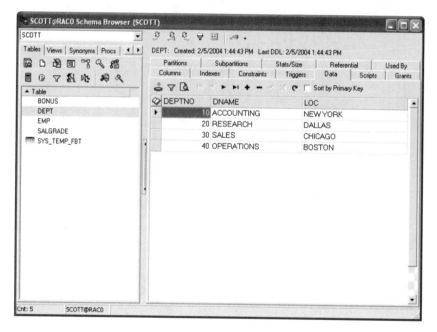

ODBC/JDBC

Many tools in the Windows (and Unix) environment can take advantage of a common framework known as *ODBC*, which stands for Open Database Connectivity. In a nutshell, ODBC allows applications that are ODBC-compliant to connect to virtually any database without knowing the details of how to connect directly to the database. All of the details are hidden in the *ODBC driver* itself. The driver may

ODBC (Open Database Connectivity)
A set of standards that allow applications that are not dependent on any one specific database to process SQL statements against any database that supports SQL.

be written by the database vendor or by a third-party developer that specializes in ODBC connectivity. Here is an example of the Oracle ODBC Driver Configuration dialog box for setting up an ODBC connection to a database.

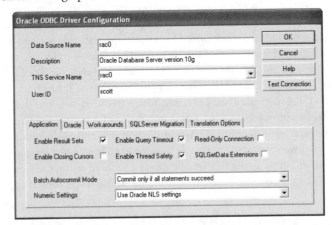

ODBC driver
An interface, usually at the operating-system level, that supports the connection of an ODBC-compliant application to a specific database platform.

After the ODBC connection is made, you can run queries. Shown below are the results of the DEPT table query from a Microsoft Access session.

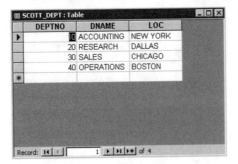

Applications that use ODBC are not limited to tools such as Microsoft Access, which also has its own client-based database engine in addition to the capability to connect to other databases. Spreadsheets, financial applications, and statistical analysis packages are among the many types of applications that need to connect to a database for their source data. ODBC gives the end user the freedom to choose which external database to use and frees the application vendor from needing to develop a special connection routine for every possible database source.

JDBC (Java Database Connectivity)
A set of library routines specific to the Java language that allows a Java application to easily connect to and process SQL statements against an Oracle database.

JDBC, which stands for Java Database Connectivity, is very similar to ODBC in that JDBC provides a common set of routines to allow a Java developer to connect to any SQL-compliant database without knowing the specifics of the target database. The key difference between ODBC and JDBC is that JDBC is specifically for Java applications and ODBC is application-neutral.

OCI

Finally, we have *OCI*, which stands for Oracle Call Interface. OCI is a set of library routines for C developers (on any operating system platform) that can provide all the functionality available from a SQL command-line session and more. Below are some code fragments in the C language that include OCI calls:

```
text *username = (text *) "SCOTT";
text *password = (text *) "TIGER";
...
text *insert = (text *) "INSERT INTO emp(empno, \
    ename, job, sal, deptno)\
    VALUES (:empno, :ename, :job, :sal, :deptno)";
...
/*
 * Connect to ORACLE and open two cursors.
 * Exit on any error.
 */
    if (olog(&lda, (ub1 *)hda, username, -1, password, -1,
            (text *) 0, -1, (ub4)OCI_LM_DEF))
    {
        err_report(&lda);
        exit(EXIT_FAILURE);
    }
    printf("Connected to ORACLE as %s\n", username);
...
/* Parse the INSERT statement. */
    if (oparse(&cda1, insert, (sb4) -1, FALSE, (ub4) VERSION_
7))
    {
        err_report(&cda1);
        do_exit(EXIT_FAILURE);
    }
...
```

For more OCI code samples, check the ORACLE_BASE\ORACLE_HOME\oci directory under Microsoft Windows Oracle installations.

OCI (Oracle Call Interface)
A set of library routines that allows a C application on virtually any development platform to easily connect to and process SQL statements against an Oracle database. The OCI routines are called as native C library functions; therefore, no preprocessor is necessary when compiling a C application using OCI.

The Ubiquitous *SELECT* Statement

In the examples of tools for running SQL, you've seen the following simple SELECT statement:

```
select * from dept;
```

In its most basic form, the SELECT statement has a list of columns to select from a table, using the SELECT ... FROM syntax. The * means "all columns." To successfully retrieve rows from a table, the user running the query must either own the table or have the permissions granted to the user by the owner or a DBA. The most basic SELECT syntax can be described as follows:

```
SELECT {* | [DISTINCT] column | expression [alias], ...}
    FROM tablename;
```

This type of statement representation is typical of what you'll see in Oracle documentation, and it can be very complex. Here is a summary of what the elements in the syntax representation mean:

Element	Meaning
|	Pick one or the other
{ }	One within this list is required

Element	Meaning
[ ]	Item is optional
...	May repeat
Uppercase	Keyword or command
italics	Variable

We will explore many more advanced features of the SELECT statement throughout this book. However, to begin with, let's look at some examples of the *column*, *alias*, DISTINCT, and *expression* parts of a SELECT statement.

Column Specification

As you've seen, you can use the * character to view all columns in a table. But if the table contains too many columns to view at once, or your query needs only a small number of the total columns, you can pick the columns you need. For example, suppose that you want to view some information in the EMP table. How could you find out which columns are in this table without doing a SELECT * statement? You could use the DESCRIBE command in iSQL*Plus, as shown below.

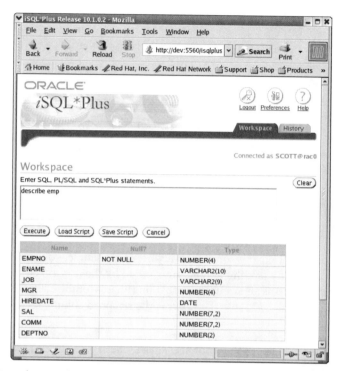

Now that you know which columns exist in the EMP table, you realize that you really need to see only the employee number, name, and salary. Therefore, your SELECT statement should be something like this:

```
select empno, ename, sal from emp;
```

It produces results similar to the following:

```
EMPNO       ENAME          SAL
---------- ---------- ----------
     7369 SMITH          800
     7499 ALLEN         1600
     7521 WARD          1250
     7566 JONES         2975
     7654 MARTIN        1250
     7698 BLAKE         2850
     7782 CLARK         2450
```

```
7788  SCOTT              3000
7839  KING               5000
7844  TURNER             1500
7876  ADAMS              1100
7900  JAMES               950
7902  FORD               3000
7934  MILLER             1300


14 rows selected.
```

Column Renaming

alias

An alternate name for a column, speci-fied right after the column name in a SELECT statement, seen in the results of the query.

In one of our earlier SQL*Plus examples, we wanted the column headers to be more readable, and we used some of the built-in features of SQL*Plus to do this. However, if your requirements for readability are fairly simple, you can use SQL's built-in capability of column renaming, noted by the [*alias*] element of the SELECT syntax. Here is an example of providing aliases for the EMPNO, ENAME, and SAL columns in the EMP table. The *alias* is the renamed column seen in the results of the query.

```
select empno "Employee Number", ename "Name", sal "Salary"
from emp;


Employee Number Name        Salary
--------------- ----------  ----------
           7369 SMITH          800
           7499 ALLEN         1600
           7521 WARD          1250
           7566 JONES         2975
           7654 MARTIN        1250
           7698 BLAKE         2850
           7782 CLARK         2450
           7788 SCOTT         3000
           7839 KING          5000
           7844 TURNER        1500
           7876 ADAMS         1100
           7900 JAMES          950
           7902 FORD          3000
           7934 MILLER        1300


14 rows selected.
```

Duplicate Removal

The DISTINCT keyword removes all duplicate rows from the results of a query. For example, what if you wanted to see the department numbers for the employees in the EMP table? Your query might be something like this:

```
select deptno from emp;
```

```
DEPTNO
----------
        20
        30
        30
        20
        30
        30
        10
        20
        10
        30
        20
        30
        20
        10
```

```
14 rows selected.
```

But what you probably want is one row for each of the departments found in the EMP table. In this case, use the DISTINCT keyword:

```
select distinct deptno from emp;
```

```
DEPTNO
----------
        10
        20
        30
```

```
3 rows selected.
```

That's much easier to read. You now know that all of the employees belong to one of three departments. However, there may be many other departments, which would be listed in the department (DEPT) table. Some departments may not have any employees right now. In Chapter 5, "Using Multiple Tables," you'll learn how to execute queries on joined tables to get this kind of information.

Expressions

To finish off our analysis of the SELECT syntax, let's look at the *expression* part of the SELECT statement. Let's say we would like to see how salaries would look if everyone got a 15 percent pay increase. All of the information we need to see is still in one table, the EMP table, but we need to perform some kind of calculation on one of the existing fields. To calculate a 15 percent pay increase, we need to not only see the existing salary but also multiply the SAL column by 1.15:

```
select empno, ename, sal, sal*1.15 from emp;
```

EMPNO	ENAME	SAL	SAL*1.15
7369	SMITH	800	920
7499	ALLEN	1600	1840
7521	WARD	1250	1437.5
7566	JONES	2975	3421.25
7654	MARTIN	1250	1437.5
7698	BLAKE	2850	3277.5
7782	CLARK	2450	2817.5
7788	SCOTT	3000	3450
7839	KING	5000	5750
7844	TURNER	1500	1725
7876	ADAMS	1100	1265
7900	JAMES	950	1092.5
7902	FORD	3000	3450
7934	MILLER	1300	1495

```
14 rows selected.
```

To make the proposed salary column more readable, we could use either a column alias or iSQL*Plus column-formatting commands. We might also want to show a total for the SAL and SAL*1.15 columns or show each salary increase to exactly two decimal places. Some of these more advanced formatting techniques will be covered in Chapter 9, "Reporting Techniques."

DML for Making Changes

DML stands for Data Manipulation Language. DML commands are the SQL statements that can change the values in database tables, as opposed to merely reading them, as SELECT statements do.

NOTE

It could be argued that SELECT statements do technically manipulate data when a query is performed, but in this book, we will differentiate between reading database tables and changing database tables. DBAs may configure and tune a mostly read-only database differently than they configure a frequent read-write database. An online transaction processing (OLTP) database would be considered a mostly read-write database. A decision support system (DSS) or data warehouse database would be considered a mostly read-only database.

The following sections provide an introduction to the DML statements UPDATE, INSERT, DELETE, and MERGE.

The *UPDATE Statement*

An UPDATE statement will change one or more rows in a database table. The basic form of an UPDATE statement must specify which table to update, which column(s) to change, and, optionally, whether to change all the rows in the table or just a few. The syntax is as follows:

```
UPDATE  tablename SET column = value [ , column = value, ...]
    [WHERE condition];
```

As with any SQL statements that access a table, the table to be updated must be owned by the user running the query or have the permissions granted to the user by the owner or a DBA. Chapter 11, "Users and Security," will cover privileges and permissions in more detail.

Since a table may have a large number of columns, you don't necessarily want to update every column. To follow up on an earlier example, let's say that the boss has decided to give a 15 percent salary increase across the board. We can use an UPDATE statement that looks very similar to the SELECT statement we wrote earlier. Here are what the UPDATE statement and the result of executing that statement in iSQL*Plus look like:

DML (Data Manipulation Language)
Includes INSERT, UPDATE, DELETE, and MERGE statements that operate specifically on database tables. Occasionally, SELECT statements are included in the SQL DML category.

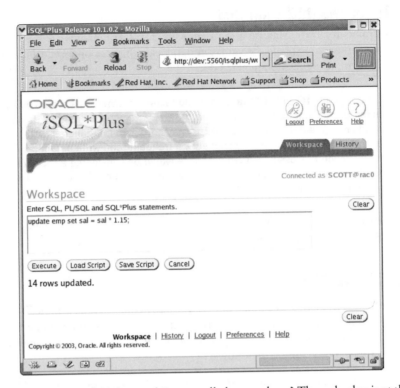

But wait, you ask, did something actually happen here? The only clue is at the bottom of the screen, where it indicates that 14 rows were updated. DML statements such as UPDATE will perform the action requested (or produce an error message on occasion), but only SELECT statements will return rows to the user. To see if the rows were updated correctly, the user SCOTT will need to rerun the SELECT query on the EMP table.

Now that all the employees have been granted their raise, the boss decides that there are still some employees who need an even bigger raise. For example, employee FORD had a lot more bright ideas last year than the average employee, so he deserves another 10 percent raise above and beyond the 15 percent raise that he already received. Also, the boss notices that the employee file has not yet been updated with her employee information after the previous boss left late last month. Both of these changes require UPDATE statements that contain a WHERE clause to narrow down the number of changed records based on the employee name. Using iSQL*Plus, we can perform these two updates at once. Here are the results of the two UPDATE operations.

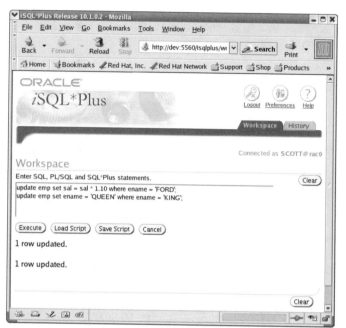

Notice that the results of both UPDATE statements appear at the bottom of the iSQL*Plus browser window.

The *INSERT* Statement

Whenever new employees are hired in Scott's widget company, new rows must be added to the EMP table. The INSERT statement does just that. Here's the basic INSERT syntax:

```
INSERT INTO tablename [(column1 [, column2 ...])]
    VALUES (value1 [, value2 ... ]);
```

This format of the INSERT statement inserts only one row at a time. In Scott's company, the boss realizes that she should probably leave the old boss's employee information intact and just add herself as a new row in the table. To handle this for her, we need to perform both an UPDATE and an INSERT on the EMP table. The two statements and their results are as follows:

```
update EMP set ENAME = 'KING' where ENAME = 'QUEEN';

insert into EMP (EMPNO, ENAME, JOB, MGR, HIREDATE,
```

```
        SAL, COMM, DEPTNO)
values (7878, 'QUEEN', 'PRESIDENT', NULL, '15-AUG-2004',
        7500, NULL, 10);
```

```
1 row updated.
```

```
1 row created.
```

Notice that while the case of the keywords and column names is important only for readability, the text within the single quotation marks is case sensitive and must represent the exact text to be searched or the exact text to be inserted into the table's column.

<table>
<tr><td>

WARNING

</td><td>

It is technically possible to create a column name with mixed case, but this technique is not recommended. This is because the column name must be specified with the same exact case in double quotation marks whenever it is referenced in any SQL command.

</td></tr>
</table>

What does the NULL value mean? NULL is a special keyword that means literally *nothing*. It is not the same as a blank or an empty string. It means that the value inserted for this column in this row is unknown or not applicable. When this value is displayed as the result of a SELECT statement, it displays with blanks. In the case of the MGR column, the PRESIDENT employee has no boss, so this column is NULL for the former employee KING and the current employee QUEEN. The format for date columns—in this case, for the column HIREDATE—will be explained in Chapter 3, "Oracle Database Functions."

The *DELETE* Statement

As the name implies, the DELETE statement will remove rows from a database table. You can delete all rows or use a WHERE clause to specify rows, similar to the UPDATE statement. Here's the syntax:

```
DELETE [FROM] tablename
    [WHERE condition];
```

The FROM keyword is optional, but it makes the DELETE statement more readable (otherwise, it looks like you're deleting the table itself!). In the case of Scott's company, all of the employees hired in the last recruitment drive on March 25, 2004 and added to the EMP table will be working for the company's subsidiary instead, so they must be deleted from the EMP table. Here's the DELETE statement to accomplish this:

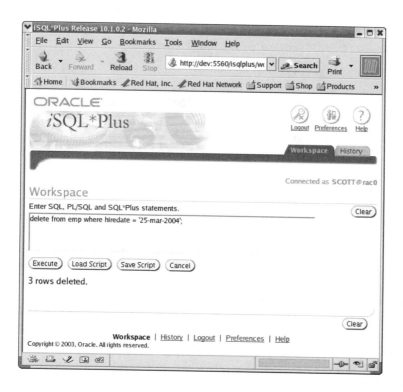

The *MERGE* Statement

The MERGE statement was introduced in Oracle9i, and it performs an operation that could be called an "upsert." It combines two operations that would normally need to be performed separately—an INSERT or an UPDATE—depending on whether the row already exists in the table.

Combining these two operations not only makes the application developer's coding more straightforward (by not needing to perform an explicit compare operation with multiple UPDATE and INSERT statements), but it also reduces the number of operations performed on the table. These operations are also performed internally to the database, which makes the operation even more efficient because the additional statement parsing does not need to occur. The syntax is as follows:

```
MERGE INTO tablename alias
    USING (tablename2 | view | subquery) alias2
    ON (join_condition)
    WHEN MATCHED THEN
        UPDATE SET
```

```
            col1 = col1_value [, col2 = col2_value ... ]
      WHEN NOT MATCHED THEN
          INSERT (column_list) VALUES (column_values);
```

The basic syntax is fairly straightforward and easy to use. When the source table and the target table match on one or more columns (in the *join_condition*), the row is updated with an UPDATE statement; otherwise, the row is inserted with an INSERT statement. Many of the components of the MERGE statement, such as *view* and *subquery*, will be covered in later chapters.

DDL for Handling Database Objects

DDL (Data Definition Language)
Includes statements such as CREATE, ALTER, and DROP to work with objects such as tables. DDL modifies the structure of the objects in a database instead of the contents of the objects.

DDL stands for Data Definition Language. This class of statements allows the user or DBA to add, change, or drop database objects, such as tables, indexes, views, and so forth. While most ordinary users and developers can create their own tables in a development environment, the DBA must still provide a solid infrastructure for these tables by providing the appropriate location and disk space allocation parameters. This will ensure that database tables are created efficiently, regardless of who is creating them.

The following sections introduce the key DDL statements: CREATE, ALTER, DROP, RENAME, and TRUNCATE. For the ALTER, DROP, RENAME, and TRUNCATE DDL operations, the table to be modified must either be owned by the user executing the DDL statement or the user must have the privilege to perform that operation in any schema.

The *CREATE* Statement

Tables are probably the most frequently created objects in the database, second only to indexes (depending on the type of database, as discussed in Chapter 12, "Making Things Run Fast (Enough)"). The basic CREATE TABLE statement has the following syntax:

```
CREATE TABLE [schema.]tablename
    (column1 datatype1 [DEFAULT expression]
      [, ...]);
```

schema
A group of related database objects assigned to a database user. A schema contains tables, views, indexes, sequences, and SQL code. The schema name can be used to qualify objects that are not owned by the user referencing the objects.

A *schema* is a group of related tables and other objects that is owned by a single user, whose username is the same as the schema name. In the context of the CREATE TABLE statement, if the table itself will not be created in the schema of the user executing the CREATE TABLE statement, the schema name must be specified. In addition, the user creating the table must have the correct privileges to create the table in a different schema. (Permissions and privileges are covered in Chapter 11.)

At the simplest level, a table must have one or more columns, and each of these columns must be of a specified type: a character string, a numeric type, a date type, a long binary value, and so forth. These columns can all have NULL values, or they can be specified as being required for every row. If the user does not specify a value for a column in an INSERT statement, a DEFAULT value can be specified for this column when the table is created.

It turns out that Scott's company is going to segregate the part-time employees into a new table. The new table will be very similar to the existing EMP table, except that the new table will have an hourly wage rate instead of a salary and a commission. Starting with the existing structure of the EMP table, we can construct a new CREATE TABLE statement as follows:

```
CREATE TABLE EMP_HOURLY (
    EMPNO       NUMBER (4)     NOT NULL,
    ENAME       VARCHAR2 (10),
    JOB         VARCHAR2 (9),
    MGR         NUMBER (4),
    HIREDATE    DATE,
    HOURRATE    NUMBER (5,2)  NOT NULL DEFAULT 6.50,
    DEPTNO      NUMBER (2),
    CONSTRAINT PK_EMP
    PRIMARY KEY ( EMPNO ) );
```

Notice that only the employee number and the hourly rate are required fields. In addition, the hourly rate defaults to $6.50 an hour if it is not specified in the INSERT statement. Below are the results of the CREATE TABLE statement in iSQL*Plus, along with a confirmation of the table structure using the iSQL*Plus DESCRIBE command.

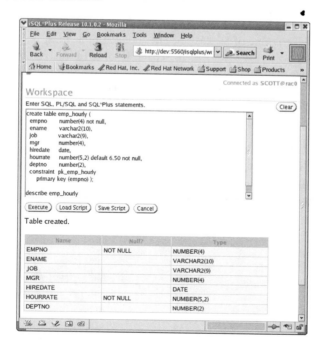

The CONSTRAINT and PRIMARY KEY clauses ensure that every table should have one column, or a combination of columns, that makes the table's row unique within the table. This makes the identification of a row much easier and less ambiguous when you're doing an UPDATE, a DELETE, or a SELECT operation. You'll learn more about ensuring unique values in Chapter 10, "Creating and Maintaining Database Objects."

TIP You can also use the CREATE TABLE AS SELECT (CTAS) version of CREATE TABLE to quickly create a new version of an existing table, with some or all of the rows from the source table. CTAS is covered in Chapter 10.

The *ALTER* Statement

The ALTER statement allows the user to make some kind of change to some object in the database. The ALTER statement's full syntax is very complex. For the purposes of this book, the ALTER statement will be used to add, delete, or change a column in a table. The ALTER statement's syntax can then be simplified to one of three statements:

```
ALTER TABLE tablename
    ADD (column1 datatype1 [DEFAULT expression] [, ...]);
ALTER TABLE tablename
    MODIFY (column1 datatype1 [DEFAULT expression] [,...]);
ALTER TABLE tablename DROP COLUMN column1;
```

A new company policy has been implemented at Scott's company that mandates a new default hourly rate of $7.25. The EMP_HOURLY table must be modified to reflect this new policy. We can use the second form of the ALTER TABLE statement shown above to accomplish this task. It also turns out that there is one manager for all hourly employees; therefore, we do not need a MGR column in the EMP_HOURLY table. We can use the third form of the ALTER TABLE statement shown above to accomplish this additional task.

```
ALTER TABLE EMP_HOURLY
    MODIFY (HOURRATE  NUMBER(5,2) DEFAULT 7.25);
ALTER TABLE EMP_HOURLY
    DROP COLUMN MGR;
DESCRIBE EMP_HOURLY;

Table altered.

Table altered.
```

Name	Null?	Type
EMPNO	NOT NULL	NUMBER(4)
ENAME		VARCHAR2(10)
JOB		VARCHAR2(9)
HIREDATE		DATE
HOURRATE	NOT NULL	NUMBER(5,2)
DEPTNO		NUMBER(2)

If columns are dropped or modified in a table, the values of the other columns in the table, as well as the total number of rows in the table, remain the same. If a new column is added to a table with existing rows, the value for this column in the existing rows is NULL, unless the column is required. If the column is required, a DEFAULT value must be specified when the column is added.

The *DROP* Statement

When a table is no longer needed, it can be dropped. Both the table definition and the rows in the table are dropped, and the space allocated for the table is made available for other database objects. The syntax for the DROP statement is about as simple as it gets:

```
DROP TABLE tablename;
```

The HR department at Scott's company was maintaining the list of retirees in an EMP_RETIRED table. Once the new management came in a couple of months ago, the retiree-tracking function was outsourced, so the EMP_RETIRED table is no longer needed. Here is how it is dropped:

```
DROP TABLE EMP_RETIRED;

Table dropped.
```

As with most other DDL operations, either the table to be dropped must be owned by the user executing the DROP statement or the user must have the privilege to drop a table in any schema.

The *RENAME* Statement

The RENAME statement is also very straightforward. A table name can be changed to another name; references by other database objects, such as indexes that refer to the renamed table, are automatically adjusted. The syntax is as follows:

```
RENAME old_tablename TO new_tablename;
```

Scott's company is changing the employee categorization method to differentiate between temporary part-time workers and permanent part-time workers. Therefore, a new table, EMP_HOURLY_TEMP, must be created, and the existing EMP_HOURLY table must be renamed to EMP_HOURLY_PERM:

```
RENAME EMP_HOURLY TO EMP_HOURLY_PERM;


Table renamed.
```

WARNING **Any references to the old table in program code (such as C code using OCI) or in stored SQL scripts must be changed manually to reflect the new table name.**

The *TRUNCATE* Statement

From the perspective of the user, the TRUNCATE statement is similar to the DELETE statement. Both of the statements will delete rows from a table. The main difference is that the DELETE can be more selective (in other words, using a WHERE clause). The TRUNCATE statement simply removes all rows from a table. The TRUNCATE statement will also appear to run faster than a DELETE in most cases.

From a DBA's point of view, however, the TRUNCATE and DELETE statements are very different. The TRUNCATE statement will immediately free any space from the deleted rows. The space from any rows deleted with DELETE will remain allocated to the table, and it may possibly be reused by future INSERT operations into the table. Also, the TRUNCATE statement is not recoverable; rows removed with DELETE can be recovered with a ROLLBACK statement. (Rolling back transactions is discussed in Chapter 7, "Logical Consistency.")

The syntax for TRUNCATE is very straightforward:

```
TRUNCATE TABLE tablename;
```

In Scott's corporate database, one of the developers inadvertently loaded the EMP_HOURLY table with 50,000 rows from the wrong table. The developer realizes that the DELETE statement would fix this, but that the DBAs would be concerned about the space that would not be reclaimed. The table didn't have any rows to begin with, so the developer determines that TRUNCATE would be the best option. Here is the command to remove all the rows, so that the table is now empty:

```
TRUNCATE TABLE EMP_HOURLY;


Table truncated.
```

The table to be truncated must be in the user's schema or the user must have the privilege to drop a table in another user's schema (the same privilege that allows the user to completely drop the table).

DCL for Handling Privileges

DCL stands for Data Control Language. DCL statements can give or take away privileges to database objects or privileges to perform certain actions. At a minimum, most users are granted the right to connect to the database. Many users may not need to create tables, so they are not granted that privilege.

Privileges can also be granted to a *role*. A role is a way to bundle together multiple privileges into a single entity. This makes it easier to grant a group of privileges to one or more users in one easy step, rather than needing to enumerate each of those privileges every time you want to grant them to a new user (or to another role). The converse is also true: It's easier to revoke a role from a user than to remove the individual privileges that make up the role. System privileges, object privileges, and roles are discussed in more detail in Chapter 11. The following sections provide an overview of the GRANT and REVOKE statements.

DCL (Data Control Language)
Includes statements such as GRANT and REVOKE to provide or deny users or roles system or object privileges.

The *GRANT Statement*

The GRANT statement is almost self-explanatory. GRANT will give a privilege (either object or system) to a user, a role, or to all users. The basic syntax for granting both system and object privileges is as follows:

```
GRANT sys_privilege [, sys_privilege ...]
   TO user | role | PUBLIC [, user | role | PUBLIC ...];
GRANT obj_privilege [(column_list)] ON object
   TO user | role | PUBLIC
[WITH GRANT OPTION];
```

role
A group of related privileges that is referenced by a single name. Privileges can be assigned to a role, and a role can be assigned to a database user or to another role. Roles ease the maintenance issues with managing privileges for a large number of users who can be grouped into a relatively small number of categories based on job function.

Granting object privileges with the WITH GRANT OPTION clause allows the user or users granted that role the ability to pass those rights onto yet another user or role.

Suppose that Scott has acquired additional responsibilities and now must help to maintain the tables in the order-entry system, specifically the ORDER_ITEMS table owned by the user OE. The DBA grants the rights on this table to user SCOTT using the following command:

```
GRANT INSERT, UPDATE, DELETE, SELECT ON
   OE.ORDER_ITEMS TO SCOTT;

Grant succeeded.
```

Scott can now add, delete, update, and view rows in the OE.ORDER_ITEMS table. He cannot, however, grant these privileges to other users or roles, since the WITH GRANT OPTION clause was not used by the DBA.

The *REVOKE* Statement

As you would expect, the REVOKE statement is the opposite of the GRANT statement. Either system privileges or object privileges can be revoked with the following basic syntax:

```
REVOKE obj_privilege | ALL [, obj_privilege] ON object
    FROM user | role | PUBLIC [, user | role | PUBLIC ...];
REVOKE sys_privilege | ALL [, sys_privilege ...]
    FROM user | role | PUBLIC [, user | role | PUBLIC ...];
```

When the DBA granted the rights to SCOTT to work with the ORDER_ITEMS table, he noticed that the user OE had the DBA role assigned! This was obviously an oversight, so he corrected the situation immediately by using the REVOKE statement to remove the DBA role from OE:

```
REVOKE DBA FROM OE;

Revoke succeeded.
```

The user OE retains all other object and system privileges granted by the DBA and other users.

Terms to Know

alias	ODBC (Open Database Connectivity)
connection identifier	ODBC driver
DCL (Data Control Language)	OEM (Oracle Enterprise Manager)
DDL (Data Definition Language)	role
DML (Data Manipulation Language)	schema
host string	SQL (Structured Query Language)
JDBC (Java Database Connectivity)	thin client
OCI (Oracle Call Interface)	tiers

Review Questions

1. What are the three types of DML (Data Manipulation Language) statements?

2. If the user SCOTT is granted the privilege to insert records on the OE.WAREHOUSES table using the command GRANT INSERT ON OE.WAREHOUSES WITH GRANT OPTION, what does the WITH GRANT OPTION clause allow SCOTT to do?

3. Under which tiers of a three-tier Oracle environment does iSQL*Plus run?

4. What two methods are used to rename a column in the report output of a SQL SELECT statement?

5. ODBC provides what capability to client applications?

6. Which SELECT statement keyword removes duplicate rows from the result of the query?

7. What is the name of the set of library routines that allows a developer to send SQL statements from a C program?

8. What are some of the differences between a DELETE and a TRUNCATE statement?

9. The new MERGE statement combines the functionality of which two other DML statements?

10. What function does the DESCRIBE command perform in SQL*Plus or iSQL*Plus?

Chapter 3

Oracle Database Functions

Every DBA needs to know about built-in functions. Many of the day-to-day tasks of a DBA involve queries, and these queries often need to transform or summarize information in database tables and views. Many DBAs will also create and maintain a library of customized functions (also known as user-defined functions) for business areas in the company and help to deploy these user-defined functions.

This chapter covers the built-in functions and provides an introduction to user-defined functions. However, before we dig into the functions themselves, we'll talk about some of the general rules for building queries, including how the DUAL table is used, how NULL values work, and how numbers and strings are constructed.

Query Basics

In order to use functions, you need to know how to call them and how to construct their arguments. This section begins by explaining how the DUAL table allows you to use queries that don't involve a real table. Next, you'll learn about the ubiquitous NULL value and how it acts as a double-edged sword at times. Then we'll cover string literals and how to construct larger strings from one or more other strings and columns. Finally, you'll learn about numeric literals and operator precedence.

Once you know how to use the SELECT statement with the DUAL table, along with how string and numeric literals work, you'll be ready to explore the built-in functions. You'll see that they are potent tools to put into your DBA bag of tricks.

The *DUAL* Table

Because Oracle SQL is table-centric, most operations performed with SQL must reference some kind of table or view. For example, consider the following SQL statement:

```
SELECT NAME;

SELECT NAME
       *
ERROR at line 1:
ORA-00923: FROM keyword not found where expected
```

This returns an error, because the basic syntax of a SELECT statement requires that you select FROM something—in this case, a table.

DUAL

A special table, owned by the Oracle SYS user, that has one row and one column. It is useful for ad hoc queries that don't require rows from a specific table.

But what if you want to use the SELECT statement to perform some calculations or do some other operation that doesn't involve a particular table, such as check the system date and time? The *DUAL* table makes this possible. You reference the DUAL table when you need a table for syntactical reasons, not necessarily for the data in the table.

The DUAL table is a real table. It's owned by the user SYS and has one row. The table has only one column, which is named DUMMY and has a string with a length of 1. The value of DUMMY in the one and only row is X. You can see the DUAL table's structure in the iSQL*Plus output shown below.

It's true that anyone could create a table like this, with one row, and accomplish the same thing. But it's good practice to have one place where you always have one row and you always know the table name.

Since DUAL is a real table, you could certainly do something like this:

```
select sysdate, dummy from dual;
```

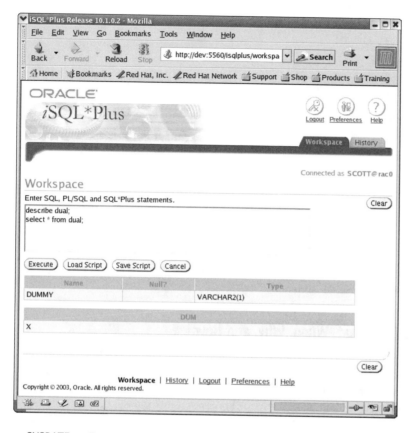

```
SYSDATE     D
--------- -
31-AUG-04 X

1 row selected.
```

But you already know what the value of DUMMY is in DUAL, so you really don't need to include this field on a query with DUAL.

And to make it clear that DUAL is a table just like any other, you could also do something like this:

```
select sysdate from dept;

SYSDATE
---------
31-AUG-04
```

```
31-AUG-04
31-AUG-04
31-AUG-04

4 rows selected.
```

Since the DEPT table has four rows, you get the SYSDATE four times.
Since you really need only one row, the DUAL table will fill the bill nicely:

```
select sysdate from dual;

SYSDATE
---------
31-AUG-04

1 row selected.
```

The DUAL table originally had two rows in early versions of Oracle, thus the
origin of the table name.

NULLs: What, When, Why, and How

NULL
A possible value for any Oracle column
that indicates the absence of any known
value for that column. A NULL is usually
used to represent a value that is unknown,
not applicable, or not available.

Simply put, a *NULL* value in an Oracle table is nothing. A NULL is not zero, a
blank character, or an empty string. It is no value whatsoever. NULLs can be the
source of much consternation when a query is not returning the expected results.

Using a NULL in an arithmetic expression returns a NULL, regardless of what
other operands and operations are in the expression. As an example, consider the
following query:

```
select 5+8, 5+0, 5+null, null+null from dual;

5+8          5+0          5+NULL      NULL+NULL
---------- ---------- ---------- ----------
          13           5

1 row selected.
```

NULL values are useful, however, to indicate when a value is unavailable,
unknown, or not applicable. For example, the commission for an employee who
is not in the Sales department would be NULL, or the department assigned to a
new employee could be NULL.

NOTE In certain functions—for example NVL, NVL2, and COALESCE—a NULL value as an
argument to the function will return a non-NULL result. This result is the exception, not
the rule.

String Literals and Concatenating Strings

A *string literal* in a SQL query is a sequence of zero, one, or more characters enclosed in single quotation marks (called *quotes* for short). Here are some valid string literals:

- `'JOHN SMITH'`
- `' '`
- `'123 Main St.'`

String literals may be combined with other string literals or table columns, and they may also be arguments to a function. Note that a zero-length string is not the same as a NULL string. You may use a NULL string to indicate that a value is missing or not yet known, and a zero-length string to indicate that the value is blank but known. For example, a new employee may not have a middle initial, and therefore their middle initial would be set to a zero-length string. But until we find out that they don't have a middle initial, it will temporarily be set to a NULL string.

Concatenation is the process of combining two or more string literals or columns into a single result. The concatenation operator || (two vertical bars) is used between the strings or columns to be combined. Alternatively, you can use the built-in string function CONCAT.

The following query demonstrates how string literals and database columns may be concatenated and act as arguments of a function:

```
select
    'Employee: ' || initcap(ename),
    concat('Dept: ',deptno)
    from emp;


'EMPLOYEE:'||INITCAP CONCAT('DEPT:',DEPTNO)
-------------------- -------------------------
Employee: Smith      Dept: 20
Employee: Allen      Dept: 30
Employee: Ward       Dept: 30
Employee: Jones      Dept: 20
Employee: Martin     Dept: 30
Employee: Blake      Dept: 30
Employee: Clark      Dept: 10
Employee: Scott      Dept: 20
Employee: King       Dept: 10
Employee: Turner     Dept: 30
Employee: Adams      Dept: 20
Employee: James      Dept: 30
```

string literal
A constant that can consist of any string of letters, digits, and special characters enclosed in single quotation marks.

concatenation
The process of combining two or more data elements into a single element. In Oracle SQL, concatenation can be accomplished by using the concatenation operator (a pair of vertical bars, | |) or the CONCAT function.

```
Employee: Ford      Dept: 20
Employee: Miller    Dept: 10

14 rows selected.
```

In the above query, there are two columns in the output: the string literal `'Employee: '` concatenated with the result of a string function on the employee name and the string literal `'Dept: '` concatenated with the department number of the employee. Notice how the case of a string is preserved within the single quotes. This example demonstrates both the concatenation operator `||` and the CONCAT function. Which you use depends on how many strings are to be concatenated, as well as your programming style. If you have more than two or three strings to concatenate, using vertical bars is more readable than using the CONCAT function over and over. However, if you are dealing with translating your queries from one character set to another on a different platform, vertical bars may not translate correctly; in this case, using the CONCAT function would be the best option for concatenating any number of strings.

Numeric Literals

numeric literal
A constant that can consist of numeric digits, plus the characters +, -, ., and E.

Numeric literals in Oracle are very straightforward and are similar to what is allowed in many programming languages: the digits 0–9, an optional decimal point, an optional sign, and an optional exponent using the letter *E* with its own optional sign. Here are some valid numeric literals:

- ◆ 1.456
- ◆ −.01
- ◆ 00000052
- ◆ +12.10
- ◆ −3.774E−16

Numbers are stored internally in scientific notation, with up to 20 bytes for the mantissa and 1 byte for the exponent. This results in a maximum precision of up to 38 digits.

Operators and Operator Precedence

Operator precedence specifies the order in which the operators are applied to the arguments of a mathematical expression when there is more than one operator in the expression. Think back to your middle school algebra class when you had to answer questions such as "A man bought 20 chickens and ducks, with a $2 discount per chicken and 50 cent discount per duck..." and you'll probably remember a few things about the order in which you had to evaluate an expression, once you figured out why a man was buying the chickens and ducks.

For example, the expression 5 * 6 + 10 is typically evaluated in most programming languages by multiplying 5 by 6, then adding 10 to the result. The expression 10 + 5 * 6 is typically evaluated in a similar manner. Because multiplication has a higher precedence than addition, 5 is multiplied by 6 first, then 10 is added to the result. If you want to add 10 to 5 first and then multiply that result by 6, write the expression with parentheses to override the assumed precedence: (10 + 5) * 6.

For operators that have an equal precedence, such as addition and subtraction or multiplication and division, the expression is evaluated from left to right. The expression 10 / 6 * 5 is evaluated by dividing 10 by 6 first and then multiplying the result by 5. When two operators have the same precedence, it's a good idea to use parentheses to eliminate any possible ambiguity: (10 / 6) * 5.

The rules for operator and conditional operator precedence in Oracle SQL are very similar to the rules in other programming languages such as C++ and Visual Basic. All standard operators have precedence over conditional operators.

Oracle's standard and conditional operators are presented in Table 3.1, listed in order of precedence (from highest to lowest).

Table 3.1   Standard and Conditional Operators and Precedence

Operator/Conditional	Description
+, – (unary), PRIOR	Positive, negative, tree traversal
*, /	Multiplication, division
+, – (binary), ||	Addition, subtraction, concatenation
=, !=, <, >, <=, >=	Comparison operators
IS [NOT] NULL, LIKE, [NOT] BETWEEN, [NOT] IN, EXISTS, IS OF	SQL-specific comparison operators
**, NOT	Exponentiation, logical negation
AND	True if both operands are true
OR	True if either operand is true
UNION, UNION ALL, INTERSECT, MINUS	Set operators

The use of the standard and conditional operators will be explained throughout the rest of this book.

Built-In Single-Row Functions

The previous sections covered all the basics of a SELECT statement using DUAL and how strings and numbers are constructed, compared, and combined. Now we can start looking at some of Oracle's built-in single-row functions that operate on strings and numbers in database table columns.

function
A named set of predefined programming language commands that performs a specific task given zero, one, or more arguments and returns a value.

In both Oracle SQL and most programming languages, a *function* is a predefined set of steps that can be accessed using a common name. A function may include zero, one, or more arguments that are passed to the function, and it may return a result. For example, the SQRT function calculates the square root of a number and returns a value of 1.414214 when called with an argument of 2: SQRT(2) = 1.414214.

single-row function
A function that may have zero, one, or more arguments and will return one result for each row returned in a query.

Single-row functions are functions that may have zero, one, or more arguments and will return one result for each row returned in the query. Functions can be called in the SELECT, WHERE, and ORDER BY clauses of a SELECT statement. (The WHERE and ORDER BY clauses are used to restrict and organize query output, as explained in the next chapter.)

NOTE

All of these functions are available for use in both SQL and PL/SQL (Oracle's SQL-based programming language). As of Oracle9*i*, SQL and PL/SQL share the same core SQL engine.

In this section, we'll cover the highlights of Oracle's string functions, numeric functions, date functions, conversion functions, and general functions that don't fall neatly into any of the other categories.

String Functions

String functions are functions that perform some kind of transformation on a string literal, a column containing a string, or an expression consisting of string literals and table columns. String functions will return a string as the result of the transformation. Table 3.2 briefly describes the built-in string functions.

Table 3.2   Built-In String Functions

Function	Description
ASCII	Returns the decimal equivalent of the first character of a string
CHR	Given a decimal number, returns the ASCII equivalent character
CONCAT	Concatenates two strings
INITCAP	Converts the first letter of each word in a string to uppercase
INSTR	Searches a string for an occurrence of another string
LENGTH	Returns the length of a string
LOWER	Converts all characters in a string to lowercase
LPAD	Left-fills a character string with a given character for a specified total length

Table 3.2   Built-In String Functions *(continued)*

Function	Description
LTRIM	Trims a specific character from the front of a string
REGEXP_INSTR	Searches a string for an occurrence of a regular expression
REGEXP_REPLACE	Replaces occurrences of a specified regular expression with another string
REGEXP_SUBSTR	Returns a substring of another string matching a regular expression
REPLACE	Replaces occurrences of a specified string within another string
RPAD	Right-fills a string with a given character for a specified total length
RTRIM	Trims a specific character from the end of a string
SOUNDEX	Returns a phonetic equivalent of a string
SUBSTR	Returns a specified portion of a string
TRANSLATE	Converts single characters to alternate single characters in a string
TREAT	Changes the declared type of an expression
TRIM	Removes leading, trailing, or both leading and trailing characters from a string
UPPER	Converts all characters in a string to uppercase

Let's consider some practical uses for string functions. Now that Scott's widget company is off the ground, Scott regrets some of the shortcuts he took when creating the initial version of the database. The users don't find the reports very readable, and it would look a lot better if the names were in uppercase and lowercase letters.

The INITCAP function offers a quick way to clean up names and addresses that may be in all uppercase, all lowercase, or mixed case. It will work for a first pass over the data to at least make the names and addresses somewhat readable. Until Scott can overhaul the database, he can use the INITCAP function and column aliases to make things look a bit better:

string function
A function that operates on string literals, columns containing strings, or an expression containing string literals and table columns, returning a string as the result.

```
select empno "Empl#", initcap(ename) "EmplName" from emp;

     Empl# EmplName
---------- ----------
      7369 Smith
      7499 Allen
```

```
7521 Ward
7566 Jones
7654 Martin
7698 Blake
7782 Clark
7788 Scott
7839 King
7844 Turner
7876 Adams
7900 James
7902 Ford
7934 Miller
```

```
14 rows selected.
```

NOTE The INITCAP function cannot capitalize mixed-case names correctly. For example, if one of the employee names were McDonald, the INITCAP function would not capitalize that name correctly (unless there was a space between *MC* and *DONALD*, which wouldn't be right either).

The next day, the Publications department wants to put the employee numbers and names on an intranet web page. The web page designers would like the employee number left justified and the employee name right justified, for a total width of 40 characters. Between the employee number and name must be a series of dots (or periods). To provide the complete 40-character field, Scott must use the LENGTH and LPAD functions in addition to what he already had from the example above:

```
select empno || lpad(initcap(ename),40-length(empno),'.')
"Employee Directory" from emp;
```

```
Employee Directory

7369.............................Smith
7499.............................Allen
7521..............................Ward
7566............................Jones
7654...........................Martin
7698............................Blake
7782............................Clark
7788............................Scott
7839.............................King
7844...........................Turner
```

```
7876............................Adams
7900............................James
7902.............................Ford
7934...........................Miller
```

14 rows selected.

This query uses three string functions: two of them are nested within another function, plus a concatenation operation. Let's break down the query to clarify how it works.

As you've seen, the function call INITCAP(ename) changes the first letter of each word to uppercase. The function call LENGTH(empno) returns the length of a character string. In this case, there is an implicit conversion of a numeric type to a string type. An *implicit conversion* occurs automatically when Oracle evaluates an expression; conversely, an *explicit conversion* occurs when the SQL statement makes no assumptions about how Oracle will convert one datatype to another and uses one or more of the built-in functions to perform the conversion. The column is converted to a character string, and the length of the converted character string is returned.

The LPAD function will left-pad a character string to a specified number of characters with the character you specify. Scott wants to end up with a total of 40 characters, so he subtracts the number of characters that the employee number would take up. Here, he will left-pad the employee name with periods, less the amount of space taken up by the employee number. Once the LPAD function is evaluated, he will concatenate the employee number at the front, and once again, he will allow the implicit conversion of the employee number from numeric to string.

Finally, Scott wants the title for the report to look readable, so he assigns a column alias to the result of the concatenated function calls. The column alias can act as a report title.

implicit conversion
Conversion of one datatype to another that occurs automatically when columns or constants with dissimilar datatypes appear in an expression.

explicit conversion
Conversion of one datatype to another in an expression using function calls such as TO_CHAR instead of relying on automatic conversion rules (implicit conversion).

Numeric Functions

Numeric functions are functions that perform some kind of transformation on a numeric literal, a column containing a number, or an expression consisting of numeric literals and table columns. Numeric functions will return a number as the result of the transformation. Table 3.3 briefly describes the built-in numeric functions.

numeric function
A function that operates on numeric literals, columns containing numbers, or an expression containing numeric literals and table columns, returning a number as the result.

Table 3.3   Built-In Numeric Functions

Function	Description
ABS	Returns the absolute value of the argument
ACOS	Returns the arc cosine

Table 3.3   Built-In Numeric Functions *(continued)*

Function	Description
ASIN	Returns the arc sine
ATAN	Returns the arc tangent
ATAN2	Returns the arc tangent of two values
BITAND	Performs a bitwise AND on two arguments
CEIL	Returns the next highest integer
COS	Returns the cosine
COSH	Returns the hyperbolic cosine
EXP	Raises e (2.718281828…) to the specified power
FLOOR	Returns the next lowest integer
LN	Returns the natural logarithm (base e)
LOG	Returns the base 10 logarithm
MOD	Returns the remainder of the first argument divided by the second, using FLOOR in the calculation
NANVL	Returns an alternate value if the first argument is non-numeric
POWER	Raises a number to an arbitrary power
REMAINDER	Returns the remainder of the first argument divided by the second, similar to MOD except that REMAINDER uses ROUND
ROUND	Returns a rounded value to an arbitrary precision
SIGN	Returns -1 if the argument is negative, 0 if 0, or 1 if positive
SIN	Returns the sine
SQRT	Returns the square root of the argument
TAN	Returns the tangent
TRUNC	Truncates a number to an arbitrary precision

Scott's company has survived its first month and has even turned a small profit. Scott wants to find a way to distribute the first month's profit in a fair manner, so he turns to the company mathematician and statistician, Julie. She suggests that the employees get a one-time bonus that is based on the square root of their current salary. Scott can run the following query to see what the potential bonuses might be using the SQRT function:

```
select ename, sal, sqrt(sal) from emp;
```

ENAME	SAL	SQRT(SAL)
SMITH	700	26.4575131
ALLEN	1600	40
WARD	1250	35.3553391
JONES	2975	54.5435606
MARTIN	1250	35.3553391
BLAKE	2850	53.3853913
CLARK	2450	49.4974747
SCOTT	3000	54.7722558
KING	5000	70.7106781
TURNER	1300	36.0555128
ADAMS	1100	33.1662479
JAMES	950	30.82207
FORD	3000	54.7722558
MILLER	1600	40

```
14 rows selected.
```

Scott seems to like this idea, since the bonuses for the highest paid workers are not as big of a percentage of their base wage as they are for the lowest paid workers.

The report is a bit unreadable; Scott wants the bonus rounded to two digits with a better heading for the bonus. The new query looks something like this, using the ROUND function:

```
select ename, sal, round(sqrt(sal),2) "Bonus" from emp;
```

ENAME	SAL	Bonus
SMITH	700	26.46
ALLEN	1600	40
WARD	1250	35.36
JONES	2975	54.54
MARTIN	1250	35.36
BLAKE	2850	53.39
CLARK	2450	49.5
SCOTT	3000	54.77
KING	5000	70.71
TURNER	1300	36.06
ADAMS	1100	33.17
JAMES	950	30.82
FORD	3000	54.77

```
MILLER            1600            40
```

```
14 rows selected.
```

The report is looking better, but the Bonus column is still not formatted quite right. We'll look at ways to fix this in the section on conversion functions later in this chapter.

Since a lot of employees are on commission, Scott may want to base the bonus on both the salary and commission. We'll look at how to do this in the section on general functions.

Date Functions

Date functions are functions that perform some kind of transformation on a date literal, a column containing a date, or an expression consisting of date literals and table columns. Date functions will return a date or a string containing a portion of the date as the result of the transformation. Table 3.4 describes the date-related functions.

Table 3.4   Built-In Date Functions

Function	Description
ADD_MONTHS	Increments a date value by a number of months
CURRENT_DATE	Returns the current date for the session's time zone
CURRENT_TIMESTAMP	Returns the current date and time in the session's time zone to a particular precision
DBTIMEZONE	Returns the database time zone as an offset in hours and minutes from UTC
EXTRACT	Returns a portion of the date and time (e.g., hour, month) from a timestamp value
FROM_TZ	Returns a timestamp with the time zone for a given combination of an individual timestamp and time zone
LAST_DAY	Returns the last day of the month for a given date
LOCALTIMESTAMP	Returns the current date and time in the session's time zone to a given precision
MONTHS_BETWEEN	Returns the numeric number of months between two date arguments
NEW_TIME	Returns a date in a second time zone given a date in the first time zone
NEXT_DAY	Finds the next occurrence of a specific day of the week given a date

Table 3.4   Built-In Date Functions *(continued)*

Function	Description
ROUND	Rounds a date value to a specific unit of time
SESSIONTIMEZONE	Returns the database time zone (DBTIMEZONE) unless altered during the session
SYS_EXTRACT_UTC	Returns the UTC for a timestamp with time zone value
SYSDATE	Returns the current date and time
SYSTIMESTAMP	Returns a timestamp with the time zone for the database date and time
TRUNC	Truncates a date value to a specified unit of time
TZ_OFFSET	Converts a text time zone to a numeric offset

Date and time handling has been greatly enhanced since Oracle9*i*. Not only can the precision of Oracle's timestamp datatypes support fractions of a second to nine decimal places, other functions and system parameters smooth the process of handling Oracle servers and sessions across multiple time zones. This is handy for companies with national and international business.

NOTE

When Scott started his widget company, he hired most of the people away from a competitor. As part of the employment agreement, he kept the new employees' original hire date for the new company. He wants to see how many employees have been working for the company (or competitor) more than 250 months. He can run this query to get the answer:

```
select ename, hiredate, months_between(sysdate,hiredate)
      "Months" from emp;
```

```
ENAME      HIREDATE    Months
---------- --------- ----------
SMITH      17-DEC-80 260.608914
ALLEN      20-FEB-81  258.51214
WARD       22-FEB-81 258.447624
JONES      02-APR-81 257.092785
MARTIN     28-SEP-81 251.254076
BLAKE      01-MAY-81 256.125043
CLARK      09-JUN-81 254.866979
SCOTT      19-APR-87 184.544398
KING       17-NOV-81 249.608914
TURNER     08-SEP-81 251.899237
ADAMS      23-MAY-87 183.415366
```

date function

A function that performs some kind of transformation on a date literal, a column containing a date, or an expression consisting of date literals and table columns. Date functions return a date or a string containing a portion of the date as the result of the transformation.

```
JAMES       03-DEC-81 249.060527
FORD        03-DEC-81 249.060527
MILLER      23-JAN-82 247.415366
```

14 rows selected.

Note that there are two functions being called: SYSDATE and MONTHS_ BETWEEN. SYSDATE has no arguments; it merely returns the current date and time, so the parentheses must be omitted. The MONTHS_BETWEEN function returns the difference between dates in months. If you wanted to know the number of days instead, you would not need the MONTHS_BETWEEN function and could use the expression SYSDATE-HIREDATE instead. Date arithmetic returns values in units of days.

Conversion Functions

As the name implies, conversion functions convert between numbers, strings, and date values. The common conversion functions are described in Table 3.5.

Table 3.5   Built-In Conversion Functions

Function	Description
ASCIISTR	Converts non-ASCII characters to ASCII
CAST	Converts one datatype to another
NUMTODSINTERVAL	Converts a number and a character string representing a unit of time to an INTERVAL DAY TO SECOND type
NUMTOYMINTERVAL	Converts a number and a character string representing a unit of time to an INTERVAL YEAR TO MONTH type
TO_CHAR	Converts a date or a number to character format
TO_DATE	Converts a character format date to a DATE datatype
TO_DSINTERVAL	Converts a character string to an INTERVAL DAY TO SECOND datatype
TO_NUMBER	Converts a character string to an internal numeric format
TO_YMINTERVAL	Converts a character string to an INTERVAL YEAR TO MONTH datatype

Scott knows he can improve on the query he used to see which employees have been with the company more than 250 months. Rather than see the number of months since the original hire date, he wants to see the dates when the employee will reach or has reached the 250-month mark. For this result, he will use the NUMTOYMINTERVAL function to add 250 months to the hire date:

```
select ename, hiredate, hiredate +
      numtoyminterval(250,'month') "250 Months" from emp;
```

```
ENAME       HIREDATE  250 Month
----------  --------- ---------
SMITH       17-DEC-80 17-OCT-01
ALLEN       20-FEB-81 20-DEC-01
WARD        22-FEB-81 22-DEC-01
JONES       02-APR-81 02-FEB-02
MARTIN      28-SEP-81 28-JUL-02
BLAKE       01-MAY-81 01-MAR-02
CLARK       09-JUN-81 09-APR-02
SCOTT       19-APR-87 19-FEB-08
KING        17-NOV-81 17-SEP-02
TURNER      08-SEP-81 08-JUL-02
ADAMS       23-MAY-87 23-MAR-08
JAMES       03-DEC-81 03-OCT-02
FORD        03-DEC-81 03-OCT-02
MILLER      23-JAN-82 23-NOV-02

14 rows selected.
```

Scott could have used the function TO_YMINTERVAL('20-10') to add 20 years and 10 months (250 months total) to the hire date. Whether to use one method or another depends on how you want to specify the format—as a discrete number of months or years or as a combination of months and years.

Now that Scott knows more about the conversion functions, he wants to revisit one of the queries he wrote previously:

```
select ename, sal, round(sqrt(sal),2) "Bonus" from emp;
```

The problem with this query was that the default numeric formatting didn't look good, even after applying the ROUND function. Scott can apply another function here, TO_CHAR, to force the bonus to have two decimal places, even if the bonus does not have any significance beyond the first decimal point. The TO_CHAR function specifies the value to be formatted and the desired format, and it can be used to format both numbers and date values. Here, Scott wants to fix that rounded number:

```
select ename, sal, to_char(round(sqrt(sal),2),'9999.99')
      "Bonus" from emp;
```

```
ENAME             SAL Bonus
----------  ----------  --------
SMITH             700     26.46
ALLEN            1600     40.00
WARD             1250     35.36
JONES            2975     54.54
MARTIN           1250     35.36
BLAKE            2850     53.39
CLARK            2450     49.50
SCOTT            3000     54.77
KING             5000     70.71
TURNER           1300     36.06
ADAMS            1100     33.17
JAMES             950     30.82
FORD             3000     54.77
MILLER           1600     40.00
```

14 rows selected.

In addition to the '9' digit in the format, you can use '0' to force leading zeros, a '$' to show dollar amounts, a '-' for leading or trailing signs, commas to make large numbers more readable, or even roman numerals. Table 3.6 shows a few sample numeric formats and how the value 7322.8 would look in that format.

Table 3.6   Numeric Format Examples Using *TO_CHAR*

Format	Result
99999.99	7322.80
$999.999	#########
00999.90	07322.80
99,999.99	7,322.80
S9999	+7323
9.9999EEEE	7.3228E+03

Notice that when a number will not fit into the format provided, it is displayed as all #s. Notice also that rounding will automatically occur if there are not enough positions to the right of the decimal to accommodate the entire number.

General Functions

The category of general functions covers all of the functions that don't fit neatly into a single category. Many of them are shortcuts that allow the DBA or developer to avoid needing to use PL/SQL for certain types of processing, such as a conditional operation that would normally require more than one statement. Table 3.7 briefly describes the general functions.

Table 3.7   Built-In General Functions

Function	Description
CASE	Allows embedded IF–THEN–ELSE logic in a SQL statement
COALESCE	Returns the first non-NULL value from a list of values
DECODE	Compares an expression to a list of possible values and returns a specified corresponding return value
DUMP	Displays the internal value of an Oracle datatype
GREATEST	Returns the highest value in a list of values given the sort order
LEAST	Returns the lowest value in a list of values given the sort order
NULLIF	Given two expressions, returns NULL if they are equal
NVL	Given two expressions, returns the second if the first one is NULL
NVL2	Given three expressions, returns the third if the first one is NULL, and returns the second if the first one is not NULL
VSIZE	Returns the number of bytes for the internal representation of the expression

Scott is continuing to analyze the profitability versus expenses in his widget company by looking at the total compensation for each employee. Most employees are salaried, but a few are salaried with a commission. Scott's first attempt at a total compensation calculation is something like this:

```
select ename, sal+comm from emp;

ENAME        SAL+COMM
----------   ----------
SMITH
ALLEN            1900
WARD             1750
JONES
MARTIN           2650
BLAKE
CLARK
```

```
SCOTT
KING
TURNER              1300
ADAMS
JAMES
FORD
MILLER
```

```
14 rows selected.
```

Wait a minute, what happened to the salaries for the other employees? As noted earlier in the chapter, NULL values provide a great benefit in that they can indicate that a value is unknown, unavailable, or not applicable. However, when combined in some kind of calculation with non-NULL values, the result will always be NULL. For example, adding 15 to an unknown value will result in a new value that is also unknown.

In the case of the employee salaries and commissions, however, Scott wants to treat the commissions as zero if they are NULL for the purpose of calculating total compensation. For this, he will use the NVL function. NVL takes two arguments. The first argument is compared to NULL, and if it is NULL, it returns the second argument; otherwise, it returns the first argument. Scott's query can be modified with the NVL function to produce the correct results:

```
select ename, sal+nvl(comm,0) from emp;
```

```
ENAME        SAL+NVL(COMM,0)
----------   ---------------
SMITH                    700
ALLEN                   1900
WARD                    1750
JONES                   2975
MARTIN                  2650
BLAKE                   2850
CLARK                   2450
SCOTT                   3000
KING                    5000
TURNER                  1300
ADAMS                   1100
JAMES                    950
FORD                    3000
MILLER                  1600
```

```
14 rows selected.
```

That looks a lot better. Other, more esoteric functions such as VSIZE are more often used by DBAs to determine how much space a particular column for a particular row is using, in bytes:

```
select ename, vsize(ename), sal, vsize(sal) from emp;

ENAME      VSIZE(ENAME)        SAL VSIZE(SAL)
---------- ------------ ---------- ----------
SMITH                 5        700          2
ALLEN                 5       1600          2
WARD                  4       1250          3
JONES                 5       2975          3
MARTIN                6       1250          3
BLAKE                 5       2850          3
CLARK                 5       2450          3
SCOTT                 5       3000          2
KING                  4       5000          2
TURNER                6       1300          2
ADAMS                 5       1100          2
JAMES                 5        950          3
FORD                  4       3000          2
MILLER                6       1600          2

14 rows selected.
```

The lengths for the employee names make sense, but why would a salary of 3000 take up less space than a salary of 2450? This is because all numbers are stored internally in scientific notation. Only the 3 from the 3000 salary needs to be stored with an exponent of 3, whereas the salary 2450 is stored as 2.45 with an exponent of 3. More digits of precision require more storage space in Oracle's variable internal numeric format.

User-Defined Functions

Even though many functions come prewritten and packaged with the default installation of the Oracle software, sometimes you need some functionality that cannot be provided by those built-in functions. Oracle's programming language, PL/SQL, which stands for Programming Language SQL, can come to the rescue.

The advanced techniques on how functions, procedures, and packages are constructed and used are beyond the scope of this book. Here, you'll get an introduction to *user-defined functions*, including a look at how you could write a custom function that's available to all database users.

user-defined function
A function that is written by an analyst, user, or database administrator and does not come as part of the default installation of the Oracle server software.

stored function

A sequence of PL/SQL variable declarations and statements that can be called as a unit, passing zero or more arguments and returning a single value of a specified datatype. Built-in stored functions are created when the database software is installed. Customized or user-defined functions are defined by application developers or DBAs.

Using PL/SQL, a database analyst, database user, or database administrator can construct a user-defined function. A user-defined function has the same characteristics as a built-in function. It will take zero, one, or more values and return a single value as its result. Functions in Oracle, whether they are built-in or written by a developer or DBA, are often known as *stored functions*, since the source code and the compiled code are both stored in the database.

As an example, let's once again consider Scott's burgeoning widget company. Since the company is still small, Scott must perform the duties of both an application developer and a DBA. The HR department appears to frequently run queries that combine the employee name, job, and department into a formatted string for display on both web pages and corporate documents. To standardize the format of this string throughout the organization, Scott wrote a function called FORMAT_EMP that can be used by any department to display the employee name, job, and department, as follows:

```
Department: 10    Employee: Smith    Title: Shipping
```

Scott creates his stored function like this:

```
create or replace function
  FORMAT_EMP (DeptNo IN number,
              EmpName IN varchar2,
              Title IN varchar2) return varchar2
is
  concat_rslt   varchar2(100);
begin
  concat_rslt :=
    'Department: ' || to_char(DeptNo) ||
    '   Employee: ' || initcap(EmpName) ||
    '   Title: ' || initcap(Title);
  return (concat_rslt);
end;
```

The first line of this command will create the function if it doesn't exist or replace it if it already exists. The next three lines define what kinds of values are going to be provided as input to the function, as well as what kind of value will be returned. In this example, Scott will provide the FORMAT_EMP function with a number and two strings, and he expects a string to be returned. He needs to create the function only once. By default, only the user who created the function can use it.

Line 6 declares a local variable called concat_rslt, which will temporarily hold the formatted string result. In a stored procedure or function, all of the actual processing occurs between the begin and the end keywords. In lines 8 to 11, the variable concat_rslt is assigned the formatted value using some of the

Oracle built-in functions. Finally, in line 12, the function returns the result to the calling program, which, in this case, is a SQL statement similar to the following:

```
select format_emp(deptno,ename,job) from emp;
```

```
Department: 20    Employee: Smith    Title: Clerk
Department: 30    Employee: Allen    Title: Salesman
Department: 30    Employee: Ward     Title: Salesman
Department: 20    Employee: Jones    Title: Manager
Department: 30    Employee: Martin   Title: Salesman
Department: 30    Employee: Blake    Title: Manager
Department: 10    Employee: Clark    Title: Manager
Department: 20    Employee: Scott    Title: Analyst
Department: 10    Employee: King     Title: President
Department: 30    Employee: Turner   Title: Salesman
Department: 20    Employee: Adams    Title: Clerk
Department: 30    Employee: James    Title: Clerk
Department: 20    Employee: Ford     Title: Analyst
Department: 10    Employee: Miller   Title: Clerk
```

```
14 rows selected.
```

Note that the names you give for the parameters in the function need not be the same as the names of the columns in the table you're using. In fact, you could use this function just as well with some values that aren't even in a table:

```
select format_emp(180,'JOHNSEN','OP MGR') from dual;
```

```
Department: 180    Employee: Johnsen    Title: Op Mgr
```

```
1 row selected.
```

Notice how you can use objects such as stored functions for standardization within an organization. An Accounting department employee does not need to remember how to format the employee information, because the formatting is kept in a common location via the stored function.

Scott can grant rights for other departments to use this function also. As an added bonus for the DBA, only a single copy of this function is stored in the *shared pool* for use by an unlimited number of users. This reduces the overall memory requirements for the database and can improve the response time for a query.

shared pool
An area of memory within the total amount of memory allocated for the Oracle database that can hold recently executed SQL statements, PL/SQL procedures and packages, as well as cached information from the system tables.

NOTE
It's important for the DBA to keep track of how many stored procedures and functions are running during the course of a business day, because there are memory and performance implications for the objects that share space in the database's shared pool. If there are too many other SQL statements and frequent accesses to database control structures, then the stored functions and procedures may be temporarily removed from the shared pool, thus affecting the response time the next time the user calls the stored function or procedure because it must be reread from disk.

Terms to Know

concatenation

date function

DUAL

explicit conversion

function

implicit conversion

NULL

numeric function

numeric literal

shared pool

single-row function

stored function

string function

string literal

user-defined function

Review Questions

1. What is another way to write the following SQL statement by using another function?

    ```
    select empno || lpad(initcap(ename),
    40-length(empno),'.')
    "Employee Directory" from emp;
    ```

2. Which function would you use to perform an explicit conversion from a number to a string?

3. How can you rewrite the function call NUMTOYMINTERVAL(17, 'year') using the function TO_YMINTERVAL?

4. What is the result of a number added to a NULL value?

5. What is the result of formatting the number –232.6 using the format mask '9999.99S'?

6. Rank the following operators or conditionals based on priority, from highest to lowest: *, OR, ||, >=

7. The DUAL table has how many rows and how many columns?

8. True or false: Strings and numbers can be concatenated.

9. Write a SELECT statement with a built-in function or functions that will format the string 'Queen' with the '!' character padded for a total of 20 characters on the left side and with the '?' character padded for a total of 30 characters on the right. (Hint: Use nested functions.)

10. What functionality does the Oracle TIMESTAMP datatype have over the DATE datatype?

Chapter 4

Restricting, Sorting, and Grouping Data

Unless your database tables are very small, or your data reporting needs are very limited, you will want to restrict the rows returned from your queries. In cases where you want to see the results of the queries in a particular order, you will want to sort the results. Grouping the data—for example, grouping sales figures by month, salary totals by department, and so forth—can be done in conjunction with restricting and sorting the data in a SQL statement.

Scott's widget company has been growing by leaps and bounds over the past few months, and it has expanded to international locations. While Scott has enjoyed being the data analyst and DBA, he has turned over these roles to Janice. The employee-related database tables have been redesigned and turned over to the HR department. All of our examples from this point on will use the HR schema, which contains the following tables: COUNTRIES, DEPARTMENTS, EMPLOYEES, JOBS, JOB_ HISTORY, LOCATIONS, and REGIONS. The names of these tables should be self-explanatory.

The *WHERE* Clause

A lot happens in the WHERE clause. This is the place where the rows (with columns both actual and derived) from the list specified in the SELECT clause are trimmed down to only the results you need to see. Starting with the syntax described in Chapter 2, "SQL*Plus and iSQL*Plus Basics," we can expand the SELECT statement syntax as follows:

```
SELECT * | {[DISTINCT] column | expression [alias], ...}
   FROM tablename
[WHERE condition ... ];
```

The WHERE clause may have one or more conditions, separated by AND and OR and optionally grouped in parentheses to override the default precedence.

From the perspective of the table, the SELECT clause slices a table vertically, and the WHERE clause slices it horizontally.

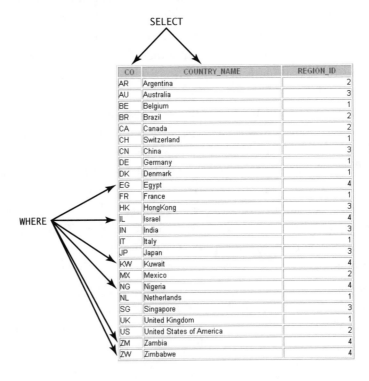

CO	COUNTRY_NAME	REGION_ID
AR	Argentina	2
AU	Australia	3
BE	Belgium	1
BR	Brazil	2
CA	Canada	2
CH	Switzerland	1
CN	China	3
DE	Germany	1
DK	Denmark	1
EG	Egypt	4
FR	France	1
HK	HongKong	3
IL	Israel	4
IN	India	3
IT	Italy	1
JP	Japan	3
KW	Kuwait	4
MX	Mexico	2
NG	Nigeria	4
NL	Netherlands	1
SG	Singapore	3
UK	United Kingdom	1
US	United States of America	2
ZM	Zambia	4
ZW	Zimbabwe	4

Comparison Conditions

A WHERE clause will often compare one column's value to a constant or compare two of the columns to each other in some way. Table 4.1 lists the comparison operators that are valid within a WHERE clause.

Table 4.1   Comparison Operators

Comparison Operator	Definition
=	Equal to
>	Greater than
>=	Greater than or equal to
<	Less than
<=	Less than or equal to
<>, !=, ^=	Not equal to

In Chapter 3, "Oracle Database Functions," you learned about operator precedence. The comparison operators are lower in precedence only to the arithmetic operators *, /, +, and − and the concatenation operator | |. This makes a lot of sense when you consider how expressions are typically used in WHERE clauses: Some kind of arithmetic operation is performed on one or more columns or constants, and that result is compared to another constant, column, or arithmetic operation on one or more columns or constants. For instance, consider this WHERE clause:

```
where salary * 1.10 > 24000
```

This example will evaluate SALARY * 1.10 first and then do the comparison to 24000.

In Scott's widget company, another corporate shakeup has occurred, and King is once again the president of the company. Janice, in her analyst role, is running some reports against the EMPLOYEES table for King, whose first task is to do a thorough salary review for all employees who have salaries that are within $10,000 of his salary. Janice knows that King's salary is $24,000, so she will specify this numeric literal in the query, along with the $10,000 for the difference in salary:

```
select employee_id "Emp ID", last_name "Last Name",
    salary "Salary" from employees
    where salary + 10000 > 24000;
```

```
Emp ID Last Name                    Salary
---------- ------------------------ ----------
       100 King                       24000
       101 Kochhar                    17000
       102 De Haan                    17000
```

3 rows selected.

A few things come to mind right away. First, King himself is in the list. You will learn how to remove his name in the next section. Janice could have also written the WHERE clause the other way around:

```
where 24000 < salary + 10000;
```

and the results of the query would be the same. Janice could have also saved a bit of processing time by calculating the salary cutoff number before writing the query:

```
where salary > 14000;
```

How you write your WHERE clause may be about style, readability, and documentation more than it is about processing speed, which is why the first version of the WHERE clause might be the best choice.

NOTE   Column aliases are not allowed in the WHERE clause. The actual column names must be used.

AND, OR, and NOT

The WHERE clause using comparison operators is really powerful, but in reality, you usually have more than one condition for selecting rows. Sometimes you need all of the conditions to be true, sometimes you need only one of the conditions to be true, and sometimes you want to specify what you don't need. You can accomplish this by using AND, OR, and NOT in your WHERE clauses.

Using an AND between two comparison conditions will give you rows from the table that satisfy both conditions. In one of the queries above, Janice noticed that King's name was returned in the query that was looking for other employees who had salaries close to King's. There is no need to include King in this query. Since Janice knows King's employee ID, she can remove him from the results of those queries by adding an AND condition, as follows:

```
select employee_id "Emp ID", last_name "Last Name",
    salary "Salary" from employees
    where salary + 10000 > 24000
    and employee_id != 100;
```

```
Emp ID Last Name                        Salary
---------- ------------------------ ----------
       101 Kochhar                      17000
       102 De Haan                      17000
```

```
2 rows selected.
```

The rules of precedence tell us that AND is very low on the list, and therefore the AND operation is performed last in the WHERE clause. However, for clarity, it doesn't hurt to add parentheses to make the conditional expressions more obvious:

```
where (salary + 10000 > 24000)
    and (employee_id != 100);
```

There are other ways to remove King from the query. We'll discuss some of these methods in Chapter 6, "Advanced SQL Queries."

Now King decides that he wants to include anyone who works in the IT department, in addition to those whose salaries are close to his. Janice recognizes that this is a job for the OR operator. She modifies the query to include those employees who are in the IT department, using the JOB_ID column:

```
select employee_id "Emp ID", last_name "Last Name",
    salary "Salary" from employees
    where (salary + 10000 > 24000)
    and (employee_id != 100)
    or job_id = 'IT_PROG';
```

```
Emp ID Last Name                        Salary
---------- ------------------------ ----------
       101 Kochhar                      17000
       102 De Haan                      17000
       103 Hunold                        9000
       104 Ernst                         6000
       105 Austin                        4800
       106 Pataballa                     4800
       107 Lorentz                       4200
```

```
7 rows selected.
```

Since the AND has a higher priority than the OR, the salary and employee ID comparisons are evaluated to see if they are both true; if so, the row is returned. If either one or the other is not true, the row might still be returned if the employee is in the IT department. Janice can make this WHERE clause more readable by putting in the parentheses, even if they're not needed:

```
where ((salary + 10000 > 24000)
and (employee_id != 100))
or (job_id = 'IT_PROG');
```

TIP When in doubt about operator precedence, use parentheses. Extra parentheses add a negligible amount of processing time and provide additional documentation benefits.

Janice expects that the other shoe will drop in a month or two, when King will ask for a report that has everyone else in it. This is a good place to use NOT. Janice can use this operator to negate the entire set of conditions that gave the first set of rows, thus returning the rest of the rows:

```
select employee_id "Emp ID", last_name "Last Name",
   salary "Salary" from employees
   where not
   (
      (salary + 10000 > 24000)
      and (employee_id != 100)
      or job_id = 'IT_PROG'
   )
;
      Emp ID Last Name                         Salary
   ---------- ------------------------- ----------
         100 King                              24000
         108 Greenberg                         12000
         109 Faviet                             9000
         110 Chen                               8200

   ...
         203 Mavris                             6500
         204 Baer                              10000
         205 Higgins                           12000
         206 Gietz                              8300
```

100 rows selected.

Note how Janice merely put the entire previous WHERE clause into parentheses and added a NOT in the front. One query returns a given set of rows, and a second query returns everything but the given set of rows. So, between the two queries, she has covered the entire table. Janice will have this report ready for King when he asks for it.

BETWEEN, IN, and LIKE

The BETWEEN, IN, and LIKE operators provide more ways to trim down the number of rows returned from a query. BETWEEN gives you an easy way to check for a value that falls within a certain range. The IN operator can help you find values in a list. LIKE can help you find character strings that match a certain pattern. Adding NOT to these will give you just the opposite set of rows.

BETWEEN a Rock and a Hard Place

The BETWEEN operator in a WHERE clause will limit the rows to a range that is specified by a beginning value and an ending value; the range is inclusive. The values can be dates, numbers, or character strings. The column values to be compared will be converted to the datatypes of the values in the BETWEEN operator as needed.

Each quarter at Scott's widget company, employees are recognized for years of service to the company. Janice is in charge of generating the report that lists the employees who have their anniversary within the next three months. Her query will use one of the functions mentioned in the previous chapter, EXTRACT, which returns one of the individual components of a DATE datatype.

```
select employee_id "Emp ID", department_id "Dept ID",
   hire_date "Hire Date",
   last_name || ', ' || first_name "Name" from employees
   /* Oct to Dec */
   where extract(month from hire_date) between 10 and 12;
```

Emp ID	Dept ID	Hire Date	Name
113	100	07-DEC-99	Popp, Luis
114	30	07-DEC-94	Raphaely, Den
116	30	24-DEC-97	Baida, Shelli
118	30	15-NOV-98	Himuro, Guy
123	50	10-OCT-97	Jasper, Susan Abigail
124	50	16-NOV-99	Mourgos, Kevin
130	50	30-OCT-97	Atkinson, Mozhe
135	50	12-DEC-99	Gee, Ki
138	50	26-OCT-97	Stiles, Stephen
141	50	17-OCT-95	Rajs, Trenna
145	80	01-OCT-96	Russell, John
148	80	15-OCT-99	Cambrault, Gerald
154	80	09-DEC-98	Cambrault, Nanette
155	80	23-NOV-99	Tuvault, Oliver
160	80	15-DEC-97	Doran, Louise

```
161           80 03-NOV-98 Sewall, Sarath
162           80 11-NOV-97 Vishney, Clara
191           50 19-DEC-99 Perkins, Randall
```

```
18 rows selected.
```

There is a lot going on in this query. First, notice that the columns are all aliased to make the output much more readable.

Janice also used the concatenation operator || to make the output more readable. She could have used the CONCAT function here, although she would need to use it twice to get the same results.

comment
Documentation for SQL statements. Comments are specified by using the pair /* and */ or by using --.

There is also something else new in this example: the /* and */. These characters denote a *comment* in Oracle SQL. A comment is used to help document the SQL code that you're writing. Documenting your SQL code is good not only for other developers who may need to modify your code in the future, but also for you when, months from now, you can't quite remember why you used a particular table or function!

Alternatively, you can use -- to specify a comment, like this:

```
select * from employees -- All columns needed for finance
```

The main difference between using /* */ and -- is that the latter form treats everything to the end of the line as a comment, whereas the former treats everything as a comment until the closing */ is reached, which may be on the same line or several lines later.

NOTE Although both /* */ and -- can be used almost interchangeably, the /* */ form must be used after the SELECT keyword when specifying optimizer hints. See Chapter 12, "Making Things Run Fast (Enough)," for details on how to specify hints to the optimizer.

Finally, the query has the BETWEEN operator. The EXTRACT function will return a value from 1 to 12 because the function is called with MONTH, and if this value falls in the range of 10 to 12, then the row is returned from the query.

What happens if you change the BETWEEN operator slightly and reverse the order of the months?

```
where extract(MONTH from HIRE_DATE) between 12 and 10;
```

Your intuition might tell you that this form of the WHERE clause would work, since 11 would still be between 12 and 10, just as 11 is between 10 and 12. But it doesn't work. This is because of how Oracle's SQL engine translates the arguments of the BETWEEN operator. When processing the query, Oracle changes BETWEEN to a pair of comparisons joined with an AND, as follows:

```
where extract(MONTH from HIRE_DATE) >= 12 and
      extract(MONTH from HIRE_DATE) <= 10;
```

Since no number can be at the same time greater than or equal to 12 and less than or equal to 10, no rows will be returned from a query with this WHERE clause.

IN the Thick of Things

The IN operator makes it easy to specify a list of values to search for in a WHERE clause. The IN clause contains a list of one or more values, separated by commas and enclosed in parentheses:

```
IN (value1, value2, ...)
```

It is ideal for situations where the values to be selected aren't in a range that the BETWEEN operator (or a pair of comparisons with an AND) can easily handle.

At Scott's widget company, one of the vice presidents, one of the store managers, and one of the purchasing managers will be temporarily moving to Chicago to open a new branch office. The employees who report to them will also move. The manager IDs for these positions are 102, 114, and 121. Janice writes a query to identify the people who are moving along with their managers:

```
select employee_id "Emp ID", manager_id "Mgr ID",
   last_name || ', ' || first_name "Name" from employees
   where manager_id in (102, 114, 121);
```

```
    Emp ID     Mgr ID Name
---------- ---------- ---------------------------
       103        102 Hunold, Alexander
       115        114 Khoo, Alexander
       116        114 Baida, Shelli
       117        114 Tobias, Sigal
       118        114 Himuro, Guy
       119        114 Colmenares, Karen
       129        121 Bissot, Laura
       130        121 Atkinson, Mozhe
       131        121 Marlow, James
       132        121 Olson, TJ
       184        121 Sarchand, Nandita
       185        121 Bull, Alexis
       186        121 Dellinger, Julia
       187        121 Cabrio, Anthony

14 rows selected.
```

The IN operator could be rewritten with a series of OR conditions, but once you need to use more than two or three values, the advantages of using IN become apparent.

NOTE

The Oracle SQL engine converts the IN operator to a series of OR conditions at runtime.

As you might expect, NOT IN is also valid. If the query you want to write sounds something like, "I want all the values except for these two or three…", then NOT IN is probably a good choice.

What's Not to Like about *LIKE*?

pattern matching
Comparing a string in a database column to a string containing wildcard characters. These wildcard characters can represent zero, one, or more characters in the database column string.

The LIKE operator lets you do *pattern matching* in a query. You know how to search for exact strings and numbers, but in some cases, you know only a few digits of the number or a portion of the string you need to find.

The LIKE operator can be used interchangeably with an equal sign, except that the string specified with LIKE can contain wildcard characters. The wildcard characters allowed in LIKE are %, which represents zero or more characters, and _, which represents exactly one character.

For example, the pattern 'Sm_th%' will match 'Smith' and 'Smythe' but not 'Smooth'. The pattern '%o%o%' will match any string that contains at least two lowercase *o* characters.

Janice is writing an ad-hoc query for Employee Services that will retrieve the job titles that have the word "Manager" somewhere in the title. She uses the LIKE operator:

```
select job_id, job_title from jobs
   where job_title like '%Manager%';


JOB_ID      JOB_TITLE
----------  ------------------------------------
FI_MGR      Finance Manager
AC_MGR      Accounting Manager
SA_MAN      Sales Manager
PU_MAN      Purchasing Manager
ST_MAN      Stock Manager
MK_MAN      Marketing Manager

6 rows selected.
```

NOTE

When numbers or dates are used with the LIKE operator, they are converted to character strings using the default conversion rules before comparing to the LIKE string.

What happens when you want to search for the _ or % characters themselves? The job IDs in Scott's corporate database use underscores, so Janice would get erroneous results if she specified 'ST_' in the LIKE string to find store-related jobs. This would also return jobs that had 'ASSISTANT' or 'COSTMGR' in the job ID. To solve this problem, she uses the ESCAPE option of the LIKE clause. The ESCAPE option lets you define a special character—one that you don't expect to find in your strings—to use before _ or % to indicate that you're actually looking for a _ or % character. To find all the job descriptions for jobs that are store-related, and therefore begin with 'ST_', Janice uses the following query:

```
select job_id, job_title from jobs
where job_id like 'ST\_%' escape '\';


JOB_ID      JOB_TITLE
----------  ------------------------------------
ST_MAN      Stock Manager
ST_CLERK    Stock Clerk

2 rows selected.
```

The ESCAPE option is used only with LIKE, and it tells the SQL engine to treat the character that follows literally instead of as a wildcard character. Notice in the above example that the underscore is "escaped," but the % acts as it normally does and specifies that zero or more characters follow.

> DBAs should keep an eye out for queries that use LIKE extensively. While this operator is very easy and intuitive for the user, queries with LIKE will scan the entire table, rather than use an index, unless there are no wildcards at the beginning of the string in the LIKE operator.

WARNING

IS NULL and IS NOT NULL

As mentioned in previous chapters, NULLs can be very useful in the database for saving disk space and for identifying values that are unknown, as opposed to being blank or zero. The key to understanding NULLs is to know that they are not equal to anything. Therefore, NULLs won't work with the standard comparison operators, such as +, /, >, =, and so forth. Janice learned this the hard way when she wanted to identify employees who made a commission of less than 15 percent or no commission at all. Here is the query she used:

```
select employee_id "Emp ID", last_name "Name", commission_pct
"Comm%"
from employees where commission_pct < 0.15;
```

```
Emp ID Name                              Comm%
---------- ------------------------- ----------
       164 Marvins                        .1
       165 Lee                            .1
       166 Ande                           .1
       167 Banda                          .1
       173 Kumar                          .1
       179 Johnson                        .1

6 rows selected.
```

This list appears to be way too short. That is because the rows in the
EMPLOYEES table with NULL values for the commission do not pass the criteria of
being less than 0.15; they don't compare to any value because they are unknown.

This is where the IS NULL and IS NOT NULL operators come to the rescue.
These two operators are the only ones that can do a direct comparison to values
that are NULL in a database row. For Janice to fix her query, she needs to add an
IS NULL condition to her WHERE clause:

```
select employee_id "Emp ID",
       last_name "Name", commission_pct "Comm%"
from employees
     where commission_pct < 0.15
     or commission_pct is null;

Emp ID Name                              Comm%
---------- ------------------------- ----------
       100 King
       101 Kochhar
       102 De Haan
...
       164 Marvins                        .1
       165 Lee                            .1
       166 Ande                           .1
       167 Banda                          .1
       173 Kumar                          .1
       179 Johnson                        .1
       180 Taylor
...
       205 Higgins
       206 Gietz

78 rows selected.
```

Be careful when constructing queries that operate on columns that can contain NULL values. A NULL is not the same as FALSE; it is the absence of a known value. This is a by-product of three-valued logic, where we have not just TRUE and FALSE, but TRUE, FALSE, and UNKNOWN.

WARNING

You'll see in the section on GROUP BY how multirow functions handle NULL values in a reasonable and expected way.

The *ORDER BY* Clause

You often need to see the results of a query in some kind of order, in other words, sorted by the values in one or more columns, either in ascending order or descending order. By default, columns are sorted in ascending order, but for completeness, you can use the ASC keyword. You use the DESC keyword to specify that a column should be sorted in descending order.

The syntax diagram for SELECT is expanded for ORDER BY as follows:

```
SELECT * | {[DISTINCT] column | expression [alias], ...}
  FROM tablename
  [WHERE condition ... ]
  [ORDER BY column [ASC | DESC], column [ASC | DESC], ...];
```

The Web Intranet group has requested that the list of employees from HR arrive sorted in ascending order. Janice is able to produce this report quickly by adding an ORDER BY to the existing query:

```
select employee_id || lpad(last_name,40-length(employee_
id),'.')
"Employee Directory" from employees
order by last_name;


Employee Directory


174...............................Abel
166...............................Ande
130...........................Atkinson
105.............................Austin
204..............................Baer
116.............................Baida
167.............................Banda
172.............................Bates
...
155..........................Tuvault
```

```
112..................................Urman
144..................................Vargas
162..................................Vishney
196..................................Walsh
120..................................Weiss
200..................................Whalen
149..................................Zlotkey
```

107 rows selected.

The column or columns to be sorted don't necessarily need to be in the SELECT clause. If there are NULL values in a column to be sorted, they will appear at the end if the sort is ascending, and they will appear first if the sort is descending.

As you might expect, you can combine both ascending and descending sorts in the same ORDER BY clause. The president, King, needs a monthly report that shows the salaries for each department, in ascending order of department number but in descending order for the salary amount. Janice comes up with the following query for King:

```
select department_id "Dept",
  last_name || ', ' || first_name "Employee",
  salary "Salary" from employees
order by department_id asc, salary desc;
```

```
Dept Employee                             Salary
----- ------------------------------  ----------
   10 Whalen, Jennifer                      4400
   20 Hartstein, Michael                   13000
   20 Fay, Pat                              6000
   30 Raphaely, Den                        11000
   30 Khoo, Alexander                       3100
   30 Baida, Shelli                         2900
   30 Tobias, Sigal                         2800
   30 Himuro, Guy                           2600
   30 Colmenares, Karen                     2500
   40 Mavris, Susan                         6500
...
   90 King, Steven                         24000
   90 Kochhar, Neena                       17000
```

90	De Haan, Lex	17000
100	Greenberg, Nancy	12000
100	Faviet, Daniel	9000
100	Chen, John	8200
100	Urman, Jose Manuel	7800
100	Sciarra, Ismael	7700
100	Popp, Luis	6900
110	Higgins, Shelley	12000
110	Gietz, William	8300
	Grant, Kimberely	7000

107 rows selected.

Unlike a WHERE clause, an ORDER BY clause can contain a column alias.

――――――――― *TIP* ―――――――――

The ASC keyword is not required, but it is specified here for clarity. Notice also how an employee with a NULL department number will end up at the bottom of the list in an ascending sort.

Group Functions and the *GROUP BY* Clause

This section explains how you can group rows together and perform some kind of *aggregate operation* on them. For example, you may want to count the rows for a given condition, calculate the averages of numeric columns, or find the highest or lowest value for a given column in a query result.

The GROUP BY clause fits into the SELECT statement as follows:

aggregate
A type of function in Oracle SQL that performs a calculation or transformation across multiple rows in a table, rather than just on a single row.

```
SELECT * | {[DISTINCT] column | expression [alias]
        | group_function(column), ...}
  FROM tablename
  [WHERE condition ... ]
  [GROUP BY group_expression, group_expression ...]
  [ORDER BY column [ASC | DESC], column [ASC | DESC], ...];
```

All group functions ignore NULLs by default. If you wanted to calculate the average commission across employees, you would most likely not want to consider employees who are not in the sales area (and therefore have a NULL commission value). On the other hand, you might want to treat NULL values numerically in other situations. You will see later in this chapter how you can convert NULL values with the NVL function.

Group Functions

Table 4.2 lists some of the most commonly used group functions in SQL statements. The COUNT function is the only aggregate function that will count rows with NULL values in any column when * is used as an argument.

Table 4.2   Common Group Functions

Function	Description
COUNT	Counts the number of rows, either all rows or for non-NULL column values
AVG	Calculates the average value of a column
SUM	Returns the sum of values for a column
MIN	Returns the minimum value for all column values
MAX	Returns the maximum value for all column values
STDDEV	Calculates the standard deviation for a specified column

All of the functions listed in Table 4.2 have a calling sequence as follows:

```
function([DISTINCT | ALL] expression)
```

As mentioned earlier, the COUNT function allows for * as its only argument, to specify that rows are to be counted, whether or not they have NULL values. The COUNT, MIN, and MAX functions apply to date and string expressions in addition to numeric expressions; the rest must have numeric arguments only.

The DISTINCT keyword indicates that duplicates are to be removed before the aggregate calculation is done. For example, calculating AVG(SALARY) versus AVG(DISTINCT SALARY) would be quite different if most of the employees are at one end of the pay scale. ALL is the default.

The boss, King, wants to get more information on salary distribution by department, so he asks Janice to give him the count of employees and the average salary and commission for his department, which has a department ID of 90. Janice runs the following query:

```
select count(*), avg(salary),
  avg(commission_pct) from employees
  where department_id = 90;


  COUNT(*) AVG(SALARY) AVG(COMMISSION_PCT)
---------- ----------- --------------------
         3  19333.3333

1 row selected.
```

Notice that the average commission in this case is not zero but NULL; there were *no* employees in department 90 with a commission. The result would have been non-NULL, if there were at least one employee who worked on a commission for part of their salary.

The next morning, the boss asks the same question for department 80, which has the bulk of the commissioned employees. Janice gets the answer with this query:

```
select count(*), avg(salary),
  avg(commission_pct) from employees
  where department_id = 80;

  COUNT(*) AVG(SALARY) AVG(COMMISSION_PCT)
---------- ----------- -------------------
        34  8955.88235                .225

1 row selected.
```

Janice hears rumors that King is going to ask for a breakdown of the number of employees, how many are on commission, and how many distinct commission percentages there are. She comes up with this query:

```
select count(*), count(commission_pct) "Comm Count",
  count(distinct commission_pct) "Distinct Comm"
  from employees;

  COUNT(*) Comm Count Distinct Comm
---------- ---------- -------------
       107         35             7

1 row selected.
```

What does this tell King? The total number of employees is 107, regardless of whether there are any NULL values in any of the columns. Of those employees, 35 are on commission (have a non-NULL value for COMMISSION_PCT), and out of those 35, there are seven different commission levels in force at the company.

Janice also suspects that King will be asking for some statistics for other departments. Rather than run the same query for different department numbers, she decides that it might be worthwhile to use the GROUP BY function to give King all the information he needs in a single query.

The *GROUP BY* Clause

The GROUP BY clause is used to break down the results of a query based on a column or columns. Once the rows are subdivided into groups, the aggregate functions described earlier in this chapter can be applied to these groups. Note the following rules about using the GROUP BY clause:

- ◆ All columns in a SELECT statement that are not in the GROUP BY clause must be part of an aggregate function.

- ◆ The WHERE clause can be used to filter rows from the result before the grouping functions are applied.

- ◆ The GROUP BY clause also specifies the sort order; this can be overridden with an ORDER BY clause.

- ◆ Column aliases cannot be used in the GROUP BY clause.

Janice has been busy preparing a report for King that will break down the salary and commission information by department. Her first query looks like this:

```
select department_id "Dept", count(*), avg(salary),
  avg(commission_pct) from employees
  group by department_id;
```

```
  Dept   COUNT(*) AVG(SALARY) AVG(COMMISSION_PCT)
  ----- ---------- ----------- --------------------
    10         1        4400
    20         2        9500
    30         6        4150
    40         1        6500
    50        45  3475.55556
    60         5        5760
    70         1       10000
    80        34  8955.88235                   .225
    90         3  19333.3333
   100         6        8600
   110         2       10150
               1        7000                    .15
```

```
12 rows selected.
```

This gives King a breakdown, by department, of the employee count, the average salary, and the average commission. NULLs are not included in the calculation for commission or salary. King likes this report, but Janice suspects that he will be asking for something different tomorrow.

One of the departments has a NULL value. There is one employee who has not yet been assigned to a department, but this employee does have a salary and a commission.

As expected, King calls the next day with another request. He wants to see how the salaries and commissions break out within department by job function. Janice realizes that all she needs to do is to add the job ID to the query in both the SELECT clause and the GROUP BY clause:

```
select department_id "Dept", job_id "Job", count(*),
  avg(salary), avg(commission_pct) from employees
  group by department_id, job_id;
```

Dept	Job	COUNT(*)	AVG(SALARY)	AVG(COMMISSION_PCT)
	SA_REP	1	7000	.15
10	AD_ASST	1	4400	
20	MK_MAN	1	13000	
20	MK_REP	1	6000	
30	PU_MAN	1	11000	
30	PU_CLERK	5	2780	
40	HR_REP	1	6500	
50	ST_MAN	5	7280	
50	SH_CLERK	20	3215	
50	ST_CLERK	20	2785	
60	IT_PROG	5	5760	
70	PR_REP	1	10000	
80	SA_MAN	5	12200	.3
80	SA_REP	29	8396.55172	.212068966
90	AD_VP	2	17000	
90	AD_PRES	1	24000	
100	FI_MGR	1	12000	
100	FI_ACCOUNT	5	7920	
110	AC_MGR	1	12000	
110	AC_ACCOUNT	1	8300	

```
20 rows selected.
```

As a side benefit, this also gives King the breakdown of jobs within each department.

Using *NVL* with Group Functions

As mentioned earlier in this chapter, group functions will ignore NULL values in their calculations. In most cases, this makes a lot of sense. For example, if only a small handful of employees worked on commission, and you calculated the average commission with the assumption that a NULL commission was essentially a zero commission, then the average commission would be quite low!

How you should interpret NULL values in a column depends on the business rules of the company and what NULL values represent. An average commission is usually based on only those employees who work on commission, and, in this case, the default behavior of Oracle's grouping functions makes sense.

However, there may be times when it makes sense to convert NULL values to something that can be aggregated. Let's assume for the moment that there is a column called COMMISSION_AMT in the EMPLOYEES table that records the latest monthly commission received by that employee. Just as with the COMMISSION_PCT column, the COMMISSION_AMT field is NULL for all employees except those in the Sales department. If King wanted a report of the average salary and commission (if any) by department, the expression

```
avg(salary + commission_amt)
```

in the SELECT clause would give results for only those rows with non-NULL commissions. That would not be what King was looking for. Janice would need to essentially convert any NULL values to zero. This is what NVL will do, and the expression above can be rewritten as

```
avg(salary + nvl(commission_amt,0))
```

For each row, if the COMMISSION_AMT is NULL, it is converted to zero (or any other amount you want) and added to SALARY, and the average is returned after all rows have been read.

The *HAVING* Clause

The HAVING clause is analogous to the WHERE clause, except that the HAVING clause applies to aggregate functions instead of individual columns or single-row function results. A query with a HAVING clause still returns aggregate values, but those aggregated summary rows are filtered from the query output based on the conditions in the HAVING clause.

The HAVING clause fits into the SELECT syntax as follows:

```
SELECT * | {[DISTINCT] column | expression [alias]
  | group_function(column), ...}
  FROM tablename
  [WHERE condition ... ]
  [GROUP BY group_expression, group_expression ...]
  [HAVING group_condition, ...]
  [ORDER BY column [ASC | DESC], column [ASC | DESC], ...];
```

The queries that Janice wrote for King have the information he needs, but his time is limited and he wants to see only the breakdowns for the department and job combinations that have average salaries over $10,000. Janice takes the original query

```
select department_id "Dept", job_id "Job", count(*),
  avg(salary), avg(commission_pct) from employees
group by department_id, job_id;
```

and adds a HAVING clause that removes the lower average salaries:

```
select department_id "Dept", job_id "Job", count(*),
  avg(salary), avg(commission_pct) from employees
group by department_id, job_id
having avg(salary) > 10000;
```

Dept	Job	COUNT(*)	AVG(SALARY)	AVG(COMMISSION_PCT)
20	MK_MAN	1	13000	
30	PU_MAN	1	11000	
80	SA_MAN	5	12200	.3
90	AD_VP	2	17000	
90	AD_PRES	1	24000	
100	FI_MGR	1	12000	
110	AC_MGR	1	12000	

```
7 rows selected.
```

Janice becomes proactive again, and she anticipates that King will want to see only certain jobs in the report. She can easily add a WHERE clause to select only administrative and sales positions. She uses the LIKE clause to select these job functions:

```
select department_id "Dept", job_id "Job", count(*),
  avg(salary), avg(commission_pct) from employees
where job_id like 'AD%' or job_id like 'SA%'
group by department_id, job_id
having avg(salary) > 10000;
```

Dept	Job	COUNT(*)	AVG(SALARY)	AVG(COMMISSION_PCT)
80	SA_MAN	5	12200	.3
90	AD_VP	2	17000	
90	AD_PRES	1	24000	

```
3 rows selected.
```

The order of the WHERE, GROUP, and HAVING clauses does not change how the query is run or the results; however, the ordering shown here is indicative of how the SQL engine processes the command. If an ORDER BY clause was needed in the above query, it could be placed anywhere after the SELECT clause but would most logically belong at the end of the query.

Terms to Know

aggregate   pattern matching

comment

Review Questions

1. Rewrite the following expression using the CONCAT function.

    ```
    last_name || ', ' || first_name
    ```

2. What are two ways that you can indicate a comment in a SQL command?

3. The SQL engine converts the IN operator to a series of _____.

4. Rewrite the following WHERE clause to be case insensitive.

    ```
    where job_title like '%Manager%';
    ```

5. What is the only group function that counts NULL values in its calculation without using NVL or other special processing?

6. The query results from using aggregate functions with a GROUP BY clause can be filtered or restricted by using what clause?

7. Identify the two special characters used with the LIKE operator and describe what they do.

8. Name two aggregate functions that work only on numeric columns or expressions and two other aggregate functions that work on numeric, character, and date columns.

9. Put the clauses of a SQL SELECT statement in the order in which they are processed.

10. Which operator can do valid comparisons to columns with NULL values?

11. The SQL engine converts the BETWEEN operator to _____.

12. Where do NULL values end up in a sort operation?

Chapter 5

Using Multiple Tables

So far, we have been dealing with only one table at a time in our SQL query examples. But typically the information needed to satisfy a user query requires more than one table. For example, the EMPLOYEES table has a column with a department number but not a department name; the department name must be retrieved from the DEPARTMENTS table. You can get this information by joining the two tables on a common column, in this case, the DEPARTMENT_ID column. Two or more tables can also be joined in situations where the columns may not be equal.

The boss at Scott's widget company has realized that data can be pulled from more than one table at a time. Now the application developer and DBA, Janice, has been busy trying to keep up with his requests for reports. Each of the join types will be discussed in this chapter, as we follow Janice's work.

Join Syntax: Out with the Old and In with the New (SQL:1999)

join
To combine two or more tables in a query to produce rows as a result of a comparison between columns in the tables.

Not only can you *join* two or more tables in a number of different ways, but you can also use two different syntax forms to perform these joins. As of Oracle9*i*, the full ANSI SQL:1999 standard for join syntax is supported. Prior to Oracle9*i*, Oracle used a proprietary syntax that wasn't always compatible with the ANSI standard.

Oracle's proprietary syntax, which is still supported in Oracle9*i* and Oracle 10*g* for backward compatibility with existing code, put all of the join conditions in the SELECT statement's WHERE clause. It also relied on relatively obscure methods to indicate certain types of join operations. The newer syntax relies more heavily on concise yet descriptive keywords to clearly indicate what operation is being performed. We'll cover both the old and new syntax in this chapter; as a DBA or developer, you'll most likely see new applications using the new syntax and plenty of existing applications that use the old syntax.

TIP All new SQL code should use the SQL:1999 or SQL:2003 standard syntax for readability and cross-platform compatibility.

There is no performance benefit to using one syntax over the other; the same kind of join using either syntax will translate into the same internal SQL engine operation. One of the biggest benefits is the ease with which the new syntax can be written and understood. The join conditions are now separated from the WHERE clause and placed in the FROM clause. The WHERE clause, if one even exists, ends up being much cleaner because it's used only for filtering the rows being returned from the query, instead of being intertwined with table join conditions.

In each section of this chapter, you'll see how the database analyst, Janice, uses both formats for each new query she develops for the boss.

Equijoins

equijoin
A join between two tables where rows are returned if one or more columns in common between the two tables are equal and not NULL.

Equijoins are also commonly known as simple joins, or *inner joins*. Given two or more tables, an equijoin will return the results of these tables where a common column between any given pair of tables has the same value (an equal value). Equijoins are typically joins between foreign keys in one table to a primary key in another table.

Pre-Oracle9*i* Equijoin Syntax

inner join
See *equijoin*.

The boss, King, gets his employee report with only the department ID on it, because the query used for the report is based on only the EMPLOYEES table. When the company was smaller, he knew automatically that department 100 was the Finance department, and so on. But now, with almost 30 departments in the company, he needs to see the department name in the report. That information is in the DEPARTMENTS table. Janice will join the two tables on the common column, DEPARTMENT_ID, and produce a report that is much more readable:

```
select employee_id "Emp ID", last_name || ', ' ||
     first_name "Name", department_name "Dept"
from employees e, departments d
where e.department_id = d.department_id;
```

```
    Emp ID Name                         Dept
    ---------- ------------------------ --------------------
       100 King, Steven                 Executive
       101 Kochhar, Neena               Executive
       102 De Haan, Lex                 Executive
       103 Hunold, Alexander            IT
       104 Ernst, Janice                IT
       105 Austin, David                IT
...
       201 Hartstein, Michael           Marketing
       202 Fay, Pat                     Marketing
       203 Mavris, Susan                Human Resources
       204 Baer, Hermann                Public Relations
       205 Higgins, Shelley             Accounting
       206 Gietz, William               Accounting

    106 rows selected.
```

Notice that table aliases are used. You've already seen quite a few column aliases in previous examples, and tables can be aliased also, either for clarity or for performance reasons. In this case, the aliases are necessary to identify which columns in which table are to be compared in this query. Typically, the column names match, but that is not a requirement for columns that are matched in a WHERE clause.

King tells Janice that the report looks good, but he also wants to see the full job description for each employee. Janice adds another table to the query and expands the WHERE clause. She also adds an ORDER BY clause to ensure that the report stays in employee ID order:

```
select employee_id "Emp ID",
   last_name "Name", department_name "Dept",
   job_title "Job"
from employees e, departments d, jobs j
where e.department_id = d.department_id
```

```
    and e.job_id = j.job_id
order by employee_id;

Emp ID Name        Dept        Job
------ ----------  ----------  ----------------------------
   100 King        Executive   President
   101 Kochhar     Executive   Administration Vice President
   102 De Haan     Executive   Administration Vice President
   103 Hunold      IT          Programmer
   104 Ernst       IT          Programmer
   105 Austin      IT          Programmer
   106 Pataballa   IT          Programmer
...
   205 Higgins     Accounting Accounting Manager
   206 Gietz       Accounting Public Accountant

106 rows selected.
```

TIP — To join together *n* tables, you need at least *n-1* join conditions to avoid undesired Cartesian products, resulting from combining every row of one table with every row of one or more other tables. Cartesian products are discussed later in this chapter.

King is still not satisfied with the report because it's too long. He wants to see only information about the Finance and Purchasing department people on a regular basis. Janice updates the query one more time to add another WHERE condition to the query:

```
select e.employee_id "Emp ID",
  e.last_name "Name", d.department_name "Dept",
  j.job_title "Job"
from employees e, departments d, jobs j
where e.department_id = d.department_id
  and e.job_id = j.job_id
  and e.department_id in (30, 100)
order by e.employee_id;

Emp ID Name          Dept          Job
------- ------------  ------------  --------------------
   108 Greenberg     Finance       Finance Manager
   109 Faviet        Finance       Accountant
   110 Chen          Finance       Accountant
```

```
111 Sciarra      Finance     Accountant
112 Urman        Finance     Accountant
113 Popp         Finance     Accountant
114 Raphaely     Purchasing  Purchasing Manager
115 Khoo         Purchasing  Purchasing Clerk
116 Baida        Purchasing  Purchasing Clerk
117 Tobias       Purchasing  Purchasing Clerk
118 Himuro       Purchasing  Purchasing Clerk
119 Colmenares   Purchasing  Purchasing Clerk
```

12 rows selected.

Janice already knew the department numbers to use with the IN operator.

Oracle9*i* Equijoin Syntax

The query that Janice wrote in the previous section works great. However, with all of the conditions specified in the WHERE clause, including both the table joins and the result filter, it gets cluttered fast. Most of the new options available in the Oracle9*i* and later syntax for joins will help make the query look cleaner, so that it is easier to read and understand. Equijoins can be constructed using the syntax NATURAL JOIN, JOIN USING, and JOIN ON.

Natural Join

Janice is quickly figuring out how to use the new Oracle9*i* syntax. She rewrites one of the first queries she wrote in this chapter, joining just the EMPLOYEES and DEPARTMENTS tables. She uses the NATURAL JOIN clause, since this method will implicitly join the two tables on columns with the same name:

```
select employee_id "Emp ID", last_name || ', ' ||
    first_name "Name", department_name "Dept"
from employees natural join departments;


    Emp ID Name                 Dept
---------- -------------------- --------------------
       101 Kochhar, Neena       Executive
       102 De Haan, Lex         Executive
       104 Ernst, Janice        IT
       105 Austin, David        IT
       106 Pataballa, Valli     IT
       107 Lorentz, Diana       IT
       109 Faviet, Daniel       Finance
...
```

```
155 Tuvault, Oliver      Sales
184 Sarchand, Nandita    Shipping
185 Bull, Alexis         Shipping
186 Dellinger, Julia     Shipping
187 Cabrio, Anthony      Shipping
202 Fay, Pat             Marketing
206 Gietz, William       Accounting
```

```
32 rows selected.
```

Janice is scratching her head, because her first query returned 106 rows, while this one returns only 32. She realizes that the simplicity of the NATURAL JOIN method is a double-edged sword. NATURAL JOIN matches on *all* columns that have the same name and datatype between the tables. On closer inspection, it turns out that the EMPLOYEES and the DEPARTMENTS tables have both the DEPARTMENT_ID and MANAGER_ID columns in common. The query she wrote is effectively the same as writing this query in Oracle8*i*:

```
select employee_id "Emp ID", last_name || ', ' ||
    first_name "Name", department_name "Dept"
from employees e, departments d
where e.manager_id = d.manager_id and
    e.department_id = d.department_id;
```

This is clearly not what she is looking for. It doesn't make much sense to join on the MANAGER_ID column because the MANAGER_ID column in the EMPLOYEES table is the MANAGER_ID of the employee, whereas the MANAGER_ID column in the DEPARTMENTS table is the manager of the department itself. The query does return the employees whose manager is a department manager, but this is not what King requested (yet!).

WARNING

Use NATURAL JOIN only for ad hoc queries where you are very familiar with the column names of both tables. Adding a new column to a table that happens to have the same name as a column in another table will cause unexpected side effects with existing queries that use both tables in a NATURAL JOIN.

Join Using

Janice decides to scale back a bit and use another form of the Oracle9*i* join syntax that still saves some typing but is more explicit on which columns to join: JOIN ... USING. This form of an equijoin specifies the two tables to be joined and the column that is common between the tables. Janice's new query looks like this:

```
select employee_id "Emp ID", last_name || ', ' ||
    first_name "Name", department_name "Dept"
```

```
from employees join departments using (department_id);
```

```
    Emp ID Name                     Dept
---------- ------------------------ --------------------
       100 King, Steven             Executive
       101 Kochhar, Neena           Executive
       102 De Haan, Lex             Executive
       103 Hunold, Alexander        IT
       104 Ernst, Janice            IT
       105 Austin, David            IT
       106 Pataballa, Valli         IT
...
       201 Hartstein, Michael       Marketing
       202 Fay, Pat                 Marketing
       203 Mavris, Susan            Human Resources
       204 Baer, Hermann            Public Relations
       205 Higgins, Shelley         Accounting
       206 Gietz, William           Accounting

106 rows selected.
```

Join On

This particular form of an equijoin appears to be a good compromise between simplicity and accuracy, but Janice knows that she'll sooner or later use another form of an equijoin, the JOIN ... ON syntax. She rewrites the query once more as follows:

```
select employee_id "Emp ID", last_name || ', ' ||
  first_name "Name", department_name "Dept"
from employees e join departments d
  on e.department_id = d.department_id;
```

```
    Emp ID Name                     Dept
---------- ------------------------ --------------------
       100 King, Steven             Executive
       101 Kochhar, Neena           Executive
       102 De Haan, Lex             Executive
       103 Hunold, Alexander        IT
...
       203 Mavris, Susan            Human Resources
       204 Baer, Hermann            Public Relations
```

```
            205 Higgins, Shelley          Accounting
            206 Gietz, William            Accounting


        106 rows selected.
```

TIP

The JOIN ... ON clause is the only SQL:1999 equijoin clause that supports joining columns with different names.

Join Using with Three Tables

Later in the afternoon, one more request comes in from King: He wants to see a list of employees similar to the query Janice just ran, but instead of departments, he wants to see the city where the employee is working, and only employees in department 40, Human Resources. Looking at the EMPLOYEES table, the DEPARTMENTS table, and the LOCATIONS table, you can see that there is no direct route from EMPLOYEES to LOCATIONS. Janice must "go through" the DEPARTMENTS table to fulfill King's request. She must take the following route to get from EMPLOYEES to LOCATIONS:

EMPLOYEES

Name	Null?	Type
EMPLOYEE_ID	NOT NULL	NUMBER(6)
FIRST_NAME		VARCHAR2(20)
LAST_NAME	NOT NULL	VARCHAR2(25)
EMAIL	NOT NULL	VARCHAR2(25)
PHONE_NUMBER		VARCHAR2(20)
HIRE_DATE	NOT NULL	DATE
JOB_ID	NOT NULL	VARCHAR2(10)
SALARY		NUMBER(8,2)
COMMISSION_PCT		NUMBER(2,2)
MANAGER_ID		NUMBER(6)
DEPARTMENT_ID		NUMBER(4)
COMMISSION_AMT		NUMBER(9,2)

DEPARTMENTS

Name	Null?	Type
DEPARTMENT_ID	NOT NULL	NUMBER(4)
DEPARTMENT_NAME	NOT NULL	VARCHAR2(30)
MANAGER_ID		NUMBER(6)
LOCATION_ID		NUMBER(4)

LOCATIONS

Name	Null?	Type
LOCATION_ID	NOT NULL	NUMBER(4)
STREET_ADDRESS		VARCHAR2(40)
POSTAL_CODE		VARCHAR2(12)
CITY	NOT NULL	VARCHAR2(30)
STATE_PROVINCE		VARCHAR2(25)
COUNTRY_ID		CHAR(2)

Since the join will use common column names between each pair of tables, Janice's query uses the JOIN ... USING clause as follows:

```
select employee_id "Emp ID", last_name || ', ' ||
   first_name "Name", city "City"
from employees
      join departments using (department_id)
            join locations using (location_id)
where department_id = 40;


    Emp ID Name                        City
---------- -------------------------- --------------------
       203 Mavris, Susan               London
```

1 row selected.

The EMPLOYEES table is joined to DEPARTMENTS on the DEPARTMENT_ID column, and then the result of that join is joined with the LOCATIONS table on the LOCATION_ID column. The result is filtered so that only the employees in department 40 are on the report.

Non-equijoins

When joining two or more tables, you usually are joining on columns that have the same value, such as department number or job ID. On occasion, however, you might join two tables where the common columns are not equal. More specifically, a column's value in one table may fall within a range of values in another table.

There is a table in the HR schema called JOBS, which lists each job in Scott's company, along with the salary ranges for a given job. Janice will query this table using both the pre-Oracle9i syntax and the Oracle9i syntax. The JOBS table is structured as follows:

```
Name                        Null?     Type
-------------------------- --------- -------------
JOB_ID                     NOT NULL  VARCHAR2(10)
JOB_TITLE                  NOT NULL  VARCHAR2(35)
MIN_SALARY                           NUMBER(6)
MAX_SALARY                           NUMBER(6)
```

Pre-Oracle9i Non-equijoin Syntax

Janice knows that the EMPLOYEES table has a salary column and a job ID column. She wants to make sure that the salary for a given employee falls within the range specified for the job assigned to that employee. The first employee she checks is the boss's daughter, Janette King, who has an employee ID of 156. The query below does a non-equijoin on the EMPLOYEES and JOBS tables to accomplish the salary range comparison:

```
select e.job_id "Empl Job", e.salary, j.job_id "Job",
  j.min_salary, j.max_salary
from employees e, jobs j
where e.salary between j.min_salary and j.max_salary
and e.employee_id = 156;
```

```
Empl Job      SALARY Job         MIN_SALARY MAX_SALARY
----------  ---------- ----------  ---------- ----------
SA_REP          10000 FI_MGR            8200      16000
SA_REP          10000 AC_MGR            8200      16000
SA_REP          10000 SA_MAN           10000      20000
SA_REP          10000 SA_REP            6000      12000
SA_REP          10000 PU_MAN            8000      15000
SA_REP          10000 IT_PROG           4000      10000
SA_REP          10000 MK_MAN            9000      15000
SA_REP          10000 PR_REP            4500      10500

8 rows selected.
```

What does this query output tell Janice? First of all, it appears that there is no nepotism going on at the company, because Janette's salary falls within the normal range for a sales representative, albeit near the high end of the range. It also is apparent that her salary is in the range for seven other positions at the company.

Oracle9i Non-equijoin Syntax

Janice wants to see if the non-equijoin query is any easier to perform using the newer Oracle9i syntax. She realizes that since she is doing a non-equijoin, she is not able to use the NATURAL JOIN or the JOIN ... USING syntax, since both of those formats assume equality between the implicit or explicit columns. It seems like the JOIN ... ON syntax will work, though, since she can specify a condition between two columns in that syntax. The query looks very similar to the previous query, but as with all Oracle9i joins, the join conditions are moved from the WHERE clause to the FROM clause:

```
select e.job_id "Empl Job", e.salary, j.job_id "Job",
  j.min_salary, j.max_salary
from employees e
```

```
join jobs j on
   e.salary between j.min_salary and j.max_salary
where employee_id = 156;
```

Empl Job	SALARY	Job	MIN_SALARY	MAX_SALARY
SA_REP	10000	FI_MGR	8200	16000
SA_REP	10000	AC_MGR	8200	16000
SA_REP	10000	SA_MAN	10000	20000
SA_REP	10000	SA_REP	6000	12000
SA_REP	10000	PU_MAN	8000	15000
SA_REP	10000	IT_PROG	4000	10000
SA_REP	10000	MK_MAN	9000	15000
SA_REP	10000	PR_REP	4500	10500

```
8 rows selected.
```

Outer Joins

Sometimes you want to join two tables and return all the rows in one table whether or not the second table contains a match on the join condition. This is known as performing an *outer join* between two tables. To illustrate why you would want to join two tables in this way, consider the EMPLOYEES and DEPARTMENTS tables for Scott's widget company. The EMPLOYEES table has a column called DEPARTMENT_ID, which can contain NULL values. If you were to join the two tables on the DEPARTMENT_ID column, the query would not return all employees. Conversely, if you had departments that did not have any employees, you would not see all of the departments represented in the query results either.

In some cases, you want to see all records in both tables, regardless of how many match on the join condition. This is known as a full outer join.

Let's look at how to perform these types of outer joins using the pre-Oracle9*i* syntax and the Oracle9*i* syntax.

outer join
A join between two or more tables returning all the rows in one table whether or not the second table contains a match on the join condition.

Pre-Oracle9*i* Outer Join Syntax

The key component of the outer join syntax for previous Oracle versions is a plus sign enclosed in parentheses: (+). In an outer join, this outer join operator is placed next to the table that may not have rows that satisfy the join condition between two tables. We'll look at some examples in the next few sections, as Janice prepares some new reports.

Outer Join

King wants Janice to produce a report listing the sales representatives and the departments in which they reside. Janice knows that at any given time, there might be employees who aren't assigned to a department. She constructs the query assuming that there might be some missing or incorrect department numbers in the EMPLOYEES table:

```
select e.employee_id "Emp ID", e.last_name || ', ' ||
    e.first_name "Name", d.department_name "Dept"
from employees e,departments d
where e.department_id = d.department_id(+)
and e.job_id = 'SA_REP';
```

```
    Emp ID Name                              Dept
---------- ------------------------------    --------------------
       179 Johnson, Charles                  Sales
       177 Livingston, Jack                  Sales
       176 Taylor, Jonathon                  Sales
       175 Hutton, Alyssa                    Sales
       174 Abel, Ellen                       Sales
...
       152 Hall, Peter                       Sales
       151 Bernstein, David                  Sales
       150 Tucker, Peter                     Sales
       178 Grant, Kimberely

30 rows selected.
```

It appears that all of the employees who have a sales position are assigned to the Sales department, except for Kimberely Grant. She has a NULL value for her department ID and therefore does not match any row in the DEPARTMENTS table.

Janice could also find out which departments don't have any employees by changing the outer join to specify the EMPLOYEES table as the table that might not have any rows corresponding to a DEPARTMENTS table row, like this:

```
select e.employee_id "Emp ID", e.last_name || ', ' ||
    e.first_name "Name", d.department_name "Dept"
from employees e,departments d
where e.department_id(+) = d.department_id;
```

```
    Emp ID Name                              Dept
---------- ------------------------------    --------------------
       100 King, Steven                      Executive
```

```
    101 Kochhar, Neena          Executive
    102 De Haan, Lex            Executive
    103 Hunold, Alexander       IT
...
    202 Fay, Pat                Marketing
    203 Mavris, Susan           Human Resources
    204 Baer, Hermann           Public Relations
    205 Higgins, Shelley        Accounting
    206 Gietz, William          Accounting
        ,                       NOC
        ,                       Manufacturing
        ,                       Government Sales
        ,                       IT Support
        ,                       Benefits
        ,                       Shareholder Services
        ,                       Retail Sales
        ,                       Control And Credit
        ,                       Recruiting
        ,                       Operations
        ,                       Treasury
        ,                       Payroll
        ,                       Corporate Tax
        ,                       Construction
        ,                       Contracting
        ,                       IT Helpdesk

122 rows selected.
```

The report includes all departments but leaves out any employees that have an invalid department number or have no department number assigned to them. Janice will be addressing this issue in the next section.

When you're not sure where the outer join operator (+) goes, place it next to the table that is missing rows. In other words, rows need to be "added" to this table for the join to succeed in a regular equijoin.

TIP

Full Outer Join

King has asked Janice to somehow combine both of the reports she just created into a single report that lists all employees and all departments, regardless of whether an employee is assigned to a department or a department has any employees. To accomplish this using the pre-Oracle9i syntax, Janice must use the UNION operator to combine two outer join queries. The UNION operator will combine the results of two outer join queries, removing duplicates found between the two queries. Her query looks like this:

```
select e.employee_id "Emp ID", e.last_name || ', ' ||
  e.first_name "Name", d.department_name "Dept"
from employees e,departments d
where e.department_id(+) = d.department_id
union
select e.employee_id "Emp ID", e.last_name || ', ' ||
  e.first_name "Name", d.department_name "Dept"
from employees e,departments d
where e.department_id = d.department_id(+);
```

```
    Emp ID Name                            Dept
    ---------- -------------------------   --------------------
       100 King, Steven                    Executive
       101 Kochhar, Neena                  Executive
       102 De Haan, Lex                    Executive
       103 Hunold, Alexander               IT
       104 Ernst, Janice                   IT
       105 Austin, David                   IT
       106 Pataballa, Valli                IT
...
       176 Taylor, Jonathon                Sales
       177 Livingston, Jack                Sales
       178 Grant, Kimberely
       179 Johnson, Charles                Sales
       180 Taylor, Winston                 Shipping
       181 Fleaur, Jean                    Shipping
...
                              ,             Payroll
                              ,             Recruiting
                              ,             Retail Sales
                              ,             Shareholder Services
                              ,             Treasury

    123 rows selected.
```

Notice that this query returns a total of 123 rows, one more than the previous version of this query that performed an outer join with the DEPARTMENTS table as the primary table. This version picked up the extra row containing Kimberely Grant from the outer join between EMPLOYEES and DEPARTMENTS in the first half of the query above.

While the query does provide the desired results, the maintenance costs are higher on a query of this type, since any changes to the first SELECT statement most likely must be reflected in the second SELECT statement. The new outer join syntax in Oracle9*i* addresses this problem.

Oracle9*i* Outer Join Syntax

As with the equijoin syntax, the outer join syntax in Oracle9*i* moves the join logic from the WHERE clause to the FROM clause. Rather than using the slightly unintuitive (+) outer join operator to specify an outer join, Oracle9*i* uses LEFT OUTER JOIN ... ON or RIGHT OUTER JOIN ... ON between the two tables to be joined. The LEFT or RIGHT specifies which table has all rows retrieved, regardless of whether there is a match in the other table.

Left Outer Join

Janice is rewriting some of the queries she wrote back when their shop was running Oracle8i. Now that they're using Oracle9i, she wants to make sure she is leveraging the full power of Oracle9*i*'s new features, not to mention the added benefits of more intuitive syntax. She starts with one of the queries for King that retrieved employees and corresponding departments:

```
select e.employee_id "Emp ID", e.last_name || ', ' ||
   e.first_name "Name", d.department_name "Dept"
from employees e,departments d
where e.department_id = d.department_id(+)
and e.job_id = 'SA_REP';
```

She rewrites the query using a LEFT OUTER JOIN, since the EMPLOYEES table is already on the "left" side of the FROM clause:

```
select e.employee_id "Emp ID", e.last_name || ', ' ||
   e.first_name "Name", d.department_name "Dept"
from employees e
   left outer join
   departments d
   on e.department_id = d.department_id
where e.job_id = 'SA_REP';
```

```
Emp ID Name                         Dept
------- ------------------------ ----------------------
    179 Johnson, Charles             Sales
    177 Livingston, Jack             Sales
    176 Taylor, Jonathon             Sales
```

```
      175 Hutton, Alyssa              Sales
      174 Abel, Ellen                 Sales
...
      152 Hall, Peter                 Sales
      151 Bernstein, David            Sales
      150 Tucker, Peter               Sales
      178 Grant, Kimberely
```

```
30 rows selected.
```

Not surprisingly, she gets the same results as she did when the query used the pre-Oracle9*i* syntax. However, this form of the query is much cleaner because the join syntax is separate from the filter criterion (employees who are sales representatives). The query is also much easier to read.

Right Outer Join

Any left outer join can be turned into a right outer join by changing the order of the tables and changing LEFT OUTER JOIN to RIGHT OUTER JOIN. The query in the previous section can be rewritten as RIGHT OUTER JOIN as follows:

```
select e.employee_id "Emp ID", e.last_name || ', ' ||
   e.first_name "Name", d.department_name "Dept"
from departments d
    right outer join
    employees e
    on e.department_id = d.department_id
where e.job_id = 'SA_REP';
```

```
Emp ID Name                          Dept
------- ---------------------------- -----------------------
      179 Johnson, Charles            Sales
      177 Livingston, Jack            Sales
      176 Taylor, Jonathon            Sales
      175 Hutton, Alyssa              Sales
      174 Abel, Ellen                 Sales
...
      152 Hall, Peter                 Sales
      151 Bernstein, David            Sales
      150 Tucker, Peter               Sales
      178 Grant, Kimberely
```

```
30 rows selected.
```

Many times, whether to use LEFT OUTER JOIN or RIGHT OUTER JOIN is simply a matter of style. As you can see, the two previous queries read differently but produce the same results.

Full Outer Join

Speaking of style and readability, the syntax for a full outer join in Oracle9*i* is greatly simplified compared to how a full outer join is performed in previous versions of Oracle. Rather than performing a UNION operation between two distinct queries, the FULL OUTER JOIN clause is specified between the two tables to be joined.

Janice is cleaning up the rest of her queries to take advantage of the new syntax, and she starts with the UNION query she wrote to display all employees and all departments in a single query. Here is the original query:

```
select e.employee_id "Emp ID", e.last_name || ', ' ||
   e.first_name "Name", d.department_name "Dept"
from employees e,departments d
where e.department_id(+) = d.department_id
union
select e.employee_id "Emp ID", e.last_name || ', ' ||
   e.first_name "Name", d.department_name "Dept"
from employees e,departments d
where e.department_id = d.department_id(+);
```

In its new format, it ends up a lot shorter and a lot more readable:

```
select e.employee_id "Emp ID", e.last_name || ', ' ||
   e.first_name "Name", d.department_name "Dept"
from employees e
     full outer join
     departments d
     on e.department_id = d.department_id;
```

```
Emp ID Name                             Dept
------- -------------------------------- ----------------------
    200 Whalen, Jennifer                 Administration
    202 Fay, Pat                         Marketing
    201 Hartstein, Michael               Marketing
  ...
              ,                          Corporate Tax
              ,                          Construction
              ,                          Contracting
              ,                          IT Helpdesk

123 rows selected.
```

self-join

A join of a table to itself where a non-primary key column in the table is related to the primary key column of another row in the same table.

hierarchical

A table design where one of the foreign keys in the table references the primary key of the same table in a parent-child relationship.

Self-Joins

You now know that you can join tables to other tables, but can you join a table to itself, producing a *self-join*? The answer is a resounding, but qualified, yes. Typically, a table will join to itself when the table is designed in a *hierarchical* manner, that is, when one particular row in a table is somehow related to another row in the table in a parent-child relationship.

At Scott's widget company, the EMPLOYEES table has a column that contains the employee number of the employee (EMPLOYEE_ID) in addition to a column that contains the employee number of the employee's immediate supervisor (MANAGER_ID). Janice will use this information to produce some new reports for the boss that essentially join the EMPLOYEES table to itself.

Pre-Oracle9*i* Self-Join Syntax

Since the EMPLOYEES table contains the employee's manager number, Janice decides to become proactive and generate a report of all employees and their managers. Her SELECT query references the EMPLOYEES table twice: once as an EMPLOYEES table and once as a MANAGERS table, since all of the managers are employees themselves. The EMPLOYEES table can be related to itself.

EMPLOYEES (Employee)

Name	Null?	Type
EMPLOYEE_ID	NOT NULL	NUMBER(6)
FIRST_NAME		VARCHAR2(20)
LAST_NAME	NOT NULL	VARCHAR2(25)
EMAIL	NOT NULL	VARCHAR2(25)
PHONE_NUMBER		VARCHAR2(20)
HIRE_DATE	NOT NULL	DATE
JOB_ID	NOT NULL	VARCHAR2(10)
SALARY		NUMBER(8,2)
COMMISSION_PCT		NUMBER(2,2)
MANAGER_ID		NUMBER(6)
DEPARTMENT_ID		NUMBER(4)
COMMISSION_AMT		NUMBER(9,2)

EMPLOYEES (Manager)

Name	Null?	Type
EMPLOYEE_ID	NOT NULL	NUMBER(6)
FIRST_NAME		VARCHAR2(20)
LAST_NAME	NOT NULL	VARCHAR2(25)
EMAIL	NOT NULL	VARCHAR2(25)
PHONE_NUMBER		VARCHAR2(20)
HIRE_DATE	NOT NULL	DATE
JOB_ID	NOT NULL	VARCHAR2(10)
SALARY		NUMBER(8,2)
COMMISSION_PCT		NUMBER(2,2)
MANAGER_ID		NUMBER(6)
DEPARTMENT_ID		NUMBER(4)
COMMISSION_AMT		NUMBER(9,2)

The query that Janice writes displays the employees who have managers:

```
select e.employee_id "Emp ID", e.last_name "Emp Name",
       m.employee_id "Mgr ID", m.last_name "Mgr Name"
from employees e, employees m
where e.manager_id = m.employee_id;
```

```
    Emp ID Emp Name              Mgr ID Mgr Name
    ---------- ---------------    ---------- ---------------
       201 Hartstein              100 King
       149 Zlotkey                100 King
       148 Cambrault              100 King
...
       177 Livingston             149 Zlotkey
       176 Taylor                 149 Zlotkey
       175 Hutton                 149 Zlotkey
       174 Abel                   149 Zlotkey
       202 Fay                    201 Hartstein
       206 Gietz                  205 Higgins

106 rows selected.
```

Notice that King is not in the list. Since the row in the EMPLOYEES table for King does not have an entry for a manager (he has no manager since he is the president of the company), his row does not match any rows in the other copy of the EMPLOYEES table and therefore does not show up as a row in the query output.

Oracle9*i* Self-Join Syntax

The Oracle9*i* syntax not only moves the join condition to the FROM clause, it also uses the familiar syntax you saw earlier for joining two different tables—the JOIN ... ON syntax. Janice rewrites the manager query using the Oracle9*i* syntax as follows:

```
select e.employee_id "Emp ID", e.last_name "Emp Name",
       m.employee_id "Mgr ID", m.last_name "Mgr Name"
from employees e
     join employees m
     on e.manager_id = m.employee_id;
```

```
    Emp ID Emp Name              Mgr ID Mgr Name
    ---------- ---------------    ---------- ---------------
       201 Hartstein              100 King
       149 Zlotkey                100 King
```

```
              148  Cambrault         100  King
    ...
              177  Livingston        149  Zlotkey
              176  Taylor            149  Zlotkey
              175  Hutton            149  Zlotkey
              174  Abel              149  Zlotkey
              202  Fay               201  Hartstein
              206  Gietz             205  Higgins

    106 rows selected.
```

Not unexpectedly, she gets the same results as she did with the pre-Oracle9*i* version of the query.

Cartesian Products: The Black Sheep of the Family

Cartesian product

A join between two tables where no join condition is specified, and as a result, every row in the first table is joined with every row in the second table.

What if you were joining two tables, or even three tables, and you left off the join conditions? The result would be a *Cartesian product*. Every row of each table in the FROM clause would be joined with every row of the other tables. If one table had 15 rows, and a second table had 21 rows, a Cartesian product of those two tables would produce 315 rows in the result set of the query. Needless to say, it can be a big problem when you have three or more tables with no join conditions specified.

———— **NOTE** ————

Partial Cartesian products are produced when a query with *n* tables has less than *n-1* join conditions between tables.

Needless to say, Cartesian products are used quite infrequently in SELECT statements, but they can be useful in very specific situations. For example, a Cartesian product of the EMPLOYEES table and the COUNTRIES table could give Janice a way to produce a checklist in a spreadsheet to note when a particular employee has visited one of the countries where Scott's widget company has a field office or distribution center. If employee visits to other offices were tallied in another table, then the Cartesian product could be joined to the new table as a running total of visits by employees to other offices.

Pre-Oracle9*i* Cartesian Product Syntax

Janice decides that the employee/country visit idea has some merit, and she experiments with some queries to generate the combinations of employees and countries using a Cartesian product query:

```
select e.employee_id "Emp ID", e.last_name "Emp Name",
       c.country_id "Cntry ID", c.country_name "Cntry Name"
from employees e, countries c;
```

```
     Emp ID Emp Name        Cn Cntry Name
     ---------- --------------- -- --------------------
          100 King            AR Argentina
          101 Kochhar         AR Argentina
          102 De Haan         AR Argentina
          103 Hunold          AR Argentina
...
          201 Hartstein       ZW Zimbabwe
          202 Fay             ZW Zimbabwe
          203 Mavris          ZW Zimbabwe
          204 Baer            ZW Zimbabwe
          205 Higgins         ZW Zimbabwe
          206 Gietz           ZW Zimbabwe

     2675 rows selected.
```

Oracle9*i* Cartesian Product Syntax

The same query using the Oracle9*i* syntax is similar, except that CROSS JOIN is used to separate the two tables that are queried to produce a Cartesian product. Janice changes the previous query to use the Oracle9*i* version:

```
select e.employee_id "Emp ID", e.last_name "Emp Name",
       c.country_id "Cntry ID", c.country_name "Cntry Name"
from employees e cross join countries c;

Emp ID Emp Name        Cn Cntry Name
---------- --------------- -- --------------------
     100 King            AR Argentina
     101 Kochhar         AR Argentina
     102 De Haan         AR Argentina
     103 Hunold          AR Argentina
...
     201 Hartstein       ZW Zimbabwe
     202 Fay             ZW Zimbabwe
     203 Mavris          ZW Zimbabwe
     204 Baer            ZW Zimbabwe
     205 Higgins         ZW Zimbabwe
     206 Gietz           ZW Zimbabwe

2675 rows selected.
```

Terms to Know

Cartesian product	join
equijoin	outer join
hierarchical	self-join
inner join	

Review Questions

1. Add a clause to the WHERE condition to make the following query return only the department names without employees:

```
select employee_id "Emp ID", last_name || ', ' ||
  first_name "Name", department_name "Dept"
from employees e,departments d
where e.department_id(+) = d.department_id;
```

2. A type of query that has either too few or no join conditions is known as a _____ query.

3. Name three kinds of equijoins.

4. A natural join makes what assumption between the columns of two or more tables to be joined?

5. The Oracle9i syntax moves the join conditions from the _____ clause to the _____ clause in a SELECT statement.

6. To avoid a Cartesian product, a query with four tables must have at least how many join conditions between tables?

7. To return all the rows in one table regardless of whether any rows in another table match on the join condition, you would use what kind of a join?

8. What is the symbol used to signify an outer join in a pre-Oracle9i query?

9. A full outer join uses what SQL set operator in a pre-Oracle9i database query?

10. A primary key in one table would frequently be joined to what in a second table?

Chapter 6

Advanced SQL Queries

In the previous chapter, you saw how you can write queries that retrieve information from multiple tables. This chapter looks at more advanced types of queries. We will begin with relatively simple subqueries, which allow you to put one query inside another, rather than running two individual queries. Subqueries can be tied even more closely to the main query using a correlated subquery, where columns in the WHERE clause of the subquery directly reference columns in the main query.

Sometimes, you need to get similar information from more than one query, and there is some overlap between the results. You might not want to see the duplicates, or you might want to see only the results that two queries have in common. As you'll learn here, you can use UNION and INTERSECT to accomplish these tasks. You'll also learn how to use ROLLUP and CUBE to summarize table information.

Subqueries

subquery
A query that is embedded in a main, or parent, query and used to assist in filtering the result set from a query.

A *subquery* places one query inside another one. The second query resides somewhere within the WHERE clause of a SELECT statement. One or more values returned by the subquery are used by the main query to return the results to the user.

The types of operators allowed in the WHERE clause depend on whether the subquery returns one row or more than one row. If only a single row is returned from a query, the comparison operators =, !=, <, >, >=, <=, and so forth are valid. If more than one row is returned from a subquery, operators such as IN, NOT IN, ANY, and ALL are valid.

Single-Row Subqueries

The boss, King, wants to do his quarterly salary analysis. He would like to see which employees in the IT department are earning more than the average salary across all employees. Janice, the database analyst and DBA, realizes that this could be written as two queries and decides to take that approach first before using a subquery. The average salary for an employee in the company is retrieved by a query you've seen in previous chapters:

```
select avg(salary) from employees;


AVG(SALARY)
-----------
 6461.68224


1 row selected.
```

Using this information as a starting point, Janice writes a second query to see which employees in the IT department (department 60) have a higher salary than the average. She must cut and paste the number returned from the previous query into this new query:

```
select employee_id, last_name, first_name, salary
from employees
where salary > 6461.68224
and department_id = 60;


EMPLOYEE_ID LAST_NAME      FIRST_NAME            SALARY
----------- -------------- ------------------ ----------
        103 Hunold         Alexander             9000


1 row selected.
```

The only employee in the IT department making more than the company average salary is Alexander Hunold, who happens to be the manager of that department.

Janice wants to streamline this reporting function for King. She realizes that this can easily be written as a *single-row subquery*. She will embed the query she used to calculate the average into the second query, replacing the constant value as follows:

single-row subquery
A subquery that returns a single row and is compared to a single value in the parent query.

```
select employee_id, last_name, first_name, salary
from employees
where salary > (select avg(salary) from employees)
and department_id = 60;
```

```
EMPLOYEE_ID LAST_NAME     FIRST_NAME              SALARY
----------- -------------  ----------------------  ----------
        103 Hunold        Alexander                 9000
```

```
1 row selected.
```

Not only is the query more readable and easier to maintain than the version with two queries, but the Oracle server also will process it much more efficiently.

As a general rule, a query, enclosed in parentheses, can take the place of a table name in the FROM **clause or a column name in the** SELECT **or** WHERE **clause of a query.**

TIP

King is starting to realize that the IT department may need some pay increases in the next fiscal year.

Multiple-Row Subqueries

Sometimes, you want to compare a column in a table to a list of results from a subquery, not just a single result. This is where a *multiple-row subquery* comes in handy. For example, King is following up on his analysis of employee salaries in the IT department, and he wants to see who else in the company is making the same salary as anyone in the IT department.

multiple-row subquery
A subquery that can return more than one row for comparison to the main, or parent, query using operators such as IN.

Janice starts out with the subquery to make sure that she starts with the right set of results to use for the main query. She wants to get the salaries for the employees in the IT department (department 60):

```
select salary
from employees
where department_id = 60;
```

```
SALARY
----------
      9000
      6000
      4800
      4800
      4200
```

```
5 rows selected.
```

So far, so good. She takes this query and makes it a subquery in the query that compares the salaries of all employees to this list by using the **IN** clause:

```
select employee_id, last_name, first_name, salary
from employees
where salary in (select salary from employees
                 where department_id = 60);
```

```
EMPLOYEE_ID LAST_NAME      FIRST_NAME             SALARY
----------- -------------  ------------------- ----------
        158 McEwen         Allan                    9000
        152 Hall           Peter                    9000
        109 Faviet         Daniel                   9000
        103 Hunold         Alexander                9000
        202 Fay            Pat                      6000
        104 Ernst          Janice                   6000
        106 Pataballa      Valli                    4800
        105 Austin         David                    4800
        184 Sarchand       Nandita                  4200
        107 Lorentz        Diana                    4200
```

```
10 rows selected.
```

But wait, something is not quite right here. King did not want to see the IT employees in this list; he wanted to include everyone *but* the IT employees. So Janice makes a slight change as follows, removing employees whose job title is not an IT job title:

```
select employee_id, last_name, first_name, salary
from employees
where salary in (select salary from employees
                 where department_id = 60)
        and job_id not like 'IT_%';
```

```
EMPLOYEE_ID LAST_NAME      FIRST_NAME              SALARY
----------- -------------- ------------------- ----------
        158 McEwen         Allan                     9000
        152 Hall           Peter                     9000
        109 Faviet         Daniel                    9000
        202 Fay            Pat                       6000
        184 Sarchand       Nandita                   4200

  5 rows selected.
```

Note that Janice also could have checked for a department ID other than 60, as you have seen in previous queries.

Correlated Subqueries

A *correlated subquery* looks very much like a garden-variety subquery, with one important difference: The correlated subquery references a column in the main query as part of the qualification process to see if a given row will be returned by the query. For each row in the parent query, the subquery is evaluated to see if the row will be returned. In Janice's situation, the salary of each individual employee is compared to the average salary for that employee's department. The check-marked rows in the parent query are returned.

correlated subquery
A subquery that contains a reference to a column in the main, or parent, query.

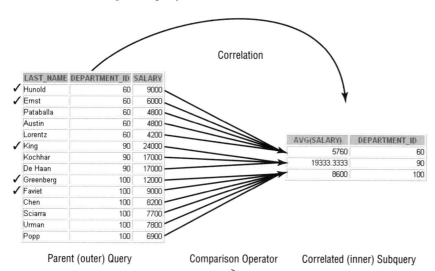

Janice knows that King will be asking for more queries regarding salaries, so she comes up with a fairly generic query that will identify employees who are

making more than the average salary for their department. As a first step, she
builds the subquery that retrieves the average salary for a department:

```
select avg(salary) from employees
    where department_id = 60;


AVG(SALARY)
-----------
       5760


1 row selected.
```

That query returns the average salary for department 60. In the correlated
subquery, she will need to generalize it so that it will correlate with any department in the parent query. Next, she builds the parent query that compares a
given employee's salary to the average she just calculated:

```
select employee_id, last_name, salary
   from employees
   where department_id = 60 and
      salary > 5760;


EMPLOYEE_ID LAST_NAME                SALARY
----------- ------------------- ----------
        103 Hunold                     9000
        104 Ernst                      6000


2 rows selected.
```

Notice that there are two queries that can now be linked together into a correlated subquery to return all employees who earn more than the average for
their department across all departments. If you're not sure how to link these two
queries, the hint is in the column names. Janice joins the two queries using the
DEPARTMENT_ID column:

```
select employee_id, last_name, department_id, salary
   from employees emp
   where
      salary > (select avg(salary) from employees
               where department_id = emp.department_id);


EMPLOYEE_ID LAST_NAME               DEPARTMENT_ID     SALARY
----------- ------------------- ------------- ----------
        100 King                           90      24000
```

103	Hunold	60	9000
104	Ernst	60	6000
108	Greenberg	100	12000
109	Faviet	100	9000
...			
193	Everett	50	3900
201	Hartstein	20	13000
205	Higgins	110	12000

```
38 rows selected.
```

As Janice expected, this query still shows that Hunold and Ernst make more than the average salary for department 60.

Multiple-Column Subqueries

There are times when you need to use a subquery that compares more than just one column between the parent query and the subquery. This is known as a *multiple-column subquery*. Typically, the IN clause is used to compare the outer query's columns to the columns of the subquery.

Multiple-column subqueries can be rewritten as a compound WHERE clause with multiple logical operators. However, this approach is not as readable or maintainable as a multiple-column subquery.

NOTE

multiple-column subquery
A subquery in which more than one column is selected for comparison to the main query using the same number of columns.

The boss, King, wants to be able to identify employees who make the same salaries as other employees with the same job. He wants to specify an employee number and have the query return the other employees who have the same job title and make the same salary. Janice immediately realizes that this could be written as a multiple-column subquery. She decides to try out the query on one of the stock clerks, Hazel Philtanker, who has an employee number of 136:

```
select employee_id, last_name, job_id, salary
  from employees
  where (job_id, salary) in
        (select job_id, salary from employees
         where employee_id = 136);
```

```
EMPLOYEE_ID LAST_NAME        JOB_ID      SALARY
----------- ---------------- ---------- ----------
        128 Markle           ST_CLERK      2200
        136 Philtanker       ST_CLERK      2200

2 rows selected.
```

The query looks good, except that Hazel is included in the results. If King decides he doesn't want to see the selected employee in the results, Janice can modify the query slightly and change it into a correlated multiple-column subquery:

```
select employee_id, last_name, job_id, salary
  from employees emp
  where (job_id, salary) in
        (select job_id, salary from employees
         where employee_id = 136
         and employee_id != emp.employee_id);
```

```
EMPLOYEE_ID LAST_NAME       JOB_ID         SALARY
----------- --------------- ---------- ----------
        128 Markle          ST_CLERK         2200
```

```
1 row selected.
```

Set Operators

Set operators combine the results of two or more queries into a single query result. The set operators in Oracle are UNION, UNION ALL, INTERSECT, and MINUS.

All of the set operators have the same precedence. To override the default left-to-right evaluation, use parentheses to group SELECT statements that you want evaluated first.

UNION and UNION ALL

The UNION operator will combine two query result sets into a single result set, sorted by the first column of the SELECT clause for both queries. The syntax for using UNION is very straightforward: Two queries that can otherwise stand alone are combined with the keyword UNION. The first query does not need a semicolon; the entire SQL statement is terminated by a single semicolon, after the second query.

There are a few rules in force when writing a compound query using UNION. The number of columns in both queries must match, and the corresponding columns must also have the same datatypes. The names of the columns need not match, though; the query result will use the column names from the first query.

A compound query using UNION removes duplicates by using a sort operation before returning the results of the query. The values of all columns must be equal for one of the rows to be removed from the query result. This is one of the few cases where a NULL value in one of the queries is considered to be equal to a corresponding NULL value in the other query.

UNION ALL operates in much the same way as UNION, except that duplicates are not removed. A row that exists in both queries will show up twice in the results. Because a UNION ALL does not need to remove duplicates, a sort operation does not occur. Therefore, a UNION ALL will usually return results faster than a UNION with the same queries. If you know ahead of time that the two queries do not have duplicates, use UNION ALL.

At Scott's widget company, the database not only keeps track of an employee's current information in the EMPLOYEES table, but it also keeps track of what jobs the employees have held in the past in the JOB_HISTORY table. The boss, King, wants to get a report that includes both the current and previous positions held by employees in the company, along with the beginning and ending dates for when the employee held that position. Janice realizes that she'll need a UNION or UNION ALL operation, plus a sort operation. She is not sure how she will retrieve the employee names from the JOB_HISTORY table, since it has only the employee's ID number.

Her first attempt at a query tries to combine the job history information with the current employment information, as follows:

```
select employee_id, last_name, hire_date, job_id, department_id
from employees
union
select employee_id, start_date, end_date, job_id, department_id
from job_history;


select employee_id, last_name, hire_date, job_id, department_id
                             *
ERROR at line 1:
ORA-01790: expression must have same datatype as
        corresponding expression
```

The two queries have the same number of columns, but the datatypes of the corresponding columns don't match. This is because the employee data doesn't have an ending date, and the JOB_HISTORY table doesn't have a column to store the employee name. To fix this problem, Janice changes the first query to include a NULL value for an ending date (since the EMPLOYEES file has only active employees):

```
select employee_id emp#, last_name, hire_date,
    NULL end_date, job_id, department_id dept#
from employees
```

She changes the second query to include a constant of an empty string to be a placeholder to match the name in the other query:

```
select employee_id, '', start_date,
    end_date, job_id, department_id
from job_history;
```

The resultant query using the UNION operator looks like this:

```
select employee_id emp#, last_name, hire_date,
    NULL end_date, job_id, department_id dept#
from employees
union
select employee_id, '', start_date,
    end_date, job_id, department_id
from job_history;
```

EMP#	LAST_NAME	HIRE_DATE	END_DATE	JOB_ID	DEPT#
100	King	17-JUN-87		AD_PRES	90
101	Kochhar	21-SEP-89		AD_VP	90
101		21-SEP-89	27-OCT-93	AC_ACCOUNT	110
101		28-OCT-93	15-MAR-97	AC_MGR	110
102	De Haan	13-JAN-93		AD_VP	90
102		13-JAN-93	24-JUL-98	IT_PROG	60
103	Hunold	03-JAN-90		IT_PROG	60
...					
201	Hartstein	17-FEB-96		MK_MAN	20
201		17-FEB-96	19-DEC-99	MK_REP	20
202	Fay	17-AUG-97		MK_REP	20
203	Mavris	07-JUN-94		HR_REP	40
204	Baer	07-JUN-94		PR_REP	70
205	Higgins	07-JUN-94		AC_MGR	110
206	Gietz	07-JUN-94		AC_ACCOUNT	110

```
117 rows selected.
```

Since the UNION of the two queries will result in adjacent employee IDs due to the default sort behavior of the UNION operator, the report makes sense to King. From this report, he can see that Kochhar was employed as both an account representative and account manager, before becoming a vice president in her current position.

Also worth noting in this report is that the columns EMPLOYEE_ID and DEPARTMENT_ID were assigned column aliases in the first query, and so those aliases applied to the entire result.

But, of course, Janice is not satisfied with the results of the report. The HIRE_ DATE column should really be a starting date for the employee in that department, but for the rows in the EMPLOYEE table, it is the employee's starting date at the company. To make the column more accurate, Janice changes the column alias for the first query to STRT_DATE and makes it a correlated subquery, so that the date is actually the date the employees started in their current department:

```
select employee_id emp#, last_name,
    coalesce(
    (select max(end_date)+1
     from job_history
     where employee_id = emp.employee_id),
     hire_date) strt_date,
   NULL end_date, job_id, department_id dept#
from employees emp
union
select employee_id, '', start_date,
   end_date, job_id, department_id
from job_history
order by emp# asc, strt_date desc;
```

EMP#	LAST_NAME	STRT_DATE	END_DATE	JOB_ID	DEPT#
100	King	17-JUN-87		AD_PRES	90
101	Kochhar	16-MAR-97		AD_VP	90
101		28-OCT-93	15-MAR-97	AC_MGR	110
101		21-SEP-89	27-OCT-93	AC_ACCOUNT	110
102	De Haan	25-JUL-98		AD_VP	90
102		13-JAN-93	24-JUL-98	IT_PROG	60
103	Hunold	03-JAN-90		IT_PROG	60
...					
201	Hartstein	20-DEC-99		MK_MAN	20
201		17-FEB-96	19-DEC-99	MK_REP	20
202	Fay	17-AUG-97		MK_REP	20
203	Mavris	07-JUN-94		HR_REP	40
204	Baer	07-JUN-94		PR_REP	70
205	Higgins	07-JUN-94		AC_MGR	110
206	Gietz	07-JUN-94		AC_ACCOUNT	110

```
117 rows selected.
```

There are two differences between this query and the previous one. A minor difference is that the query result is sorted by employee number in ascending order and by the starting date in descending order. King wants to see the employee's most recent job first.

The second difference is a bit more complex. Janice's goal was to find out if the employee had any previous jobs and, if so, return the ending date for the last job that employee had. Remember that you can have the SQL text (in parentheses) of a correlated subquery in the SELECT, FROM, or WHERE clause of the parent query. In this case, the correlated subquery is as follows:

```
(select max(end_date)+1
      from job_history
      where employee_id = emp.employee_id)
```

For each row in the EMPLOYEE table, this subquery will find the last date that the employee worked in any department and adds one day, resulting in the first date that the employee started in their current position. But if the employee has never switched departments, there will be no rows in the JOB_HISTORY table, and therefore the subquery will return a NULL result. The solution is to wrap the COALESCE function around the query.

The COALESCE function will return the first non-NULL argument in the argument list. The HIRE_DATE column is specified as the second argument to COALESCE, so if the employee has never switched departments, the original hire date will be returned from this function:

```
coalesce(
      (select max(end_date)+1
      from job_history
      where employee_id = emp.employee_id),
      hire_date) strt_date,
```

To reiterate, the above section of SQL evaluates to either the first day employees started in their current department or their hiring date, if they have never switched departments. The column alias STRT_DATE is assigned to this derived column.

The next morning, Janice realizes that she could have used UNION ALL instead of UNION in this query. There will never be any duplicate records between the two queries in this compound query, mainly because the database does not store the employee's current job position and starting date in the JOB_HISTORY table.

TIP

DBAs should be on the lookout for queries that use UNION when UNION ALL would produce the same desired results. Because UNION does a sort while removing duplicates, many UNION queries will have a much more noticeable performance impact on the system than the same queries that use UNION ALL. Oracle 10g's web-based Enterprise Manager Database Control can easily identify SQL statements or sessions with a high impact on the system using the Top SQL and Top Sessions functions.

INTERSECT

There are times when you need to know which rows two tables or queries have in common. The INTERSECT operator provides this functionality. As with the UNION operator, the number and types of the columns in the two queries to be compared must be the same, but the column names can be different. Rows are returned from an INTERSECT operation only if all columns in the two queries match.

In Scott's widget database, the current employment information is kept in the EMPLOYEES table, and the previous employment information (when employees have changed jobs) is kept in the JOB_HISTORY table. The boss wants to find out which employees have changed departments multiple times and have come back to work in the department they worked in previously, with the same job title. Janice knows that she needs to use the EMPLOYEES and JOB_HISTORY tables, and she decides to use the INTERSECT operator to see if there are current employees in a particular department and job title that are also in the JOB_HISTORY table. Janice realizes that a multicolumn join in a WHERE clause may produce similar results, but she thinks that the INTERSECT method is more straightforward and easier to use and maintain. Her first query looks like this:

```
select employee_id, job_id, department_id from employees
intersect
select employee_id, job_id, department_id from job_history;


EMPLOYEE_ID JOB_ID     DEPARTMENT_ID
----------- ---------- -------------
        176 SA_REP                80


1 row selected.
```

King looks at this report and thinks that something is amiss. He is sure that there was another employee besides employee number 176 who has changed job titles and came back to work with her original job title. Janice realizes that she is comparing too many columns, and she rewrites her query as follows:

```
select employee_id, job_id from employees
intersect
select employee_id, job_id from job_history;


EMPLOYEE_ID JOB_ID
----------- ----------
        176 SA_REP
        200 AD_ASST


2 rows selected.
```

As King suspected, employee number 200 is back working with her old job title, after previously switching departments. Because one of the three columns was different in the previous query, employee number 200 did not show up in the results.

Now that Janice has the result set that King was looking for, she decides that it would be more readable if the employee's last name and first name were in the report also. The problem is, she can't add it to the EMPLOYEES query with the INTERSECT operator, since the JOB_HISTORY table does not have the employee's last name, and as a result the compound INTERSECT query would not return any rows. Instead, she treats the last query as a subquery and joins it back to the EMPLOYEES table:

```
select e.employee_id, e.last_name, e.first_name,
   e.job_id from employees e inner join
    (select employee_id, job_id from employees
     intersect
     select employee_id, job_id from job_history) i
on e.employee_id = i.employee_id;
```

```
EMPLOYEE_ID LAST_NAME        FIRST_NAME     JOB_ID
----------- ---------------- -------------- ----------
        176 Taylor           Jonathon       SA_REP
        200 Whalen           Jennifer       AD_ASST
```

```
2 rows selected.
```

Notice that Janice is using Oracle's INNER JOIN syntax, available since Oracle9*i*. The query in parentheses is treated just as if it were another table being joined in the new query.

MINUS

The MINUS compound-query operator returns rows from the first query only if they are not in a second query. In other words, the second query is subtracted from the first query. Any rows in the second query that are not in the first query are ignored and do not affect the results of the entire compound query. As with the UNION operator, the number and types of the columns in the two queries to be compared must be the same, but the column names can be different.

The boss wants to make sure that the company's expansion plans are going well, and he wants to know which countries don't yet have a department located in that country. Janice realizes that a MINUS operator might do the trick here. She can subtract the countries with departments from a query with the COUNTRIES table. The first part of her query is straightforward. It is a SELECT from the COUNTRIES table:

```
select country_id, country_name from countries;

CO COUNTRY_NAME
-- ----------------------------------------
AR Argentina
AU Australia
BE Belgium
BR Brazil
CA Canada
CH Switzerland
CN China
DE Germany
DK Denmark
EG Egypt
FR France
HK HongKong
IL Israel
IN India
IT Italy
JP Japan
KW Kuwait
MX Mexico
NG Nigeria
NL Netherlands
SG Singapore
UK United Kingdom
US United States of America
ZM Zambia
ZW Zimbabwe

25 rows selected.
```

The second part is a bit trickier. She needs to subtract the countries in which the departments reside. The DEPARTMENTS table does not have a COUNTRY_ID column, but it does have a LOCATION_ID column. The LOCATIONS table has a COUNTRY_ID column, so Janice will need to join the DEPARTMENTS and LOCATIONS tables to get the list of countries with departments:

```
select distinct country_id
from departments d, locations l
```

```
where d.location_id = l.location_id;


CO
--
CA
DE
UK
US


4 rows selected.
```

Janice realizes that she will also need the country name in the query for the INTERSECT operation to work, so this query needs to have the COUNTRIES table as part of the join:

```
select distinct c.country_id, country_name
from departments d, locations l, countries c
where d.location_id = l.location_id
  and c.country_id = l.country_id;


CO COUNTRY_NAME
-- ----------------------------------------
CA Canada
DE Germany
UK United Kingdom
US United States of America


4 rows selected.
```

Janice can now bring it all together by using the MINUS operator to subtract this query from the first query against the COUNTRIES table:

```
select country_id, country_name from countries
minus
select distinct c.country_id, country_name
from departments d, locations l, countries c
where d.location_id = l.location_id
  and c.country_id = l.country_id;


CO COUNTRY_NAME
-- ----------------------------------------
AR Argentina
AU Australia
```

```
BE  Belgium
BR  Brazil
CH  Switzerland
CN  China
DK  Denmark
EG  Egypt
FR  France
HK  HongKong
IL  Israel
IN  India
IT  Italy
JP  Japan
KW  Kuwait
MX  Mexico
NG  Nigeria
NL  Netherlands
SG  Singapore
ZM  Zambia
ZW  Zimbabwe


21 rows selected.
```

King now realizes that the company is a long way from having a significant presence in all of the countries where there are company employees.

ROLLUP and *CUBE*

Sometimes, a simple GROUP BY clause just isn't enough in a query. Once you generate a report of, let's say, average salary by department or the standard deviation of sick days by job title, you often must run a second query that calculates the average salary or standard deviation across the entire set of employees. It gets even more complex when you break down the average salary by more than one factor, such as department and job title. In this case, you would need to run two or more additional queries to produce the average salary just by department or for the entire workforce.

The results from both CUBE and ROLLUP can be produced by multiple queries, but this requires multiple passes over the rows in the table. CUBE and ROLLUP need only one pass.

TIP

The ROLLUP operator provides rollups of aggregate functions in one direction across the fields that are aggregated. For each ROLLUP operation that uses n columns, the result set has aggregates for each combination of columns and $n+1$ groupings.

The CUBE operator takes the ROLLUP operator a step further and provides rollups of aggregate functions in both directions across the fields that are to be aggregated. For each CUBE operation that uses *n* columns, the result set has aggregates for each combination of columns plus 2*n* groupings.

ROLLUP

The boss asks Janice to give him a report that breaks down the average salary by both department and job function for departments 10 through 90. Janice wants to save time writing the query, and she knows by now that King will want to see some subtotals and grand totals. She will use ROLLUP to accomplish the task in a single query, as follows:

```
select department_id "Dept", job_id "Job",
       avg(salary) "Avg Sal"
from employees
where department_id between 10 and 90
group by rollup(department_id, job_id);
```

Dept	Job	Avg Sal
10	AD_ASST	4400
10		4400
20	MK_MAN	13000
20	MK_REP	6000
20		9500
30	PU_MAN	11000
30	PU_CLERK	2780
30		4150
40	HR_REP	6500
40		6500
50	ST_MAN	7280
50	SH_CLERK	3215
50	ST_CLERK	2785
50		3475.55556
60	IT_PROG	5760
60		5760
70	PR_REP	10000
70		10000
80	SA_MAN	12200
80	SA_REP	8396.55172
80		8955.88235

```
90  AD_VP              17000
90  AD_PRES            24000
90              19333.3333
                        6250
```

25 rows selected.

Notice that because Janice has two columns listed in her ROLLUP clause, she will have three (two plus one) types of groupings in the query output:

◆ Combinations of departments and jobs (for example, 30 and PU_CLERK, with an average salary of 2780)

◆ Summaries by departments (for example, 20 and a NULL job title, with an average salary of 9500)

◆ A grand total (NULL department number and NULL job title, with an average salary for all employees in all departments of 6250)

CUBE

The report that Janice wrote for King using the ROLLUP operator was fine—until he wanted to know summaries by job title also. Janice realizes that she should have given him the version of the query using CUBE to begin with, so she changes her previous query, substituting the keyword CUBE for ROLLUP:

```
select department_id "Dept", job_id "Job",
       avg(salary) "Avg Sal"
from employees
where department_id between 10 and 90
group by cube(department_id, job_id);


Dept Job          Avg Sal
------ ---------- ----------
                     6250
       AD_VP        17000
       HR_REP        6500
       MK_MAN       13000
       MK_REP        6000
       PR_REP       10000
       PU_MAN       11000
       SA_MAN       12200
       SA_REP    8396.55172
       ST_MAN        7280
       AD_ASST       4400
```

	AD_PRES	24000
	IT_PROG	5760
	PU_CLERK	2780
	SH_CLERK	3215
	ST_CLERK	2785
10		4400
10	AD_ASST	4400
20		9500
20	MK_MAN	13000
20	MK_REP	6000
30		4150
30	PU_MAN	11000
30	PU_CLERK	2780
40		6500
40	HR_REP	6500
50		3475.55556
50	ST_MAN	7280
50	SH_CLERK	3215
50	ST_CLERK	2785
60		5760
60	IT_PROG	5760
70		10000
70	PR_REP	10000
80		8955.88235
80	SA_MAN	12200
80	SA_REP	8396.55172
90		19333.3333
90	AD_VP	17000
90	AD_PRES	24000

```
40 rows selected.
```

Using CUBE, she has two columns listed in our ROLLUP clause and therefore will have four (two squared) types of groupings in the query output:

- Combinations of departments and jobs (for example, 30 and PU_CLERK, with an average salary of 2780)

- Summaries by jobs (for example, MK_REP having an average salary of 6000)

- Summaries by departments (for example, 20 and a NULL job title, with an average salary of 9500)

- A grand total (NULL department number and NULL job title, with an average salary for all employees in all departments of 6250)

Terms to Know

correlated subquery

multiple-column subquery

multiple-row subquery

single-row subquery

subquery

Review Questions

1. A subquery is allowed in which parts of a SQL SELECT statement?

2. True or false: A correlated subquery references a table in the SELECT clause.

3. Which set operator will not remove duplicate rows from the result of a compound query?

4. What characteristics of the columns in a compound query using INTERSECT must match?

5. How are NULL values handled using set operators in a compound UNION query?

6. Why are ROLLUP and CUBE the preferred methods for generating subtotals and grand totals for an aggregate query?

7. Which operators can be used to compare a column to a single-row subquery?

8. A compound query that needs to find only the rows that are the same between the two queries should use the _____ set operator.

9. True or false: The IN operator cannot be used with a single-row subquery.

10. Put the set operators UNION, UNION ALL, INTERSECT, and MINUS in order of precedence.

11. What can be used to change the precedence of a pair of queries in a compound query with more than two queries?

Chapter 7

Logical Consistency

In This Chapter

+ Constraints
+ Transaction processing

A key strength of any modern relational database is its ability to validate the information stored in the database. One way the database itself can perform validation is by the use of constraints on a column or columns in a table. A constraint on a table column restricts the type of information in the column. A constraint can ensure that data is not omitted from a column, is within a certain range, is unique within the table, or exists in another table.

A second way to maintain the logical consistency in a database is the ability to "group" several SQL statements together in a transaction, where either all of these SQL statements succeed or all of them fail. This group of SQL statements is considered a logical unit of work. You can control transaction processing by using the COMMIT and ROLLBACK statements.

Constraints

constraint
A condition defined against a column or columns on a table in the database to enforce business rules or relationships between tables in the database.

Constraints are a way to validate the data in a column or columns of a table. The Oracle database has five distinct types of constraints that can be defined on a column or columns in a table: NOT NULL, CHECK, UNIQUE, PRIMARY KEY, and FOREIGN KEY. Only the FOREIGN KEY constraint, as its name implies, does its validation in reference to another table within the database.

——————————————   *NOTE*   ——————————————

The end-user application frequently validates the data entered into the database, even before an INSERT or UPDATE operation occurs, and this might be the best way to implement complex business rules. The ways in which business rules are implemented in applications can be varied and complex. For more information about data validation through the use of business rules in applications, see the book *Business Rules Applied: Building Better Systems Using the Business Rules Approach* by Barbara Von Halle. Oracle separates the business rules enforcement from both the client and the server with its Business Components for Java (BC4J) product. More information on BC4J can be found at http://otn.oracle.com/products/jdev/htdocs/bc4j9irc_datasheet.html. **Oracle's Oracle Technology Network (OTN) is a free website but requires you to register with a valid e-mail address.**

Constraints, like many other database objects, can be defined when the table is defined or added to the table later. You can also remove, disable, or enable existing constraints.

Any constraint can have a name assigned to it when it is created. If you do not explicitly assign a name, Oracle will give the constraint a system-assigned name.

The NULL constraint can be defined only at the column level. All other constraints can be defined at the column level or at the table level. Some constraints, such as a constraint that compares the values of two columns, must necessarily be defined at the table level.

NOT NULL

NOT NULL constraint
A constraint that prevents NULL values from being entered into a column of a table.

The *NOT NULL constraint* is the most straightforward of all the constraints. It specifies that a column will not allow NULL values, regardless of its datatype. The syntax for a NOT NULL constraint is as follows:

```
[CONSTRAINT <constraint name>] [NOT] NULL
```

In Scott's widget database, the HR table JOBS contains the job identifier, the job description, and the minimum and maximum salary for the job. The table structure is shown here with a DESCRIBE command:

```
desc jobs


Name                              Null?    Type
```

----------------------------	--------	----------------
JOB_ID	NOT NULL	VARCHAR2(10)
JOB_TITLE	NOT NULL	VARCHAR2(35)
MIN_SALARY		NUMBER(6)
MAX_SALARY		NUMBER(6)

When a new job is added or an existing job is modified, the columns for the job identifier and the job title must contain a value. The salary range columns, however, can remain undefined—either explicitly by assigning NULL values to them or implicitly by not specifying those two column names in an INSERT statement.

The boss, King, wants to make sure that when a new job is created, a minimum salary is always entered for the job. Janice, the DBA, changes the structure of the JOBS table with the ALTER TABLE command, as follows:

```
alter table jobs modify (min_salary not null);
```

```
Table altered.
```

The next time someone from HR tries to add a new JOBS table row without a minimum salary, here is what will happen:

```
insert into jobs (job_id, job_title)
    values('IT_DBDES', 'Database Designer');
```

```
insert into jobs (job_id, job_title)
*
ERROR at line 1:
ORA-01400: cannot insert NULL into
    ("HR"."JOBS"."MIN_SALARY")
```

The MIN_SALARY field must be entered with some value, even if it is zero:

```
insert into jobs (job_id, job_title, min_salary)
    values('IT_DBDES', 'Database Designer', 12500);
```

```
1 row created.
```

At some point, the HR department may want to update this row in the JOBS table to indicate an upper range for the salary for this job position. However, it would not be unreasonable to expect that some job positions may not have any upper value, and therefore a NULL value in the MAX_SALARY field could reflect the business rule that there is no maximum salary in force for a particular position.

CHECK

CHECK constraint
A constraint that evaluates the condition defined in the constraint and permits the INSERT or UPDATE of the row in the table if the condition is satisfied.

A *CHECK constraint* can apply directly to a specific column, or it can apply at the table level if the constraint must reference more than one column. CHECK constraints are useful if you need to keep values of a column within a certain range or within a list of specific values, such as ensuring that a gender column contains either M or F.

The CONSTRAINT clause can be specified at either the column level or at the table level. The constraint can be specified at the column level if the constraint refers only to that column. The format of the CONSTRAINT clause is as follows:

```
[CONSTRAINT <constraint name>] CHECK (<condition>)
```

The HR department members are still having some problems with the JOBS table. They sometimes enter the lower and upper ranges for the salary amount backwards. As usual, Janice is tasked with finding a way to fix this problem. She considers changing the data-entry screens to check the salary amounts before they are inserted, but this might not be the best solution, since some of the people in the HR department use the INSERT statement against the database, bypassing any business logic that might be in the application that supports the data-entry screen.

Janice decides to add a CHECK constraint to the JOBS table to make sure the salaries are entered in the correct order:

```
alter table jobs
    add constraint ck1_jobs
        check (max_salary > min_salary);


Table altered.
```

TIP

It's good practice to name your constraints with a reference to both the type of constraint and the table it references. This helps both DBAs and developers when tracking down which table is causing a constraint violation in an application that might have hundreds of tables.

Now if the order of the salaries were inadvertently reversed in the INSERT statement, the INSERT would not be allowed, due to the new CHECK constraint:

```
insert into jobs
    (job_id, job_title, min_salary, max_salary)
    values
    ('IT_TECHLD', 'Technical Lead', 17500, 10000);


insert into jobs
    (job_id, job_title, min_salary, max_salary)
```

```
*
ERROR at line 1:
ORA-02290: check constraint (HR.CK1_JOBS) violated
```

The HR department decides that the new technical lead position has an open-ended upper salary, so the addition is made with the following INSERT command:

```
insert into jobs (job_id, job_title, min_salary)
    values('IT_TECHLD', 'Technical Lead', 10000);
```

```
1 row created.
```

Even though no maximum salary is specified, this INSERT operation still works. A CHECK constraint condition will allow the record to be inserted if the CHECK condition expression evaluates to either true or unknown. In this INSERT statement, the MAX_SALARY column is NULL, and therefore the CHECK condition expression (max_salary > min_salary) is (NULL > 10000), which evaluates to NULL (unknown). Therefore, the CHECK condition will not prevent this row from being inserted. However, explicit NULL checking can be performed in a CHECK constraint by using the IS NULL or IS NOT NULL operator.

Later in the week, Janice learns that the business rule for minimum and maximum salary in the JOBS table has changed; if a minimum salary is specified, then a maximum salary must also be specified. Therefore, either both salaries are NULL or both salaries are NOT NULL. Janice decides that a new CHECK constraint is needed to enforce this business rule, so her first step is to drop the existing constraint on the table:

```
alter table jobs drop constraint ck1_jobs;
```

```
Table altered.
```

The new check constraint will compare MIN_SALARY and MAX_SALARY only if both values are NOT NULL, otherwise both values must be NULL to pass the CHECK constraint:

```
alter table jobs add constraint ck1_jobs
    check ((max_salary is not null and
            min_salary is not null and
            max_salary > min_salary)
        or
        (max_salary is null and min_salary is null)
        );
```

```
Table altered.
```

In rare circumstances, there is an exception to this business rule. Occasionally, the boss still wants to enter a minimum salary without a maximum salary. Janice can temporarily disable the constraint:

```
alter table jobs disable constraint ck1_jobs;

Table altered.

insert into jobs (job_id, job_title, min_salary)
     values('IT_RSRCH', 'IT Research and Development',
                    25000);

1 row created.
```

By default, if Janice reenables the constraint, this new row in the JOBS table will fail the constraint check, so she must use the NOVALIDATE option when reenabling the constraint:

```
alter table jobs enable novalidate constraint ck1_jobs;

Table altered.
```

Using NOVALIDATE doesn't check to see if any existing rows violate the CHECK constraint; only new or updated rows are checked. As you'd expect, the default is VALIDATE when reenabling a constraint. When a constraint is reenabled with VALIDATE, the data in every row is checked to make sure it passes the CHECK constraint.

UNIQUE

UNIQUE constraint
A constraint that prevents duplicate values from being specified in a column or combination of columns in a table. NULL values may be specified for columns that have a UNIQUE constraint defined, as long as the column itself does not have a NOT NULL constraint.

The *UNIQUE constraint* can be applied at the column level or at the table level. It ensures that no two rows contain the same value for the column or columns that have the UNIQUE constraint.

The syntax for a UNIQUE constraint clause is as follows:

```
[CONSTRAINT <constraint name>]
     UNIQUE [(<column>, <column>, ...)]
```

For ensuring that a combination of two or more columns is unique within the table, the optional column specification portion of the above syntax is used at the table level.

To more easily report salaries and bonuses to the IRS, King has asked Janice, the DBA, to add a social security number column to the EMPLOYEES table. Since

no two employees can have the same social security number, Janice uses a
UNIQUE constraint when she adds this column to the EMPLOYEES table:

```
alter table employees
    add (ssn varchar2(11)
        constraint uk1_employees unique);
```

```
Table altered.
```

Janice is doing two things in one statement: adding the SSN column and adding the named constraint. The column will still allow NULL values, but when it is
populated for an employee, it must not duplicate any other SSN value in the
EMPLOYEES table.

When the HR department tries to update two records with the same social
security number, the constraint prevents the second UPDATE command from
completing successfully:

```
update employees
    set ssn = '987-65-4321'
    where employee_id = 116;
```

```
1 row updated.
```

```
update employees
    set ssn = '987-65-4321'
    where employee_id = 117;
```

```
update employees
*
ERROR at line 1:
ORA-00001: unique constraint (HR.UK1_EMPLOYEES) violated
```

PRIMARY KEY

A *PRIMARY KEY constraint* is similar to a UNIQUE constraint, with two exceptions: a PRIMARY KEY constraint will not allow NULL values, and only one PRIMARY
KEY constraint is allowed on a table. A PRIMARY KEY constraint can be defined at
either the column level or the table level. A PRIMARY KEY constraint is important
when you want to find a way to uniquely reference a row in the table with the primary key in another table. The syntax for a PRIMARY KEY constraint is similar to
that of the UNIQUE constraint:

PRIMARY KEY constraint
A constraint that uniquely defines each
row of a table and prevents NULL values
from being specified in the column or
combination of columns. Only one
PRIMARY KEY constraint may be
defined on a table.

```
[CONSTRAINT <constraint name>]
    PRIMARY KEY [(<column>, <column>, ...)]
```

If the PRIMARY KEY constraint is applied at the table level (usually due to the primary key of the table consisting of more than one column), the optional column specification portion of the above syntax is used.

Because of tighter budgets and layoffs, many employees at Scott's widget company are performing duties in other departments, but the structure of the EMPLOYEES table supports an employee assigned to only one department at a time. Janice, the DBA, has been tasked with creating a new table that can reflect the new business rule that an employee can be working in more than one department at a time.

She decides to create a table that has three columns: an employee number, a department number, and the starting date for the employee in that department. What should the primary key be? She can't use just the employee number (EMPLOYEE_ID), since this column won't be unique in this table; an employee may be associated with more than one department. The same holds true for the department number column (DEPARTMENT_ID); a department will most likely have more than one employee assigned to it. Janice realizes that the combination of the two columns in this table will always be unique and not NULL, and therefore this will be the primary key. The table definition for this new table is as follows:

```
create table employees_departments
(employee_id   number(6),
 department_id number(4),
 start_date    date,
 constraint pk_empdept
     primary key (employee_id, department_id)
);

Table created.
```

The names for the employee number and department number columns do not need to be identical to the names given in the EMPLOYEES and DEPARTMENTS tables, but it is good design practice to make them the same if the columns will hold the same type of information as the corresponding EMPLOYEES and DEPARTMENTS table columns.

The HR department staff performs the following INSERT operations on the new table:

```
insert into employees_departments
    (employee_id, department_id, start_date)
    values (103, 60, '15-sep-04');

1 row created.
```

```
insert into employees_departments
    (employee_id, department_id, start_date)
    values (104, 60, '12-sep-04');

1 row created.

insert into employees_departments
    (employee_id, department_id, start_date)
    values (104, 50, '15-sep-04');

1 row created.

insert into employees_departments
    (employee_id, department_id, start_date)
    values (103, 60, '19-sep-04');

insert into employees_departments
*
ERROR at line 1:
ORA-00001: unique constraint (HR.PK_EMPDEPT) violated
```

The fourth row is not allowed in the table, because the same combination of employee number and department number is already in the table. The PRIMARY KEY constraint of the table prevented the INSERT operation from completing successfully.

As a result of the three successful INSERT operations, employee number 103 (Hunold) is working only in department number 60 (IT), but employee number 104 (Ernst) is working in department number 60 (IT) and department number 50 (Shipping).

FOREIGN KEY

A *FOREIGN KEY* constraint helps maintain the data integrity between a parent table and a child table. It allows you to define a column in the child table that exists as a primary key or a unique key in the parent table. When a value is entered into a column with a FOREIGN KEY constraint, the value is checked against the primary key or unique value in the parent table to make sure it exists there; if not, the row cannot be inserted.

The syntax for specifying a FOREIGN KEY constraint is as follows:

FOREIGN KEY constraint
A constraint that establishes a parent-child relationship between two tables via one or more common columns. The foreign key in the child table refers to a primary or unique key in the parent table.

```
[CONSTRAINT <constraint name>]
    REFERENCES [<schema>.]<table>
        [(<column>, <column>, ...)]
    [ON DELETE {CASCADE | SET NULL}]
```

As the syntax indicates, a different user can own the parent table that contains the primary or unique key referenced, and therefore the parent table name referenced must be qualified with the owner name. The column list can be omitted if the referenced key is a primary key.

The last part of the syntax, [ON DELETE {CASCADE | SET NULL}], specifies what happens when the row in the parent table is deleted. If this clause is omitted, the row in the parent table cannot be removed until all the rows containing foreign key references in all child tables are either removed or the foreign key column is set to NULL. If ON DELETE CASCADE is specified and the parent table's row is deleted, all rows in the child table that contain the primary key of the parent table's row are deleted. If ON DELETE SET NULL is specified, a much more benign action occurs: If a parent table row is deleted, the foreign key column in all child table rows that contain the parent row's primary key value is set to NULL.

For about a month now, the HR department has been using the new SSN column in the EMPLOYEES table. Now the boss decides that this is not a good idea, because of privacy concerns. Other departments use the EMPLOYEES table, and the social security information should not be visible to the other departments.

Janice needs to create an entirely new table to hold the social security number values for the employees and remove the SSN column from the EMPLOYEES table. The new table must be linked to the EMPLOYEES table, so she wants to have a column with the employee number that is a foreign key to the EMPLOYEES table. She also needs the SSN column itself. She'll put in a date field to hold the date when the social security number was entered into this table. No other columns are necessary now (columns can always be added later).

What should be the primary key of this new table? The SSN column looks like a suitable candidate for a primary key, since it is unique and not empty. Rows will not be inserted into this table until the social security number is known. Janice creates the new table, EMPLOYEES_SSN, as follows:

```
create table employees_ssn
(ssn           varchar2(11),
 employee_id   number(6)
     constraint fk_empl_ssn
         references employees (employee_id),
 add_date      date,
 constraint pk_empl_ssn primary key (ssn)
);

Table created.
```

This new table has two constraints: a column constraint (the FOREIGN KEY constraint on the EMPLOYEE_ID column) and a table constraint (the PRIMARY KEY constraint on the SSN column, which could have also been defined as a column constraint since the primary key is only one column).

The HR department inserts the first few rows into this new table, as follows:

```
insert into employees_ssn (ssn, employee_id, add_date)
    values('987-65-4321', 101, '13-sep-04');

1 row created.

insert into employees_ssn (ssn, employee_id, add_date)
    values('123-45-6789', 102, '13-sep-04');

1 row created.

insert into employees_ssn (ssn, employee_id, add_date)
    values('222-44-6666', 303, '13-sep-04');

insert into employees_ssn (ssn, employee_id, add_date)
*
ERROR at line 1:
ORA-02291: integrity constraint (HR.FK_EMPL_SSN)
        violated - parent key not found

insert into employees_ssn (ssn, employee_id, add_date)
    values('999-99-9999', 104, '13-sep-04');

1 row created.
```

The third INSERT operation failed due to the FOREIGN KEY constraint on the table. The employee number specified (303) does not exist in the EMPLOYEES table; therefore, the row is not inserted into the EMPLOYEES_SSN table.

Once all of the social security numbers and employee numbers have been entered into the EMPLOYEES_SSN table, the SSN column in EMPLOYEES can be dropped.

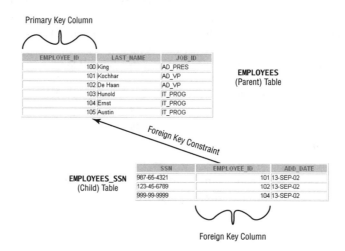

Primary Key Column

EMPLOYEES (Parent) Table

Foreign Key Constraint

EMPLOYEES_SSN (Child) Table

Foreign Key Column

Transaction Processing

transaction

A logical unit of work consisting of one or more SQL statements that must all succeed or all fail to keep the database in a logically consistent state. A transfer of funds from one bank account is a logical transaction, in that both the withdrawal from one account and the deposit to another account must succeed for the transaction to succeed.

As you've learned, constraints created on columns of a table help you to maintain integrity and consistency in the database at the statement level. *Transactions* go beyond individual INSERT or UPDATE statements and allow you to ensure that multiple DML statements against the database either all succeed or all fail.

From a DBA's perspective, the transaction concept is important to understand when allocating disk space. The more activity that occurs within a transaction, the greater the need for disk space to maintain *read consistency* in the database. If a user initiates a long-running SELECT statement, the table data seen by the user will appear to be unchanged, even if other users are subsequently making changes to the same rows while the SELECT statement is executing. As a result, additional disk space (known as undo or rollback space) must be allocated to hold both the old and new versions of the rows being read by one user and written to by another user.

Transactions begin with a single DML statement and end (successfully or unsuccessfully) when one of the following events occurs:

◆ Either a COMMIT or ROLLBACK statement is executed. A COMMIT statement makes the changes to the table permanent, while the ROLLBACK undoes the changes to the table.

◆ The user exits SQL*Plus or iSQL*Plus normally (automatic COMMIT).

◆ A DDL (Data Definition Language) or DCL (Data Control Language) statement is executed (automatic COMMIT).

◆ The database crashes (automatic ROLLBACK).

◆ The SQL*Plus or iSQL*Plus session crashes (automatic ROLLBACK).

In addition, you can use SAVEPOINT to further subdivide the DML statements within a transaction before the final COMMIT of all DML statements within the transaction. SAVEPOINT essentially allows partial rollbacks within a transaction.

The *COMMIT* Statement

There are many situations when you want a given set of DML statements—a transaction—to fail or succeed, ensuring data integrity.

Suppose that the boss decides that to keep the salary budget the same next year, all employees who get raises must be offset by employees who get pay cuts. When the updates are made to the database, it is important that the total salary paid out every month remains constant; therefore, pay increases and cuts must either all succeed or all fail.

In the iSQL*Plus example shown here, Janice performs two pay cuts and one pay increase in a single transaction. If the second SELECT statement had not generated the total the boss wanted, she could have either executed additional UPDATE statements before doing a COMMIT or performed a ROLLBACK to undo the updates and start over again.

If the database had crashed after the second UPDATE statement, the results from all statements in the transaction would be removed from the database. The following statement in the example ensures that the total of the monthly salaries is the same before and after the updates:

```
select sum(salary) from employees;
```

read consistency
A feature of the Oracle database that ensures a database reader (in a SELECT statement) will see the same data in a table regardless of changes made to the table by database writers that were initiated after the reader initiated the SELECT statement.

The *ROLLBACK* Statement

The ROLLBACK statement allows you to change your mind about a transaction. It brings back the state of the tables to the state as of the last COMMIT statement or the beginning of the current transaction.

Janice is nearing the end of a busy day. She decides to perform one more task for the boss before leaving. She wants to remove some order detail items from the OE.ORDER_ITEMS table that are more than five years old, since the ORDERS table was recently purged of all orders more than five years old. She runs the DELETE statement as follows:

```
DELETE FROM OE.ORDER_ITEMS;

665 rows deleted.
```

Janice realizes that she forgot the WHERE clause in the DELETE, so she needs to get back the rows she accidentally deleted:

```
ROLLBACK;

Rollback complete.
```

Another disaster averted. Now she won't need to restore the OE.ORDER_ITEMS table from a backup.

The *SAVEPOINT* Statement

The SAVEPOINT statement allows you to discard a subset of the DML statements within a transaction since the SAVEPOINT was issued. The SAVEPOINT itself is named, and it can be referenced in the ROLLBACK statement, as follows:

```
ROLLBACK TO SAVEPOINT savepoint_name;
```

Regardless of how many savepoints exist within a transaction, a ROLLBACK statement without a savepoint reference will automatically roll back the entire transaction. The following example shows Janice using a savepoint to conditionally undo the DML statements since the savepoint was issued:

```
insert into regions (region_id, region_name)
   values (5, 'Arctic');

1 row created.

savepoint region_5;

Savepoint created.
```

```
insert into regions (region_id, region_name)
   values (6, 'Antarctic');

1 row created.

savepoint region_6;

Savepoint created.

rollback to region_5;

Rollback complete.

commit;

Commit complete.
```

Only the REGIONS row with a REGION_ID of 5 is saved in the table after the COMMIT.

Terms to Know

CHECK constraint	PRIMARY KEY constraint
constraint	read consistency
FOREIGN KEY constraint	transaction
NOT NULL constraint	UNIQUE constraint

Review Questions

1. A COMMIT occurs under which three conditions within a transaction?

2. Under what circumstances can a foreign key column not match the defined primary key value in the parent table?

3. True or false: A CHECK constraint cannot check for NULL values.

4. How are PRIMARY KEY constraints and UNIQUE constraints different? List two ways.

5. What are the three conditions that may be specified, either implicitly or explicitly, on a foreign key column when the primary key column in the parent table is deleted?

6. Write a CHECK constraint that ensures MAX_SALARY is at least 10,000 more than MIN_SALARY.

7. What statement will allow a partial rollback of certain DML statements within a transaction?

8. True or false: A NOT NULL constraint can be defined at the table level or at the column level.

9. What kind of constraint establishes a parent-child relationship between two tables via one or more common columns?

10. If the database crashes while a user session is active, what type of transaction processing is automatically performed when the database is restarted?

Chapter 8

Installing Oracle and Creating a Database

In This Chapter

- Oracle disk and memory structures
- Installing Oracle software using OUI
- Creating an Oracle database using DBCA

When you install Oracle and create a database, you are setting up all of the facilities and components for running Oracle. These components include logical, physical, and memory structures. Every DBA needs to be intimately familiar with how Oracle's memory structures are allocated and managed. This chapter begins with a discussion of the basic components that make up Oracle's memory structures.

While the Oracle software itself is most likely already installed on one of your servers, we'll go over the basics of installing Oracle on the Microsoft Windows platform to see how the Oracle Universal Installer (OUI) does its magic and leads you through the installation process.

After you have the Oracle software in place, you can create the Oracle database itself using Oracle's Database Configuration Assistant (DBCA). You will see how a single installation of the Oracle software can support more than one copy of a database on a particular server.

Oracle Components Overview

database
The collection of all physical files on disk that are associated with a single Oracle instance.

An Oracle server consists of both a database and an instance. In Oracle terminology, *database* refers to only the physical files on disk. These are the files that store the data itself, the database state information in the control file, and the changes made to the data in the redo log files. The term *instance* refers to the Oracle processes and memory structures that reside in the server's memory and access an Oracle database on disk. One of the reasons for separating the concepts of a database and an instance is that a database may be shared by two or more different Oracle instances as part of an Oracle configuration that enhances the scalability, performance, and reliability of the Oracle server.

instance
The collection of memory structures and Oracle background processes that operates against an Oracle database.

It's also important to differentiate between the logical and physical structures of the database. The logical structures represent components such as tables—what you normally see from a user's point of view. The physical structures are the underlying storage methods on disk—the physical files that compose the database.

Logical Storage Structures

logical structures
Structures in an Oracle database that a database user would see, such as a table, as opposed to the underlying physical structures at the datafile level.

The Oracle database is divided into increasingly smaller logical units to manage, store, and retrieve data efficiently and quickly. The illustration below shows the relationships between the *logical structures* of the database: tablespaces, segments, extents, and blocks.

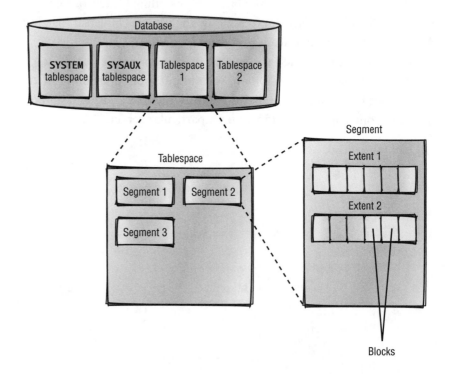

The logical storage management of the database's data is independent of the physical storage of the database's physical files on disk. This makes it possible for changes to the physical structures to be transparent to the database user at the logical level.

Tablespaces

A *tablespace* is the highest level of logical objects in the database. A database consists of one or more tablespaces. A tablespace will frequently group together similar objects, such as tables, for a specific business area or a specific function. A particular tablespace can be reorganized, backed up, and so forth with minimal impact to other users whose data may be in other tablespaces.

All Oracle databases must have at least two tablespaces: the SYSTEM tablespace and the SYSAUX tablespace. Having more than just the SYSTEM and SYSAUX tablespaces is highly recommended when creating a database. In the illustration of logical structures, you can see the SYSTEM tablespace, the SYSAUX tablespace, and two others. Oracle's Database Configuration Assistant, discussed later in this chapter, creates a total of six tablespaces for a default installation of Oracle 10*g*.

tablespace
A logical grouping of database objects, usually to facilitate security, performance, or the availability of database objects such as tables and indexes. A tablespace is composed of one or more datafiles on disk.

Segments

A tablespace is further broken down into *segments*. A database segment is a type of object that a user typically sees, such as a table. Tablespace 1 in the logical structure illustration consists of three segments, which could be tables, indexes, and so forth. It's important to note that this is the logical representation of these objects; the physical representation of these objects in the operating system files will most likely not resemble the logical representation.

segment
A set of extents allocated for a single type of object, such as a table.

Extents

The next-lowest logical grouping in a database is the *extent*. A segment groups one or more extents allocated for a specific type of object in the database. Segment 2 in the logical structure illustration consists of two extents. Note that an extent cannot be shared between two segments. Also, a segment, and subsequently an extent, cannot cross a tablespace boundary.

extent
A contiguous group of blocks allocated for use as part of a table, index, and so forth.

Database Blocks

At the other end of the spectrum of logical objects is the *database block* (also known as an *Oracle block*), the smallest unit of storage in an Oracle database. Every database block in a tablespace has the same number of bytes. Starting with Oracle9*i*, different tablespaces within a database can have database blocks with

database block
The smallest unit of allocation in an Oracle database. One or more database blocks compose a database extent.

different sizes. Typically, one or more rows of a table will reside in a database block, although very long rows may span several database blocks.

Oracle block
See *database block*.

Extents group together logically contiguous database blocks in a tablespace. All database blocks within a single extent will store the same kind of information.

A database block can have a size of 2KB, 4KB, 8KB, 16KB, or 32KB. Once any tablespace, including the SYSTEM and SYSAUX tablespaces, is created with a given block size, it cannot be changed. If you want the tablespace to have a larger or smaller block size, you need to create a new tablespace with the new block size, move the objects from the old tablespace to the new tablespace, and then drop the old tablespace.

Schemas

schema
A named group of objects associated with a particular user account, such as tables, indexes, functions, and so forth.

A *schema* is another logical structure that can classify or group database objects. A schema has a one-to-one correspondence with a user account in the Oracle database, although some schemas may be designed to hold only objects that may be referenced by other database users. For instance, in the logical structure illustration, Segments 1 and 3 may be owned by the HR schema, while Segment 2 may be owned by the SCOTT schema.

A schema is not directly related to a tablespace or any other logical storage structure; the objects that belong to a schema may be in many different tablespaces. Conversely, a tablespace may hold objects for many different schemas. A schema is a good way to group objects in the database for purposes of security and access control.

Physical Storage Structures

From the perspective of building queries and running reports, regular users don't need to know much about the underlying physical structure of the database on disk. However, DBAs do need to understand these database components.

physical structures
Structures of an Oracle database, such as datafiles on disk, that are not directly manipulated by users of the database. Physical structures exist at the operating system level.

The *physical structure* of the Oracle database consists of datafiles, redo log files, and control files. On a day-to-day basis, the DBA will deal most often with the datafiles, since this is where all of the user and system objects, such as tables and indexes, are stored. The illustration below shows the physical structure and its relationship to the Oracle memory structures and logical storage structures.

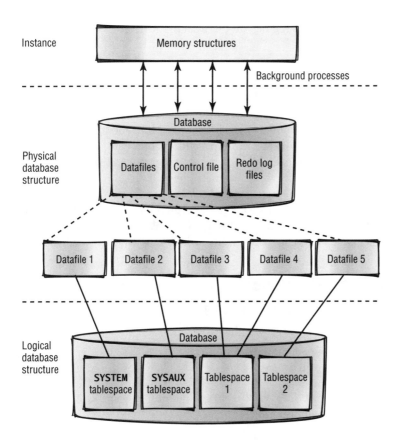

Datafiles

The *datafiles* in a database contain all of the database data that the users of the database save and retrieve. A single datafile is an operating system file on the server's disk. Each datafile belongs to only one tablespace; a tablespace can have many datafiles associated with it.

There are five physical datafiles in the database in the physical structure illustration: one is used for the SYSTEM tablespace, one is used for the SYSAUX tablespace, two datafiles are assigned to Tablespace 1, and the fifth datafile is assigned to Tablespace 2.

datafiles
Files that contain all of the database data that the users of the database save and retrieve using SELECT and other DML statements. A tablespace comprises one or more datafiles.

Redo Log Files

The *redo log files* facilitate the Oracle mechanism to recover from an instance failure or a media failure. When any changes are made to the database, such as updates to data or creating or dropping database objects, the changes are recorded to the redo log files first. A database has at least two redo log files, and it is recommended that multiple copies of the redo log files be stored on different disks. (Oracle automatically keeps the multiple copies in synch.) If the instance

redo log files
Files that contain a record of all changes made to the data in both tables and indexes as well as changes to the database structures themselves. These files are used to recover changed data that was in memory at the time of a crash.

fails, any changed database blocks that were not yet written to the datafiles are retrieved from the redo log files and written to the datafiles when the instance is started again.

Control Files

control file
A file that records the physical structure of a database, the database name, and the names and locations of datafiles and redo log files.

The *control file* maintains information about the physical structure of the entire database. It stores the name of the database, the names and locations of the tablespaces in the database, the locations of the redo log files, information about the last backup of each tablespace in the database, and much more. Because of the importance of this file, it is recommended that a copy of the control file reside on at least three different physical disks. As with the redo log files, Oracle keeps all copies of the control file in synch automatically.

The control file and redo log file contents do not map directly to any database objects, but their contents and status are available to the DBA by accessing virtual tables called data dictionary views, which are owned by the SYS schema.

Oracle Memory Structures

The memory allocated to Oracle includes the following types of data:

- Data from user reading and writing activity
- Information about database objects
- SQL commands
- Stored procedures and functions
- Transaction information
- Oracle program executables

This information is stored in three major areas: the System Global Area (SGA), the Program Global Area (PGA), and the Software Code Area.

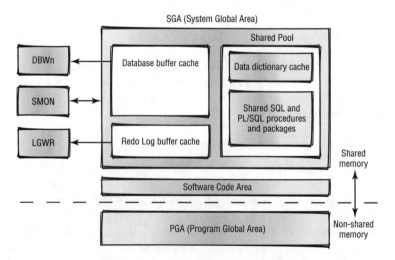

The overall memory allocated to Oracle can be divided into two categories: shared memory and nonshared memory. The SGA and the Software Code Area are shared among all database users. The PGA is considered nonshared. There is one dedicated PGA allocated for each user connected to the database.

System Global Area

The *System Global Area (SGA)* is the memory area that is shared by all connected users of the database. The SGA is broken down into many areas. We will discuss the areas that hold cached data blocks from database tables, recently executed SQL statements, and information on recent structural and data changes in the database. These areas are known as the database buffer cache, the shared pool, and the redo log buffer, respectively.

System Global Area (SGA)
A group of shared memory structures for a single Oracle instance.

Database Buffer Cache

The *database buffer cache* holds copies of database blocks that have been recently read from or written to the database datafiles. The data cached here primarily includes table and index data, along with data that supports ROLLBACK statements.

Any database block can be in one of three states: dirty, free, or pinned.

database buffer cache
The memory structure in the SGA that holds the most recently used or written blocks of data.

Dirty buffers   A dirty buffer contains data from a database block that has been changed or added because of an INSERT, an UPDATE, or a DELETE statement but has not yet been written to disk. This buffer cannot be reused until it has been successfully written to disk.

Free buffers   These buffers either never contained any data or have data that matches their corresponding database block on disk. Free buffers are available to be overwritten by another read operation from disk at any time. Oracle employs an *LRU (least recently used) algorithm* in the buffer cache; the longer a buffer has not been used, the more likely it is that it will be reused by a new database block read from disk.

LRU (least recently used) algorithm
An algorithm used to determine when to reuse buffers in the database buffer cache that are not dirty or pinned. The less frequently a block is used, the more likely it is to be replaced with a new database block read from disk.

Pinned buffers   These buffers are currently in use by DML statements or are explicitly saved for future use, and therefore they cannot be reused.

Shared Pool

The *shared pool* contains recently used SQL and PL/SQL statements (stored procedures and functions). It also contains data from system tables (the data dictionary tables), such as character set information and security information. Because objects such as PL/SQL stored functions can be cached in the shared pool, another user or process that needs the same stored functions can benefit from the performance improvement because of the stored function already being in memory.

shared pool
An area in the SGA that contains cached SQL and PL/SQL statements and cached tables owned by SYS.

Redo Log Buffer

redo log buffer

A buffer in the SGA that contains information pertaining to changes in the database.

The *redo log buffer* keeps the most recent information regarding changes to the database resulting from SQL statements. The blocks in this buffer are eventually written to the online redo log files, which are used to recover, or redo, all recent changes to the database after a failure.

Program Global Area

The *Program Global Area (PGA)* belongs to one user process or connection to the database and is therefore considered nonsharable. It contains information specific to the session, and it can include sort space and information on the state of any SQL or PL/SQL statements that are currently active by the connection.

Software Code Area

Software Code Area

A location in memory where the Oracle application software resides. The Software Code Area can be shared among several Oracle instances.

The *Software Code Area* is a shared area containing the Oracle program code or executables against the database. It can be shared by multiple database instances running against the same or different databases, and as a result, it saves a significant amount of memory on the server.

Background Processes

process

An executing computer program in memory that performs a specific task.

A *process* on a server is a section of a computer program in memory that performs a specific task. When the Oracle server starts, multiple processes are started on the server to perform various functions as part of the Oracle instance. While a detailed discussion of all Oracle background processes is beyond the scope of this book, we will discuss a few of the key processes: Database Writer (DBWn), Log Writer (LGWR), and System Monitor (SMON). These processes communicate with various areas of the SGA, such as the database buffer cache and the redo log buffer, as indicated in the earlier illustration.

Database Writer (DBWn)

Program Global Area (PGA)

A nonshared area of memory used for storing all connection information, including SQL statement information, in a dedicated server configuration for a user who is connected to the database. In a shared server configuration, a large portion of the memory for each connection is stored in the SGA instead of the PGA.

There may be anywhere from one to 20 copies (DBW0 through DBW9 and DBWa through DBWj) of the Database Writer process running in an Oracle instance. As noted earlier in the section on the SGA, new and modified data is stored in buffers in the database buffer cache, which are marked as dirty buffers. At some point (for example, when the number of free buffers is low), these buffers need to be written out to disk, which is what the DBWn process does, allowing subsequent SELECT statements and other DML statements access to those buffers in the buffer cache.

If there is enough memory and the demand on the system is high, having more than one copy of this process may dramatically improve the performance and reduce the response time when a query or DML statement is run.

Log Writer (LGWR)

The Log Writer process writes the buffers in the SGA's redo log buffer out to disk to the redo log files. The Log Writer process must be able to write redo log buffers fast enough to make sure that there is room in the redo log buffer for entries from new transactions. By writing all changes to the database to the redo log files, the changes made to the database can be recovered by reissuing the commands in the logs if an instance failure occurs.

Log Writer writes under a variety of conditions: when a user issues a `COMMIT`, when the redo log buffer is one-third full, when DBWn writes dirty buffers, or every three seconds.

System Monitor (SMON)

SMON performs a number of different functions in the database. If there is a system crash, the SMON process will apply the changes in the redo log files (saved to disk previously by the LGWR process) to the datafiles the next time the instance is started. This ensures that no committed transactions are lost because of the system crash. (SMON also performs a number of other tasks that are beyond the scope of this book.)

Installing Oracle Software

Now that you have an understanding of how the Oracle database components are structured and interoperate, you can install the software that will create and control the components.

Oracle Universal Installer (OUI)
A GUI-based tool used to install or uninstall Oracle software components and tools.

To install Oracle 10*g*, you can use the *Oracle Universal Installer (OUI)*, a GUI-based Java tool that has the same look and feel regardless of which software platform you are using to install the software. As part of most Oracle installations, you can also install the *Oracle Enterprise Manager (OEM)* toolset, which is a graphical system management tool that allows a DBA to manage and administer more than one Oracle instance from a single application. In addition, the browser-based *Oracle Enterprise Manager Database Control* interface makes it easy to administer an Oracle database from any platform that supports a web browser.

Oracle Enterprise Manager (OEM)
A GUI-based tool used to manage one or more Oracle database instances.

Here, we'll go through a basic installation of the Oracle server and review some of the key features of the OEM console.

Using the Oracle Universal Installer

One of the key concepts to understand when Oracle is installed on a server is the *Oracle Home*. An Oracle Home is simply a single directory location in the filesystem that contains all of the installed Oracle products and options for a specific version of the Oracle software. Each Oracle Home has a name assigned to it, and the value of this name is stored in the Windows Registry.

Oracle Enterprise Manager Database Control
An Internet browser-based tool used to manage one or more Oracle database instances.

Oracle Home
A common directory location used to store the associated program files for a specific release of the Oracle database software.

At Scott's widget company, the DBA, Janice, needs to install a second Oracle server on a Microsoft Windows platform. She runs the program `setup.exe` from an Oracle installation CD image on disk. The first OUI screen past the Welcome screen appears, as shown below, prompting Janice for the file locations where the Oracle software should be installed. The source for the install is already specified as a directory location on drive D:.

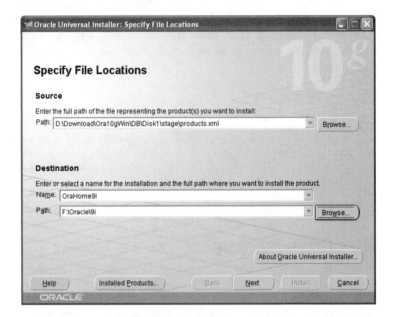

If there are previous installations of Oracle on this server, the pathnames are shown in the Destination section of this OUI screen. In this example, there is an existing installation of Oracle9*i* in the directory `F:\Oracle\9i`. Janice wants to install the newer Oracle Database 10*g* software into the directory `F:\Oracle\10g2`, so she changes the entry in the Path text box to `F:\Oracle\10g2`, changes the name in the Oracle Home text box to `OraHome10g2`, and clicks the Next button.

On nearly all of the screens in an installation using OUI, there is a button labeled Installed Products, which allows the DBA to view and uninstall other products already installed on this server.

After the product list is retrieved from the CD in drive D:, OUI displays the available products that can be installed from the CD. Janice chooses to install the Oracle Database 10*g* Enterprise Edition and clicks the Next button.

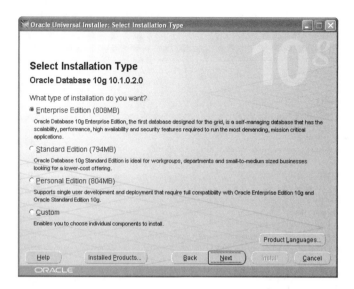

The next decision Janice must make is what kind of database she wants to have installed or whether to have only the software installed. OUI comes with several preconfigured databases, each optimized for different environments. Since none of these preconfigured databases suits Janice's needs exactly, she will install only the software now and create a database manually using the Database Configuration Assistant, discussed later in this chapter. Janice selects the Do Not Create A Starter Database option.

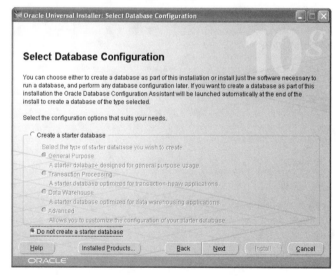

A summary screen gives Janice one more chance to change the installation options or cancel the entire installation.

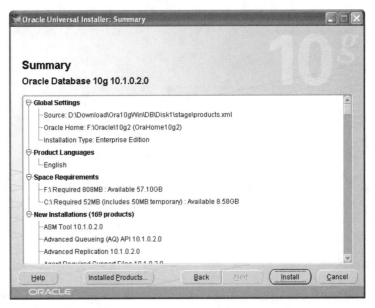

Janice clicks the Install button to begin the installation of the Oracle software. The final OUI screen shows that the installation was successful.

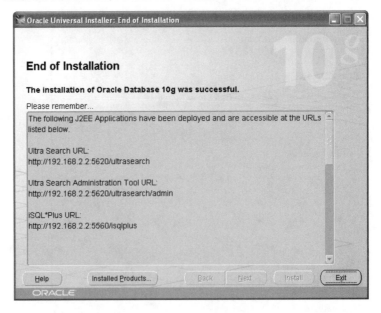

Using the Oracle Enterprise Manager Tools

One of the tools available with Oracle Enterprise Edition is OEM, which allows you to manage Oracle components and to control and configure one or more Oracle databases from one console.

The OEM console has two panes. The Navigator pane on the left provides a hierarchical view of all of the databases and other Oracle-related services on the network. Clicking one of the nodes in the Navigator pane brings up the status and contents of that node in the pane on the right. Using OEM, you can easily browse objects and characteristics of the database, such as tablespaces, user accounts, datafiles, and configuration parameters of the instance.

Janice, the DBA, wants to get a quick overview of the tablespaces that exist in the database that has a connect descriptor of or92. She starts OEM under Microsoft Windows by selecting Start ➢ All Programs ➢ Oracle - OraHome 10g2 ➢ Enterprise Manager Console. She enters her username, her password, and the connect descriptor.

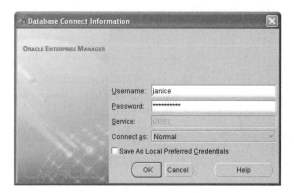

The next screen shows the different kinds of functionality available to Janice in the Navigator pane of OEM. She expands the Storage branch by double-clicking and then clicks Tablespaces. She notices that the EXAMPLE tablespace is at full capacity, which is fine since it is used for training and will not have any new objects. However, she does need to look into expanding the size of the SYSTEM tablespace, since it is 99.39 percent full.

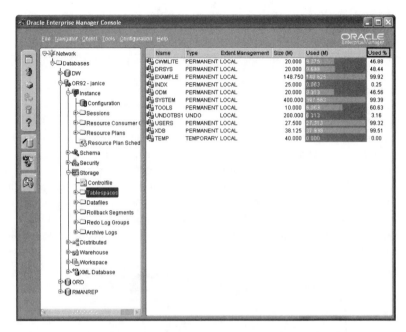

Starting with Oracle 10g, access to a database instance is available using a web browser, giving Janice functionality similar to that of the OEM console. Shown below is the home page for the ord database.

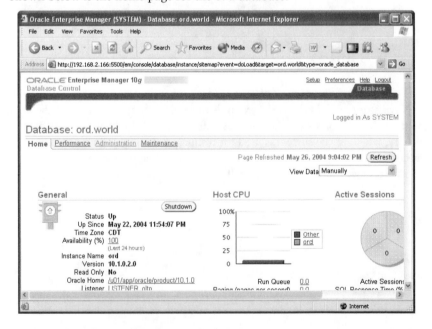

Creating an Oracle Database

Once the Oracle software is installed on a server, you can create one or more database instances using a single copy of the Oracle software. The *Database Configuration Assistant (DBCA)* is Oracle's GUI tool for creating, modifying, and deleting databases.

Database Configuration Assistant (DBCA)
A multiplatform GUI tool that allows a DBA to easily create, modify, and delete databases, as well as manage database templates.

Disk and Memory Requirements

While the software code is shared among instances, the instances themselves each must have a minimum amount of system memory and disk space for adequate performance.

For the Microsoft Windows platform, each Oracle instance requires at least 256MB of memory, plus 8GB of disk space for a fairly complete installation of Oracle Enterprise Edition. Oracle strongly recommends at least 512MB of memory. The amount of disk space needed for the datafiles depends on the application's data needs, but one of Oracle's starter databases uses approximately 1.5GB of disk space.

Using the Database Configuration Assistant

The DBA, Janice, has two big tasks ahead of her for the week. Now that the widget company is over a year old, the boss, King, wants to offload some of the analysis tasks to a second database to minimize the impact on the primary database. He suggests that this new database be designed for data warehouse use. Janice will use the Oracle DBCA to create a new instance to support the data warehousing effort.

To create a new database instance, Janice starts up DBCA by selecting Start ➢ All Programs ➢ Oracle - OraHome10g2 ➢ Configuration and Migration Tools ➢ Database Configuration Assistant. The Welcome screen is shown below.

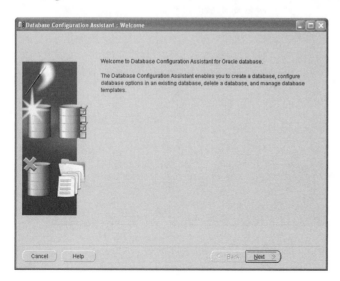

Janice clicks Next. DBCA asks for the type of operation to perform. Janice selects the first option, Create A Database, and clicks Next.

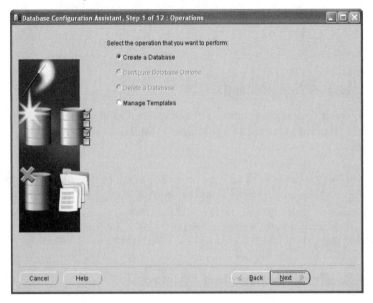

Since the boss wants a database to be used as a data warehouse, she selects Data Warehouse in the Database Templates screen, which appears below, and clicks Next.

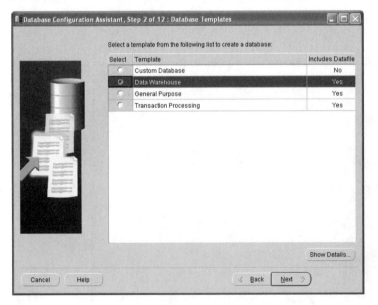

In the next step, Janice needs to label the instance. Janice gets the Global Database Name's suffix from the system administrator, but she specifies the SID as wh10g. The *SID*, or system identifier, is a unique name for the Oracle instance. This is the same as the connect descriptor that a database user uses when connecting to the database with SQL*Plus. When Janice types in the fully qualified name of the database, wh10g.widgetsRus.com, the SID is automatically extracted from the Global Database Name and placed in the SID text box.

SID

A system identifier, which is a unique name assigned to an Oracle instance. A user must supply a SID to connect to an Oracle instance.

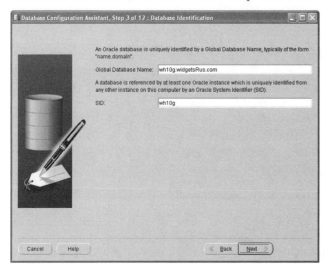

On the next screen, Janice accepts the option to use Enterprise Manager Database Control to manage her database. She also has the option to send all e-mail alerts to her e-mail account, so she specifies the name of the company's e-mail server and her e-mail address.

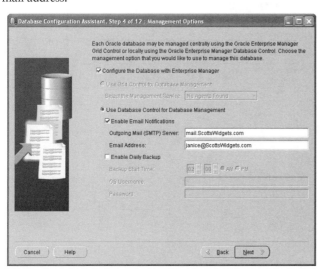

In Step 5 of the DBCA, Janice specifies the same initial password for all of the privileged user accounts in the database and clicks Next.

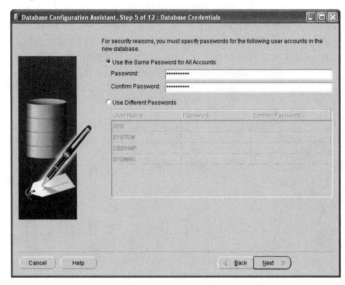

In Step 6, Janice specifies how the database files will be stored. Since she does not have many databases to manage and does not have any Unix experts in-house to configure raw devices, she chooses the default, File System, to hold the database files.

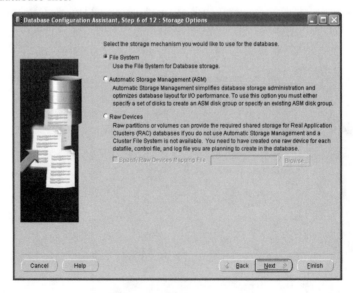

The default database file locations from the Data Warehouse template are fine for Janice's needs, so she accepts the default in Step 7. If she wants to change the template defaults, she can click the File Location Variables button. In this case, the template specifies that the database files will be stored in the same directory structure that contains the Oracle software, `F:\Oracle\10g2`.

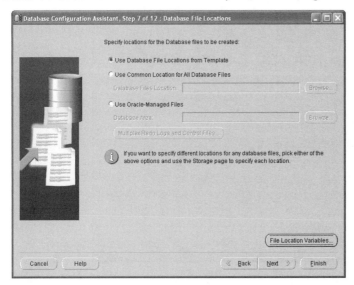

In Step 8, Janice decides that a Flash Recovery Area will help her manage backups and accepts the default. A *Flash Recovery Area* is a central location on disk used by Oracle for backup and recovery operations.

Flash Recovery Area

A central location on disk used by Oracle to contain files for backup and recovery operations.

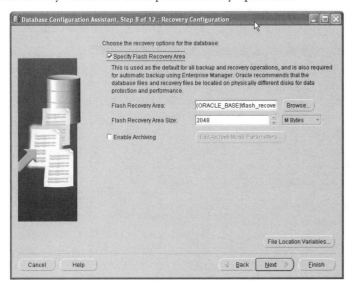

In Step 9, Janice decides to install the sample schemas. They will help her test out the new features of Oracle 10*g*. However, once the new database is put into production, she will remove the sample schemas, because they could pose a security risk in addition to putting a drain on system performance if users are training with this database.

The next screen allows Janice to further refine the memory parameters that Oracle suggests in a data warehouse environment given the server resources, but she accepts the defaults for now. She will perform some advanced tuning once the data warehouse queries have been designed and tested. She does decrease the percentage of memory allocated for this instance from 40 percent down to 25 percent, however, since there is already another Oracle instance on this server.

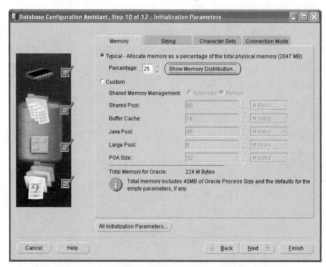

On the same screen, Janice selects the Connection Mode tab. Oracle can accept connections in one of two modes: Dedicated or Shared. Dedicated mode gives the best response time for users who run queries constantly, and Shared mode works best for users who run infrequent queries on a server that may have limited memory resources. Only a handful of users will be using this data warehouse, so Janice selects Dedicated Server Mode.

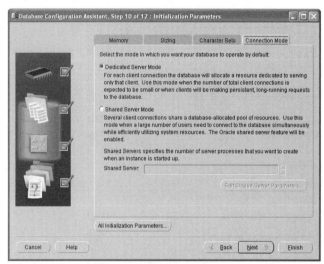

After clicking Next, Janice has the option to tweak the datafile names and locations, but she once again accepts the defaults for all file locations and clicks Next.

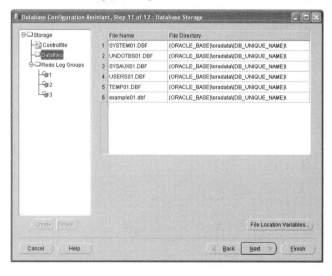

The next screen gives Janice two options. She can either create the database immediately or save everything up to this point as a template. If Janice thought that she might create many databases with identical or very similar characteristics to this one, then she would save these settings as a template for future DBCA sessions. In this case, she decides that there will not be any other databases like this one, so she leaves the default Create Database option checked and clicks Finish to start the process of creating the database.

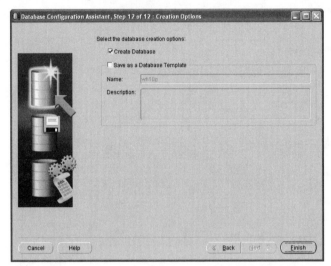

A Confirmation screen is displayed before the actual database creation begins. It allows a final review of the parameters, with the added option of saving the entire set of database characteristics as an HTML file for documentation purposes. Janice clicks OK to continue.

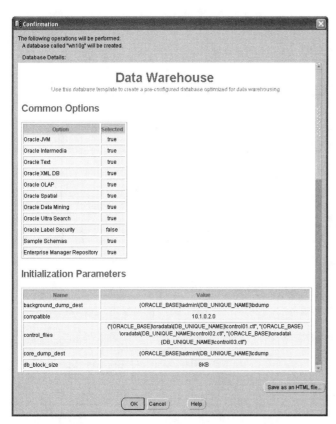

The DBCA provides the status and percentage complete while the database is being created.

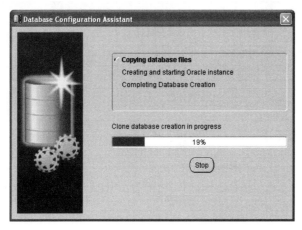

Janice clicks Exit after she reviews the summary screen. The database is ready to use.

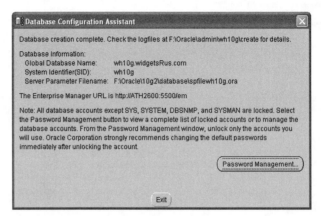

In the future, Janice can use OEM to manage both Oracle instances within the same Navigation pane. As shown here, Janice's new OEM session shows connections to both the `or92` and `wh10g` database instances.

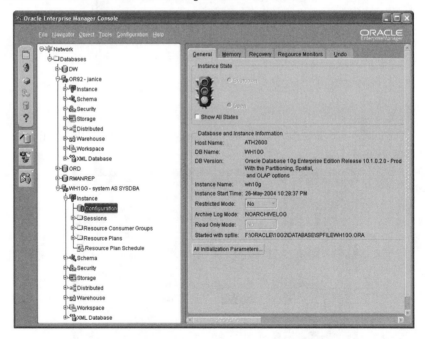

Terms to Know

control file	Oracle Universal Installer (OUI)
database	physical structures
database block	process
database buffer cache	Program Global Area (PGA)
Database Configuration Assistant (DBCA)	redo log buffer
datafiles	redo log files
extent	schema
Flash Recovery Area	instance
segment	LRU (least recently used) algorithm
shared pool	logical structures
SID	Oracle block
Software Code Area	Oracle Enterprise Manager (OEM)
System Global Area (SGA)	Oracle Enterprise Manager Database Control
Oracle Home	tablespace

Review Questions

1. What are the four functions of the Database Creation Assistant (DBCA)?

2. What is the Oracle background process that writes modified data blocks to disk?

3. What is the difference between a database and an instance?

4. An extent is composed of one or more _____.

5. True or false: The control file contains important system tables.

6. What is the GUI-based Oracle tool that can manage and monitor one or more Oracle instances?

7. DBCA can save the specified database parameters in what kind of file?

8. Which Oracle background process will apply the data in the redo log files to the datafiles in the event of a system crash?

9. A database schema is closely associated with which other database object?

10. A segment consists of one or more _____.

Chapter 9

Reporting Techniques

In This Chapter

* Configuring the iSQL*Plus environment
* Formatting an iSQL*Plus report
* Using substitution variables
* Saving and running scripts

It's important that the data returned from a query be presented in a manner that is easy to interpret. The reporting features of iSQL*Plus, SQL*Plus, and SQL*Plus Worksheet make it easy to give columns more meaningful names, as well as provide report headers and footers so that the contents of the report are clear.

In fact, changing how reports are formatted and displayed is one way that you can customize the iSQL*Plus environment to suit your needs. You can also change how the interface appears and change an account's password.

Along with formatting, another way to improve a report is by using substitution variables, which prompt the user to enter portions of the query at runtime. For example, instead of including a department number in a SELECT statement, a query can ask the user to enter a department number. Finally, after you've come up with a set of commands that you'll want to reuse, you can save them in a file and run them later.

iSQL*Plus Configuration

After you've logged in to an Oracle database using the iSQL*Plus login screen, you can make changes to your environment using the Preferences link in the upper-right area of the browser.

From the Preferences screen, you can do one of five things:

- Change how the iSQL*Plus environment appears with the Interface Configuration screen (the default Preferences screen)
- Change how reports are formatted and displayed using the Script Formatting link
- Change how the scripts are executed with the Script Execution link
- Change DBA settings for database recovery with the Database Administration link
- Change your account's password with the Change Password link.

In this section, we'll review the Interface Configuration, Script Formatting, and Change Password screens.

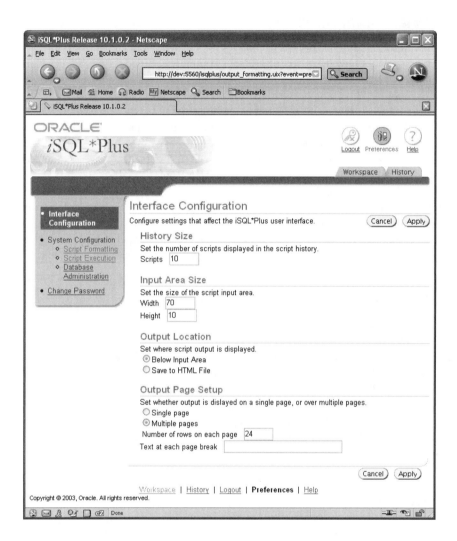

Interface Configuration

script
A set of one or more SQL or iSQL*Plus commands that is executed as a group. Scripts may be retrieved from within an iSQL*Plus session or saved to an operating system file and retrieved later in another session.

The Interface Configuration page controls the History Size. The History Size option specifies how many sets of previous commands, called scripts, are saved in an internal buffer for possible reexecution later. A *script* is a set of one or more SQL or iSQL*Plus commands that is executed as a group. Scripts are saved in the history buffer during an iSQL*Plus session or can be saved to an operating system file to be retrieved later and executed during the same or a new iSQL*Plus or SQL*Plus session. This page also allows you to adjust, in the Input Area Size section, how big a window you need to enter your SQL statements. You can also specify in the Output Location section how the output from the SQL statements will be displayed: below the input area or saved to an operating system file in HTML format. Finally, the Output Page Setup lets you control whether the output from the script appears on a single page or on multiple pages. If the output appears on multiple pages, you can also specify how many lines to display per page.

After you've adjusted the settings as desired, click Apply to save your preferences.

Script Formatting and System Variables

Executing a script and formatting its output are controlled by system variables. A *system variable* in iSQL*Plus is similar to a variable in any programming language. Like a column in a row of a table, a system variable can hold a string or a number. The string or number in the system variable controls some aspect of how iSQL*Plus will display the results of a query or a DML statement.

───── **NOTE** ─────

All of the system variables that can be set in the iSQL*Plus Script Formatting page are also available for customization in the iSQL*Plus, SQL*Plus, and SQL*Plus Worksheet environments by using the command SET `<system_variable> <value>`.

system variable
A variable maintained in the iSQL*Plus, SQL*Plus, or SQL*Plus Worksheet environment that holds a status or a setting for a particular feature in that environment. LINESIZE is an example of a system variable in iSQL*Plus.

The iSQL*Plus environment contains more than 40 variables, most of which are accessible on the Script Formatting page. The Script Formatting page contains more readable versions of these variables and makes it easy to change them using the iSQL*Plus graphical environment.

The following sections discuss a few of the key system variables and their corresponding names on the Script Formatting page in iSQL*Plus: LINESIZE, HEADING, HEADSEP, and FEEDBACK.

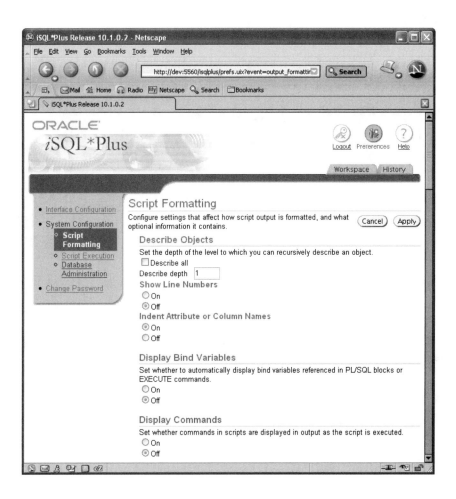

LINESIZE

The LINESIZE system variable (Line Size on the Script Formatting page) specifies how many characters will be displayed on each row of output. Any characters beyond this limit will wrap to the next line.

HEADING

The value for HEADING (Display Headings on the Script Formatting page) can either be On or Off, and it specifies whether column headings should appear in query output. Using SQL*Plus, the following command turns query headings off:

```
set heading off
```

Turning the column headings off may be useful, for example, when sending the output of a SQL query to a file for processing by another program that may not need to have the column headings.

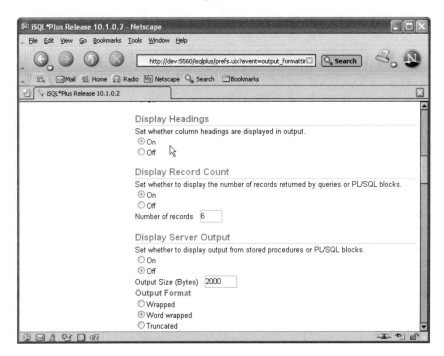

HEADSEP

The HEADSEP variable (Headings on Multiple Lines on the Script Formatting page) allows column headings to appear on multiple lines in the output. A single character, which is the vertical bar (|) by default, divides the heading onto multiple lines. You can set the HEADSEP variable to either specify the separator character or turn on or off the HEADSEP feature. We'll talk more about HEADSEP later in this chapter, in conjunction with the COLUMN command.

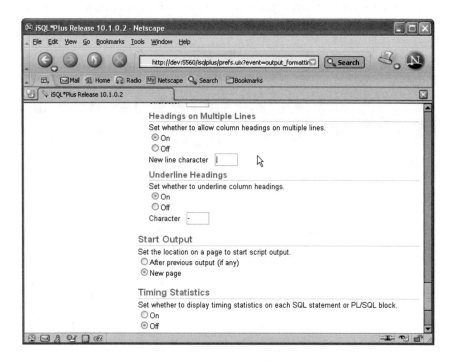

FEEDBACK

By default, if a query returns six or more rows, iSQL*Plus returns a summary of the number of rows returned from a query, as in this example.

```
select * from countries;

CO COUNTRY_NAME                        REGION_ID
-- ---------------------------------- ----------
AR Argentina                                   2
AU Australia                                   3
BE Belgium                                     1
BR Brazil                                      2
CA Canada                                      2
...
UK United Kingdom                              1
US United States of America                    2
ZM Zambia                                      4
```

```
ZW Zimbabwe                              4
```

25 rows selected.

You can set the FEEDBACK variable (Display Record Count on the Script Formatting page) to either change the number of rows that will trigger the row count or turn off this feedback entirely.

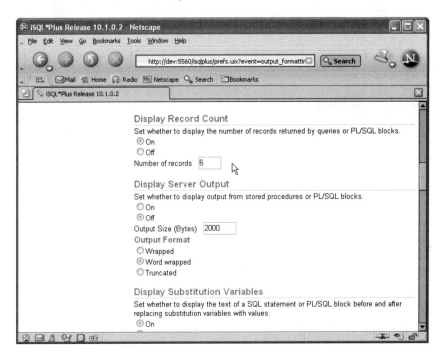

Change Password

The Change Password page allows you to change your Oracle login password. Changing your password on a regular basis reduces the risk of someone obtaining your password and gaining unauthorized access to your account. You must specify your username, old password, and your new password (twice). In SQL*Plus, you can change your password by using the SQL*Plus PASSWORD command or by using the following SQL DCL command:

```
ALTER USER <username> IDENTIFIED BY <new password>;
```

The PASSWORD command will prompt you for the old and new passwords. The ALTER USER command does not prompt you for the old password.

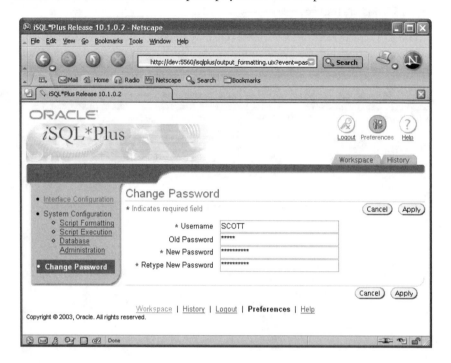

Report Formatting

While a DBA or an application developer who is familiar with the data can interpret terse column names such as MGR_NO and ST_ID, these column names may not be very intuitive for employees in the Accounting department. Similarly, consider a query like this:

```
select last_name from employees
    where department_id = 80;
```

Its output does not make it clear that the query output is only for the Sales department, unless you have all the department numbers memorized!

Reports generated from SQL queries are much more readable and understandable when you use descriptive column names and report headers and footers. The added features of the iSQL*Plus, SQL*Plus, and SQL*Plus Worksheet environment provide this functionality.

In this section, you'll learn how to add headers and footers. You'll also find another way to create descriptive column names. In previous chapters, the examples used column aliases to change column names in the SQL query output.

Using the COLUMN command, you can provide the column alias function along with other formatting. Next, you'll see how the BREAK command can suppress the output of duplicate column values, making a report much more readable. Finally, you'll learn how the COMPUTE command gives totals in a report.

Defining column aliases, changing system variables, and computing totals are settings that stay in effect only for the duration of the iSQL*Plus, SQL*Plus, or SQL*Plus Worksheet session. You'll see how to save and retrieve some of these settings later in this chapter in the "Saving and Running Scripts" section.

NOTE

Unless specified otherwise in this chapter, all command formats and options are valid in all three environments: iSQL*Plus, SQL*Plus, and SQL*Plus Worksheet. However, the examples throughout this chapter focus on the iSQL*Plus environment.

Headers and Footers

The TTITLE and BTITLE commands provide a flexible way to generate report headers and footers. In addition to specifying text to appear in the header and footer, this text can be centered, left-justified, or right-justified. Header and footer text can also extend to two or more lines.

Using *TTITLE*

The syntax of the TTITLE command is as follows:

```
TTI[TLE] [option [text] ...] [ON|OFF]
```

The *option* part of the TTITLE command specifies what you're doing with the header, such as justifying the text. The *text* part of the command is where you specify the text to be placed in the header. You can specify ON or OFF to turn the header on or off. Even if you temporarily turn off the header, the values you specified with the TTITLE command will be retained and will be in effect the next time you turn the header back on.

At Scott's widget company, Janice, the application developer and DBA, has been reviewing some of her old queries to see if she can use some of the reporting capabilities to better advantage when she generates reports for King, the boss. Janice digs up the query that produces the salary report by department, sorted by descending salary within each department:

```
select department_id "Dept",
   last_name || ', ' || first_name "Employee",
   salary "Salary" from employees
order by department_id asc, salary desc;
```

```
Dept Employee                            Salary
----- ------------------------------- ----------
   10 Whalen, Jennifer                   4400
   20 Hartstein, Michael                13000
   20 Fay, Pat                           6000
   30 Raphaely, Den                     11000
   30 Khoo, Alexander                    3100
   30 Baida, Shelli                      2900
   30 Tobias, Sigal                      2800
   30 Himuro, Guy                        2600
   30 Colmenares, Karen                  2500
   40 Mavris, Susan                      6500
...
  100 Chen, John                         8200
  100 Urman, Jose Manuel                 7800
  100 Sciarra, Ismael                    7700
  100 Popp, Luis                         6900
  110 Higgins, Shelley                  12000
  110 Gietz, William                     8300
      Grant, Kimberely                   7000

107 rows selected.
```

Janice wants to make the report more readable by using some of the reporting features of iSQL*Plus. She also knows that King usually wants to see only departments 30 and 60 in the report. She adds an IN clause to the query plus a left-justified report title:

```
ttitle left 'Department Salary Report'
select department_id "Dept",
  last_name || ', ' || first_name "Employee",
  salary "Salary" from employees
where department_id in (30,60)
order by department_id asc, salary desc;
```

Department Salary Report		
Dept	Employee	Salary
30	Raphaely, Den	11000
30	Khoo, Alexander	3100
30	Baida, Shelli	2900
30	Tobias, Sigal	2800
30	Himuro, Guy	2600
30	Colmenares, Karen	2500
60	Hunold, Alexander	9000
60	Ernst, Bruce	6300
60	Pataballa, Valli	4800
60	Austin, David	4600
60	Lorentz, Diana	4200

11 rows selected.

The LEFT option in the TTITLE command left-justified the header above the report. Notice also that there is no semicolon after the TTITLE command; since TTITLE is an iSQL*Plus command, it is terminated automatically at the end of a line, unless the – continuation character is specified.

Using *BTITLE*

The BTITLE command has the same syntax as the TTITLE command. It specifies the text to appear at the end of an iSQL*Plus report. Janice adds a report footer to the report she has been so diligently revising for the boss, in addition to removing the feedback returned from the SELECT query:

```
set feedback off
ttitle left 'Department Salary Report'
btitle left 'End Salary Report' skip 1 -
   left 'Widgets-R-Us, Inc.'
select department_id "Dept",
  last_name || ', ' || first_name "Employee",
  salary "Salary" from employees
where department_id in (30,60)
order by department_id asc, salary desc;
```

Department Salary Report		
Dept	Employee	Salary
30	Raphaely, Den	11000
30	Khoo, Alexander	3100
30	Baida, Shelli	2900
30	Tobias, Sigal	2800
30	Himuro, Guy	2600
30	Colmenares, Karen	2500
60	Hunold, Alexander	9000
60	Ernst, Bruce	6300
60	Pataballa, Valli	4800
60	Austin, David	4600
60	Lorentz, Diana	4200
End Salary Report		
Widgets-R-Us, Inc.		

In the BTITLE command, notice how Janice not only splits the iSQL*Plus command to a second line but also specifies more than one line in the report footer by using the SKIP *n* option to skip to the next line. In other words, the report output will skip to the next line before displaying additional text in the report footer. The BTITLE command would also work just fine if it were all on one line. Janice split it up so that the report specification was more readable to whoever may modify this report in the future.

Column Formatting

The COLUMN command in iSQL*Plus has the following syntax:

```
COL[UMN] [{column|expr} [option ...]]
```

You can specify aliases for column headings in a query when an alias specified as part of a SELECT statement itself is not sufficient. For example, you might want the column alias to appear on two lines above the column's data instead of on just one. The column values themselves can be formatted as left-justified, right-justified, or centered. Numeric values that represent dollar amounts can be formatted with the dollar sign character ($).

Janice makes some additional changes in the iSQL*Plus report she has been working on all morning. She adds two COLUMN commands: one to specify a new column alias for the department number column and the other to format the salary amounts with a dollar sign.

```
set feedback off
ttitle left 'Department Salary Report'
btitle left 'End Salary Report' skip 1 -
   left 'Widgets-R-Us, Inc.'
column Dept heading 'Dept|Number'
```

```
column salary format $999,999.99
select department_id "Dept",
  last_name || ', ' || first_name "Employee",
  salary "Salary" from employees
where department_id in (30,60)
order by department_id asc, salary desc;
```

Department Salary Report		
Dept Number	Employee	Salary
30	Raphaely, Den	$11,000.00
30	Khoo, Alexander	$3,100.00
30	Baida, Shelli	$2,900.00
30	Tobias, Sigal	$2,800.00
30	Himuro, Guy	$2,600.00
30	Colmenares, Karen	$2,500.00
60	Hunold, Alexander	$9,000.00
60	Ernst, Bruce	$6,300.00
60	Pataballa, Valli	$4,800.00
60	Austin, David	$4,600.00
60	Lorentz, Diana	$4,200.00
End Salary Report		
Widgets-R-Us, Inc.		

In the first COLUMN command, Janice is using a *heading separator*. When iSQL*Plus formats this column heading, the heading separator splits the heading so it appears on multiple lines. The default heading separator is the vertical bar character (|), but you can change this on the System Variables page in iSQL*Plus or by using the SET HEADSEP command in iSQL*Plus, SQL*Plus, or SQL*Plus Worksheet. Notice that the heading separator character does not appear in the output.

Note that the iSQL*Plus column alias operation is being applied to the alias in the SELECT statement itself ("Dept"). The COLUMN command does not care if the column heading coming from the SELECT statement is the actual column name or an alias applied by the SELECT statement; it will substitute its own new alias to matching column names from the SELECT statement.

The second COLUMN statement applies a numeric format to the "Salary" column, displaying it as a dollar amount.

heading separator
A single character embedded in an iSQL*Plus column alias that indicates where the alias is split to appear on multiple lines in the output. The heading separator itself does not appear in the output.

BREAK Processing

The values in a particular column may repeat, for example, in a report containing employees with their department numbers. To make the report more readable, it's often desirable to suppress duplicate values in columns like these until the value in this column changes. The iSQL*Plus BREAK command facilitates the suppression of duplicate values for a given column in a report. The syntax for the BREAK command is as follows:

```
BRE[AK] [ON report_element]
```

BREAK **commands are almost always applied to columns that are sorted.**

Janice knows that there is always room for improvement. She also knows that, at some point, the boss will be asking her to make it clearer when the department number changes on her most recent iSQL*Plus report. To remove the extra department numbers, she adds a BREAK command, as follows:

```
set feedback off
ttitle left 'Department Salary Report'
btitle left 'End Salary Report' skip 1 -
    left 'Widgets-R-Us, Inc.'
column Dept heading 'Dept|Number'
column salary format $999,999.99
break on Dept
select department_id "Dept",
   last_name || ', ' || first_name "Employee",
   salary "Salary" from employees
where department_id in (30,60)
order by department_id asc, salary desc;
```

Department Salary Report

Dept Number	Employee	Salary
30	Raphaely, Den	$11,000.00
	Khoo, Alexander	$3,100.00
	Baida, Shelli	$2,900.00
	Tobias, Sigal	$2,800.00
	Himuro, Guy	$2,600.00
	Colmenares, Karen	$2,500.00
60	Hunold, Alexander	$9,000.00
	Ernst, Bruce	$6,300.00
	Pataballa, Valli	$4,800.00
	Austin, David	$4,600.00
	Lorentz, Diana	$4,200.00

End Salary Report
Widgets-R-Us, Inc.

The report is significantly more readable, and the boss can easily spot where the rows for department 60 begin in the report.

Summary Operations (Totals)

iSQL*Plus provides the capability to provide running and final totals to any report by using the COMPUTE command. The COMPUTE command has the following format:

```
COMP[UTE] [function [LAB[EL] text] ...
    OF {expr|column|alias} ...
    ON {expr|column|alias|REPORT|ROW} ...]
```

You can attach specific labels to each subtotal by using the LABEL subclause. The *function* clause can be any of a number of aggregate functions, such as SUM, AVG, MIN, MAX, and so forth. The summary operation can occur when a column value changes or at the end of the report.

Janice is anticipating the next request from her boss and decides to modify her report further to provide the sum of salaries by department and across all departments specified in the report. She will need two new COMPUTE statements and a change to the BREAK statement:

```
set feedback off
ttitle left 'Department Salary Report'
btitle left 'End Salary Report' skip 1 -
    left 'Widgets-R-Us, Inc.'
column Dept heading 'Dept|Number'
column salary format $999,999.99
break on Dept on Report
compute sum label 'Dept Total' -
    of salary on Dept
compute sum label 'All Depts' -
    of salary on Report
select department_id "Dept",
    last_name || ', ' || first_name "Employee",
    salary "Salary" from employees
where department_id in (30,60)
order by department_id asc, salary desc;
```

Department Salary Report		
Dept Number	Employee	Salary
30	Raphaely, Den	$11,000.00
	Khoo, Alexander	$3,100.00
	Baida, Shelli	$2,900.00
	Tobias, Sigal	$2,800.00
	Himuro, Guy	$2,600.00
	Colmenares, Karen	$2,500.00
**********		------------
Dept Total		$24,900.00
60	Hunold, Alexander	$9,000.00
	Ernst, Bruce	$6,300.00
	Pataballa, Valli	$4,800.00
	Austin, David	$4,600.00
	Lorentz, Diana	$4,200.00
**********		------------
Dept Total		$28,900.00

All Depts		$53,800.00

End Salary Report		
Widgets-R-Us, Inc.		

The on Report clause was added to the BREAK command so that totals would be generated by the COMPUTE statement that follows it. Janice "breaks" on the report only once, but she still needs to specify it, because the COMPUTE statement performs the aggregate operation only at a BREAK in a report. The COMPUTE statements in Janice's revised report perform a sum of the salary amounts and provide a custom label when the department salary sum is displayed on the report.

Substitution Variables

substitution variable

A string literal with no embedded spaces, preceded by & or &&, that will prompt the user for a value when an iSQL*Plus script containing one of these variables is executed. A substitution variable preceded by & will not prompt the user for a value if the same substitution variable, preceded by &&, exists earlier in the script.

Another way to make an iSQL*Plus report more flexible is by using *substitution variables*. A substitution variable is a string preceded by either an ampersand (&) or a double ampersand (&&) in an iSQL*Plus script that will prompt the user for its value when the script is run.

A substitution variable preceded by a single ampersand will prompt for a value every time it is encountered in a script. A substitution variable preceded by a double ampersand will prompt for a value once and will save that value. Once saved, if the same substitution variable preceded by a single ampersand is encountered, it will use the value saved when the substitution variable with the double ampersand was encountered.

Janice is reviewing the script she has been working on all day and realizes that sooner or later, the boss will want to run that script for any list of departments, not just departments 30 and 60. She realizes that substitution variables would be useful in this situation, and she changes her script as follows to allow iSQL*Plus to prompt for the department numbers before the query runs:

```
set feedback off
ttitle left 'Department Salary Report'
btitle left 'End Salary Report' skip 1 -
    left 'Widgets-R-Us, Inc.'
column Dept heading 'Dept|Number'
column salary format $999,999.99
break on Dept on Report
compute sum label 'Dept Total' -
    of salary on Dept
compute sum label 'All Depts' -
    of salary on Report
select department_id "Dept",
    last_name || ', ' || first_name "Employee",
    salary "Salary" from employees
where department_id in (&DeptList)
order by department_id asc, salary desc;
```

The only change is the replacement of the specific department numbers in the original script with the substitution variable DeptList. When Janice clicks the Execute button in iSQL*Plus, she is prompted for the value of DeptList.

The script runs as before, except this time a different group of departments is returned from the query.

```
old 4: where department_id in (&DeptList)
new 4: where department_id in (20,40)
```

Department Salary Report		
Dept Number	**Employee**	**Salary**
20	Hartstein, Michael	$13,000.00
	Fay, Pat	$6,000.00
**********		------------
Dept Total		$19,000.00
40	Mavris, Susan	$6,500.00
**********		------------
Dept Total		$6,500.00

All Depts		$25,500.00

End Salary Report		
Widgets-R-Us, Inc.		

Notice that iSQL*Plus, by default, will show the substitutions that occurred before presenting the results. This can be turned off with the SET VERIFY OFF command.

As you may have noticed, Janice is somewhat of a perfectionist, and she thinks that the report would look even better if the report header contained the list of departments in the report. This gives Janice a good opportunity to use the double ampersand in her substitution variable, so that she will not need to enter the department list twice when she runs the script. Her revised script now looks like this:

```
set feedback off
ttitle left -
    'Department Salary Report, Departments: &&DeptList'
btitle left 'End Salary Report' skip 1 -
    left 'Widgets-R-Us, Inc.'
column Dept heading 'Dept|Number'
column salary format $999,999.99
break on Dept on Report
compute sum label 'Dept Total' -
    of salary on Dept
compute sum label 'All Depts' -
    of salary on Report
select department_id "Dept",
    last_name || ', ' || first_name "Employee",
    salary "Salary" from employees
where department_id in (&DeptList)
order by department_id asc, salary desc;
```

She changed the TTITLE command to include the substitution variable &&DeptList. When this script is run, the prompt for DeptList occurs only once.

(i) Input Required

Enter value for deptlist: 10,30

However, the substitution is performed twice. The first substitution variable `&&DeptList` has a double ampersand, and therefore its value is retained when `&DeptList` is encountered later in the script.

Department Salary Report, Departments: 10,30		
Dept Number	Employee	Salary
10	Whalen, Jennifer	$4,400.00
**********		------------
Dept Total		$4,400.00
30	Raphaely, Den	$11,000.00
	Khoo, Alexander	$3,100.00
	Baida, Shelli	$2,900.00
	Tobias, Sigal	$2,800.00
	Himuro, Guy	$2,600.00
	Colmenares, Karen	$2,500.00
**********		------------
Dept Total		$24,900.00

All Depts		$29,300.00

End Salary Report		
Widgets-R-Us, Inc.		

Saving and Running Scripts

If a set of SQL or iSQL*Plus commands will be used over and over again, it makes sense to save it as a script in a central location and retrieve it when it needs to be run. iSQL*Plus makes it easy to save and retrieve scripts.

Janice decides that the iSQL*Plus script she wrote for displaying salaries by department will be used by every department manager, so she will save it on a network disk drive that is accessible to all of the managers. She clicks the Save Script button at the bottom of the Workspace area.

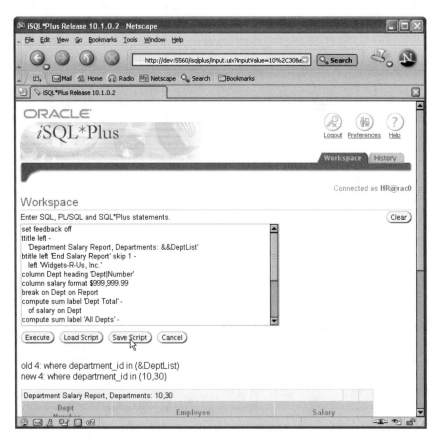

This brings up the Save As dialog box. Janice saves the contents of the Workspace area to the directory F:\Common\SQLScripts.

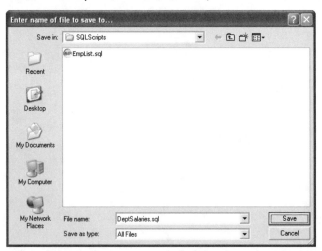

To retrieve a script, Janice clicks the Load Script button underneath the Workspace area, clicks Browse, navigates to the directory containing the script, and selects the filename to be retrieved.

Finally, she clicks the Load button.

The contents of the file are placed in the Workspace area, and Janice can run the commands right away or make further modifications to the script before running it.

Terms to Know

heading separator

substitution variable

script

system variable

Review Questions

1. An iSQL*Plus substitution variable is preceded by what character(s) in a script?

2. Identify the two iSQL*Plus commands that define the header and footer for a report.

3. On which iSQL*Plus web page can you adjust the size of the iSQL*Plus window where you enter your iSQL*Plus commands or SQL statements?

4. Write an iSQL*Plus footer command to display the text *Page 22*, right-justified on the line.

5. Sums and averages can be displayed on an iSQL*Plus report using which iSQL*Plus command?

6. Write a single iSQL*Plus COLUMN command to format the Salary column with a total of six digits, four to the left of the decimal point and two to the right. In the same COLUMN command, define the header to be Monthly Salary, with the words appearing on different lines in the column header.

7. Which iSQL*Plus command controls the row count display after a SELECT statement is executed?

8. Which iSQL*Plus command controls how duplicate column values are displayed on a report?

9. The iSQL*Plus BREAK command is almost always specified in conjunction with what SQL SELECT statement clause?

10. In both the TTITLE and BTITLE commands, what option must be used to specify more than one line in the header or footer?

Chapter 10

Creating and Maintaining Database Objects

As both a DBA and a developer, you will be responsible for creating and maintaining a variety of database objects. First and foremost, you will be creating tables. You will also need to know how to create indexes and views.

To keep track of tables, indexes, and other database objects, you can use data dictionary views, which allow you to retrieve various kinds of statistics about tables and other database objects.

Two other useful database objects covered here are sequences and synonyms. Sequences make it easy to generate a series of unique numbers that are typically used for the primary key of a table. Synonyms facilitate a consistent naming convention for database objects that may exist in the user's schema or in another schema of the same database.

In This Chapter

- Creating relational and external tables
- Using Create Table As Select (CTAS)
- Creating indexes
- Creating views
- Using data dictionary and dynamic performance views
- Creating sequences and synonyms

Creating Tables

The table is the most basic and most important object you will create in a database. Essentially, you could do without every other database object in a database except for tables. Without tables, you cannot store anything in a database.

You can create tables with the CREATE TABLE statement or "on the fly" with a method known as Create Table As Select, or CTAS.

Once you know that you need to create a table, you must decide what kind of table you want. In this section, we'll cover the most common types of tables:

◆ Relational tables

◆ Tables created directly from the result of a query

◆ Tables whose data resides outside the database

◆ Tables with a definition that is available to all sessions but whose data is local to the session that created the data

Relational Tables

relational table

The most common form of a table in the Oracle database; the default type created with the CREATE TABLE statement. A relational table is permanent and can be partitioned.

A *relational table* is the most common form of a table in the Oracle database. It is created with the CREATE TABLE statement, its data is stored in the database, and it can be partitioned. When you partition a table, the data for the table is internally stored in two or more pieces to potentially improve performance and to make the table easier for the DBA to manage if the table has many rows. Partitioning tables is covered in more detail in Chapter 12, "Making Things Run Fast (Enough)."

The basic syntax for the CREATE TABLE statement is as follows:

```
CREATE TABLE [schema.]tablename
    (column1 datatype1 [DEFAULT expression]
        [, ...]);
```

The table that Scott, the company founder, created back in Chapter 2, "SQL*Plus and iSQL*Plus Basics," was built with this statement:

```
create table emp_hourly (
  empno       number(4)     not null,
  ename       varchar2(10),
  job         varchar2(9),
  mgr         number(4),
  hiredate    date,
  hourrate    number(5,2)  not null default 6.50,
  deptno      number(2),
  constraint pk_emp
primary key ( empno ) ) ;
```

Now, the HR schema is used to manage employee information. Therefore, Janice, the DBA and senior developer, must re-create the table to match the datatypes and name of the EMPLOYEES table in the HR schema, as follows:

```
create table employees_hourly (
  employee_id     number(6)    not null,
  first_name      varchar2(20),
  last_name       varchar2(25) not null,
  email           varchar2(25) not null,
  phone_number    varchar2(20),
  job_id          varchar2(10) not null,
  manager_id      number(6),
  hire_date       date not null,
  hourly_rate     number(5,2) default 6.50 not null,
  department_id   number(4),
  ssn             varchar2(11),
  constraint pk_employees_hourly
            primary key( employee_id ) ) ;
```

Because of the PRIMARY KEY constraint on the EMPLOYEE_ID column, the values in the EMPLOYEE_ID column must be unique within the table.

Create Table As Select (CTAS)

If you want to base the contents of a new table on the results of a query of one or more other tables, you can use the statement CREATE TABLE ... AS SELECT, otherwise known as *CTAS*. It's shorthand for two or more individual statements: the traditional CREATE TABLE statement and one or more INSERT statements. Using CTAS, you can create a table and populate it in one easy step.

The syntax for CTAS varies from the basic syntax of a CREATE TABLE statement as follows:

```
CREATE TABLE [schema.]tablename
    AS SELECT <select_clauses>;
```

CTAS
Also known as Create Table As Select, a method for creating a table in the database by using the results from a subquery to both populate the data and specify the datatypes of the columns in the new table.

Notice that with CTAS you cannot specify the datatypes of the new columns; the column datatypes of the original columns, along with any NOT NULL constraints, are derived from the columns in the SELECT query. Any other constraints or indexes may be added to the table later. Column aliases in the SELECT query are used as the column names in the new table.

At Scott's widget company, the Order Entry department frequently sends out mailings to non-administrative staff, but the mailing list is becoming outdated. The manager in the Order Entry department asks Janice to grant the developers in the group the rights to access the EMPLOYEES table. However, the EMPLOYEES table contains sensitive personal information about employees, such as their salary. So, instead of granting access to the EMPLOYEES table, Janice decides to give the Order Entry department developers their own table with a limited number of columns. Using CTAS, her CREATE TABLE statement extracts the name and e-mail address for the Order Entry department as follows:

```
create table oe.non_admin_employees
    as select employee_id, last_name, first_name, email
    from hr.employees e where e.job_id not like 'AD_%';
```

Notice that Janice is copying some of the rows with only a few of the columns from the EMPLOYEES table in the HR schema, and she is creating a new table named NON_ADMIN_EMPLOYEES in the OE schema. To confirm her work, Janice checks the new table:

```
describe oe.non_admin_employees
```

Name	Null?	Type
EMPLOYEE_ID		NUMBER(6)
LAST_NAME	NOT NULL	VARCHAR2(25)
FIRST_NAME		VARCHAR2(20)
EMAIL	NOT NULL	VARCHAR2(25)

```
select * from oe.non_admin_employees;
```

EMPLOYEE_ID	LAST_NAME	FIRST_NAME	EMAIL
103	Hunold	Alexander	AHUNOLD
104	Ernst	Janice	JERNST
105	Austin	David	DAUSTIN
106	Pataballa	Valli	VPATABAL
107	Lorentz	Diana	DLORENTZ
108	Greenberg	Nancy	NGREENBE
...			
195	Jones	Vance	VJONES
196	Walsh	Alana	AWALSH
197	Feeney	Kevin	KFEENEY
198	OConnell	Donald	DOCONNEL
199	Grant	Douglas	DGRANT
201	Hartstein	Michael	MHARTSTE
202	Fay	Pat	PFAY

```
203 Mavris        Susan        SMAVRIS
204 Baer          Hermann      HBAER
205 Higgins       Shelley      SHIGGINS
206 Gietz         William      WGIETZ
```

```
103 rows selected.
```

Everyone in the EMPLOYEES table is in the new NON_ADMIN_EMPLOYEES table, except for the four administrative employees whose job ID begins with AD_.

Janice makes sure to re-create the table in the OE schema every time employees are added, deleted, or changed in HR's EMPLOYEE table. If the Order Entry department wants any other constraints or indexes other than the NOT NULL constraint on columns in the new table, Janice will need to create them manually.

External Tables

Sometimes you want to access data that resides outside the database, but you want to use it as if it were another table within the database. An *external table* is a read-only table whose definition is stored within the database but whose data stays external to the database itself.

external table
A table whose definition is stored in the database but whose data is stored externally to the database.

External Table Data

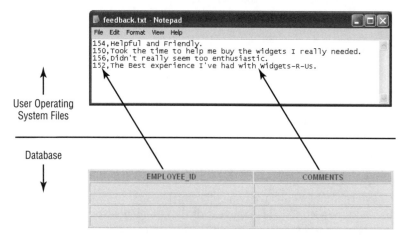

CUSTOMER_COMMENTS External Table Definition

You may ask, "Why not use one of Oracle's utilities to load the external data into an internal table, and then use the internal table?" While this is an option, there are many reasons why this may not be the best solution. One reason is that you can use the functionality of Oracle SQL against the external table to more easily load the data into other tables. Also, if the external data source is maintained by another business area in a text format, the database's copy of the data most likely will be out of synch until the next time you import it. If you treat the external data as a table, it will always be up to date every time you access it as an external table.

There are a few drawbacks to using external tables. External tables are read-only; changes cannot be made to the external data source with UPDATE statements. Also, external tables cannot be indexed. Therefore, if you need to access only a small fraction of the rows in the external table, an internal table with an index might be a better solution.

Janice, the DBA, has been assigned the task of making the customer feedback files maintained by the Customer Service group accessible from within the database. Currently, the Customer Service group receives customer feedback, which is entered on a daily basis into a text file on the shared network drive I:\Common\CustomerComments with a filename of feedback.txt.

directory
A database object that stores a reference to a directory on the host operating system's filesystem.

The first step Janice must perform is to define an Oracle object known as a *directory*. An Oracle directory is an Oracle object that contains an alias to a directory path on the operating system's filesystem. Once defined in this manner, the Oracle directory object can be used to refer to the location on the filesystem in subsequent Oracle commands, such as the CREATE TABLE ... ORGANIZATION EXTERNAL command. You need to run the CREATE DIRECTORY command only once for each filesystem pathname you want to access. Janice's command for creating this directory object is as follows:

```
create directory comment_dir as
        'I:\Common\CustomerComments';


Directory created.
```

The file that contains the data for the external table, feedback.txt, looks like this:

```
154,Helpful and Friendly.
150,Took the time to help me buy the widgets I really needed.
156,Didn't really seem too enthusiastic.
152,The Best experience I've had with Widgets-R-Us.
```

The external table will have two columns: The first field is the employee number, and the second field is the text of the comments from the customer. A comma separates the employee number from the comment. Janice uses the following CREATE TABLE statement to create the external table:

```
create table cust_comments (
   employee_id    number,
   comments       varchar2(100))
organization external
 (default directory comment_dir
```

```
access parameters
(records delimited by newline
 fields terminated by ','
  (employee_id char, comments char))
location('feedback.txt'));

Table created.
```

The first part of the CREATE TABLE statement looks familiar. It contains two columns: EMPLOYEE_ID and COMMENTS. The ORGANIZATION EXTERNAL clause specifies this table to be an external table. The operating system file is located in the directory defined by the directory object comment_dir. Each line of data corresponds to one row in the table, and each column in the external file is separated by a comma. Both of the fields are character strings in the external file, so we define those fields as CHAR. Finally, we specify the name of the external file itself with the LOCATION clause.

Janice, as well as anyone else who can access tables in the HR schema, can use the CUST_COMMENTS table in a query as easily as using any of the internal tables:

```
select * from cust_comments;

EMPLOYEE_ID COMMENTS
----------- -----------------------------------------
        154 Helpful and Friendly.
        150 Took the time to help me buy the widgets
               I really needed.
        156 Didn't really seem too enthusiastic.
        152 The Best experience I've had with
               Widgets-R-Us.

4 rows selected.
```

To produce a report that is more readable for the boss, Janice joins the external table with the internal EMPLOYEES table:

```
select employee_id "EmpID",
    last_name || ', ' || first_name "Name", comments
from employees join cust_comments using (employee_id);

EmpID Name                   COMMENTS
------ --------------------   -------------------------
   154 Cambrault, Nanette     Helpful and Friendly.
   150 Tucker, Peter          Took the time to help me
```

		buy the widgets I really needed.
156	King, Janette	Didn't really seem too enthusiastic.
152	Hall, Peter	The Best experience I've had with Widgets-R-Us.

```
4 rows selected.
```

The CUST_COMMENTS table is indistinguishable in usage from any other table in the database, as long as you don't try to perform any INSERT, UPDATE, or DELETE statements on the external table.

Temporary Tables

temporary table
A table whose definition is persistent and shared by all database users but whose data is local to the session that created the data. When the transaction or session is completed, the data is truncated from the temporary table.

A *temporary table* is a table whose definition is available to all sessions in the database but whose rows are available only to the session that added the rows to the table. Once the transaction is committed or the session is terminated, the data created during that session is removed from the temporary table. To create a temporary table, you use the familiar CREATE TABLE syntax with the addition of the GLOBAL TEMPORARY clause. An additional clause, ON COMMIT PRESERVE ROWS, retains the rows added to the table until the end of the session; otherwise, the rows are removed after each COMMIT.

A temporary table might be useful in an application that uses a table for its session data and is used by hundreds of users; the table needs to be created only once, with the proper permissions so that all application users can access it.

Janice, the DBA, is installing a travel itinerary application that employees use to plan their business trips. The application needs a table that temporarily holds the travel destinations and costs for the employee. Janice realizes a temporary table is perfect for this purpose. Her CREATE TABLE statement looks like this:

```
create global temporary table travel_dest
   (employee_id     number(6),
    destination_id  number(4),
    airfare         number(7,2),
    hotel           number(6,2))
on commit preserve rows;
```

```
Table created.
```

Once the travel itinerary application is terminated and the user disconnects from the database, any rows placed in this table by the user are automatically removed.

Creating Indexes

The purpose of indexes can be summarized in one word: performance. An *index* is a database structure designed to reduce the amount of time necessary to retrieve one or more rows from a table. Indexes can also enforce uniqueness on one or more columns of a table.

Any number of indexes may be created on a table. An index may also be built against a combination of columns in a table; this type of index is known as a *composite index.*

Indexes are maintained automatically. When new rows are added to the table, new entries are recorded in the indexes. When rows are deleted from the table, the corresponding index entries are also deleted.

Be cautious when creating indexes in an environment with frequent update, insert, and delete operations. The overhead of keeping the indexes up-to-date can have a performance impact on the database and potentially increase the response time for users.

Indexes can be either unique or nonunique. A unique index prevents duplicate values from being inserted into a table column with a unique index. For example, an employee table might have a column with a social security number. Since no two employees will have the same social security number, a unique index can be created on the column. If a primary key is defined for a table, a unique index is automatically created to enforce the uniqueness of the primary key.

Nonunique indexes, by definition, will not enforce uniqueness but can still speed processing by narrowing down the range of blocks where the desired rows of a table can be found. For example, a nonunique index on a column with a last name would likely have many entries for Smith. Each of the index entries for Smith would point to a row in the table where the last name was Smith. Using this nonunique index to find all the Smith entries will typically take much less time than scanning the entire table for Smith directly.

An index on a database table column corresponds closely to the real-world analogy of an index in a book. A topic in a book can be located much more quickly if the topic's title is located in the book's index with the corresponding page number. Without the index, you might need to search through each page of the book to locate the topic you want.

The simplest form of the CREATE INDEX statement looks like this:

```
CREATE INDEX index_name
ON table_name (column1[, column2]...);
```

The columns *column1*, *column2*, and so forth are the columns to be indexed on the table *table_name*. The index name *index_name* must be unique across all objects within the same schema.

Janice has been receiving complaints that the queries against the COUNTRIES table have been slow. She knows that there is already an index on the COUNTRY_ID

index
A database object designed to reduce the amount of time it takes to retrieve rows from a table. An index is created based on one or more columns in the table.

composite index
An index that is created on two or more columns in a table.

WARNING

column, so she is surprised that the response time would be poor when selecting a row from the COUNTRIES table. After further investigation, she discovers that a lot of users are trying to find the two-letter country code given the name of the country—the users are searching the table using a WHERE clause on the COUNTRY_NAME column. She decides that an index on the COUNTRY_NAME column might improve the response time. To create the index, she uses the following command:

```
create index countries_ie1 on countries(country_name);

    Index created.
```

The index did not necessarily need the name of the table in its name. However, Janice realizes that it's good practice to include the table name so that she can easily avoid duplicate index names in the database.

Creating and Using Views

In this section, we'll talk about views that users can create themselves, and then we'll cover views owned by SYS that contain important information about the objects in the database.

User-Defined Views

view
A database object that is based on a SELECT statement against one or more tables or other views in the database. A regular view does not store any data in the database; only the definition is stored. Views are also known as stored queries.

Views are database objects that look like tables but are instead derived from a SELECT statement performed on one or more tables. In other words, a *view* is a subset of data from one or more tables. A view does not contain its own data; the contents of a view are dynamically retrieved from the tables on which it is based. A view is sometimes referred to as a *stored query*.

Views can enhance the usability of the database by making complex queries appear to be simple. For example, users may frequently join together two or more tables in the same way. A view will make the users' lives a bit easier, allowing them to write a query against a single view instead of needing to rewrite a complex query over and over.

Views can also be used to restrict access to certain rows or columns of a table. For example, the DBA can create a view against the EMPLOYEES table that excludes the SALARY column and can make this view available to those departments that need to see employee information but should not see salary information.

The CREATE VIEW statement looks like this:

```
CREATE VIEW view_name (alias1[, alias2] ...)
    AS subquery;
```

The *subquery* clause is a SELECT statement that may join more than one table and may also have a WHERE clause. Column aliases can be specified for the resulting columns from the subquery.

After reviewing some of the SELECT statements that the users are writing, Janice, the DBA and application developer, notices that there are frequent joins between the EMPLOYEES table and the DEPARTMENTS table, similar to the following:

```
select employee_id, last_name, first_name,
       department_id, department_name
from employees join departments using(department_id);
```

Creating a view based on this query might help the users who typically don't use SQL to join tables but need to see the associated department information for each employee. Janice creates the view using the sample query above as the sub-query in a CREATE VIEW statement:

```
create view
       emp_dept(emp_id, lname, fname, dept_id, dname) as
select employee_id, last_name, first_name,
       department_id, department_name
from employees join departments using(department_id);


View created.
```

Notice that Janice has supplied column aliases so that the original column names are not visible to the users of the view. For all intents and purposes, the EMP_DEPT view looks and operates in the same way as a single table, as demonstrated below with the DESCRIBE and SELECT statements:

```
describe emp_dept;
Name                                Null?    Type
----------------------------------- -------- ------------
EMP_ID                              NOT NULL NUMBER(6)
LNAME                               NOT NULL VARCHAR2(25)
FNAME                                        VARCHAR2(20)
DEPT_ID                             NOT NULL NUMBER(4)
DNAME                               NOT NULL VARCHAR2(30)


select * from emp_dept;

EMP_ID LNAME          FNAME        DEPT_ID DNAME
------- -------------- ------------ ------- ----------------
    100 King           Steven            90 Executive
    101 Kochhar        Neena             90 Executive
    102 De Haan        Lex               90 Executive
```

```
103 Hunold        Alexander      60 IT
104 Ernst         Janice         60 IT
105 Austin        David          60 IT
106 Pataballa     Valli          60 IT
107 Lorentz       Diana          60 IT
108 Greenberg     Nancy         100 Finance
109 Faviet        Daniel        100 Finance
110 Chen          John          100 Finance
...
203 Mavris        Susan          40 Human Resources
204 Baer          Hermann        70 Public Relations
205 Higgins       Shelley       110 Accounting
206 Gietz         William       110 Accounting

106 rows selected.
```

   The EMP_DEPT view can be used in the same way as any database table. The users can add a WHERE clause to the SELECT statement above. Also, the EMP_DEPT view can be joined with a table in another query if so desired.

Data Dictionary Views

data dictionary views
Read-only views owned by the user SYS that are created when the database is created and contain information about users, security, and database structures, as well as other persistent information about the database.

Data dictionary views are predefined views that contain a variety of information about tables, users, and various other objects in the database. Like other views, data dictionary views are based on one or more tables. The main differences between data dictionary views and user-created views are that data dictionary views are owned by the user SYS and the views themselves may appear to have different results depending on who is accessing them.

Data Dictionary View Types

Data dictionary views have one of three prefixes:

   USER_   These views show information about the structures owned by the user (in the user's schema). They are accessible to all users and do not have an OWNER column.

   ALL_   These views show information about all objects that the user has access to, including objects owned by the user and objects to which other users have granted the user access. These views are accessible to all users. Each view has an OWNER column, since some of the objects may reside in other users' schemas.

   DBA_   These views have information about all structures in the database—they show what is in all users' schemas. Accessible to the DBA, they provide information on all the objects in the database and have an OWNER column as well.

Common Data Dictionary Views

Some data dictionary views are commonly used by both developers and DBAs to retrieve information about tables, table columns, indexes, and other objects in the database. The following descriptions refer to the ALL_ version of each of the views.

ALL_TABLES

The ALL_TABLES view contains information about all database tables to which the user has access. The following query, run by the user HR, identifies the table and owner of all tables that HR can access:

```
select table_name, owner from all_tables;

TABLE_NAME                    OWNER
----------------------------- ------
DUAL                          SYS
SYSTEM_PRIVILEGE_MAP          SYS
TABLE_PRIVILEGE_MAP           SYS
STMT_AUDIT_OPTION_MAP         SYS
AUDIT_ACTIONS                 SYS
...
REGIONS                       HR
COUNTRIES                     HR
LOCATIONS                     HR
DEPARTMENTS                   HR
JOBS                          HR
EMPLOYEES                     HR
JOB_HISTORY                   HR
EMP                           SCOTT
SALGRADE                      SCOTT
EMPLOYEES_DEPARTMENTS         HR
EMPLOYEES_SSN                 HR
CUST_COMMENTS                 HR
EMPTY_CUST_COMMENTS           HR

44 rows selected.
```

Many of the tables visible to HR are tables owned by SYS and SYSTEM, such as the DUAL table. The user HR can also access the EMP and SALGRADE tables owned by SCOTT.

ALL_TAB_COLUMNS

The ALL_TAB_COLUMNS view contains information about the columns in all tables accessible to the user. If the user HR wanted to find out the columns and datatypes in the COUNTRIES table, the query would be written as follows:

```
select column_name, data_type from all_tab_columns
where table_name = 'COUNTRIES';
```

```
COLUMN_NAME                   DATA_TYPE
------------------------      ------------
COUNTRY_ID                    CHAR
COUNTRY_NAME                  VARCHAR2
REGION_ID                     NUMBER
```

```
3 rows selected.
```

ALL_INDEXES

The ALL_INDEXES view contains information about the indexes accessible to the user. If the HR user wanted to find out the indexes that were created against the COUNTRIES table and whether the indexes were unique, the query would look like this:

```
select table_name, index_name, uniqueness from all_indexes
where table_name = 'COUNTRIES';
```

```
TABLE_NAME                    INDEX_NAME              UNIQUENESS
------------------------      --------------------    ---------
COUNTRIES                     COUNTRY_C_ID_PK         UNIQUE
COUNTRIES                     COUNTRIES_IE1           NONUNIQUE
```

```
2 rows selected.
```

The COUNTRIES table has two indexes, one of which is a unique index.

ALL_IND_COLUMNS

The ALL_IND_COLUMNS view contains information about the columns indexed by an index on a table. Following the previous example, the HR user can use the INDEX_NAME to help identify the indexed column or columns on the table:

```
select table_name, column_name from  all_ind_columns
where index_name = 'COUNTRY_C_ID_PK';
```

```
TABLE_NAME       COLUMN_NAME
-----------      ------------------
COUNTRIES        COUNTRY_ID
```

```
1 row selected.
```

The index COUNTRY_C_ID_PK indexes the COUNTRY_ID column in the
COUNTRIES table.

ALL_OBJECTS

The ALL_OBJECTS view combines all types of Oracle structures into one view.
This view comes in handy when you want a summary of all database objects
using one query, or you have the name of the object and want to find out what
kind of object it is. The following query retrieves all the objects accessible to HR
and owned by either the HR or JANICE schema:

```
select owner, object_name, object_type, temporary
   from all_objects
   where owner in ('HR','JANICE');
```

```
OWNER       OBJECT_NAME                  OBJECT_TYPE          T
----------  ---------------------------  -------------------  -
JANICE      TRAVEL_DEST                  TABLE                Y
HR          ADD_JOB_HISTORY              PROCEDURE            N
HR          COUNTRIES                    TABLE                N
HR          COUNTRIES_IE1                INDEX                N
HR          COUNTRY_C_ID_PK              INDEX                N
HR          CUST_COMMENTS                TABLE                N
HR          DEPARTMENTS                  TABLE                N
HR          DEPARTMENTS_SEQ              SEQUENCE             N
HR          DEPT_ID_PK                   INDEX                N
...
HR          PK_EMPL_SSN                  INDEX                N
HR          REGIONS                      TABLE                N
HR          REG_ID_PK                    INDEX                N
HR          SECURE_DML                   PROCEDURE            N
HR          SECURE_EMPLOYEES             TRIGGER              N
HR          UK1_EMPLOYEES                INDEX                N
HR          UPDATE_JOB_HISTORY           TRIGGER              N
```

```
43 rows selected.
```

The TEMPORARY (T) column in the ALL_OBJECTS view indicates whether the object is temporary. The temporary table TRAVEL_DEST, created and owned by JANICE but accessible to all users, is indicated correctly as being a temporary table in the query results.

Data Dictionary View Shorthand

Because of how frequently some of the data dictionary views are used by a typical database user, a number of short synonyms exist for these views. Here are some examples of shortened view names:

◆ TABS is a synonym for USER_TABLES.

◆ IND is a synonym for USER_INDEXES.

◆ OBJ is a synonym for USER_OBJECTS.

Dynamic Performance Views

dynamic performance views
Data dictionary views owned by the user SYS that are continuously updated while a database is open and in use and whose contents relate primarily to performance. These views have the prefix V$ and their contents are lost when the database is shut down.

Dynamic performance views are similar in nature to data dictionary views, with one important difference: Dynamic performance views are continuously updated while the database is open and in use; they are re-created when the database is shut down and restarted. In other words, the contents of these views are not retained when the database is restarted. The contents of dynamic performance views primarily relate to the performance of the database.

The names of the dynamic performance views begin with V$. Two common dynamic performance views are V$SESSION and V$INSTANCE.

V$SESSION

The dynamic performance view V$SESSION contains information about each connected user or process in the database. To find out what programs the user HR is using to connect to the database, you can query the PROGRAM column of V$SESSION:

```
select sid, serial#, username, program from v$session
where username = 'HR';
```

```
       SID    SERIAL# USERNAME              PROGRAM
---------- ---------- -------------------- ----------------
        16       6921 HR                    Toad.exe
        19         18 HR                    jrew.exe
        20         39 HR                    sqlplusw.exe
        21       6932 HR                    Toad.exe

4 rows selected.
```

In this case, the user HR has four connections open in the database using three different programs. The SID and SERIAL# columns together uniquely identify a session. This information is needed by the DBA if, for some reason, one of the sessions must be terminated.

V$INSTANCE

The V$INSTANCE view provides one row of statistics for each Oracle instance running against the database. Multiple instances running against a single database can greatly enhance the scalability of the Oracle database by spreading out the CPU resource usage over multiple servers. The following query finds out the version of the Oracle software and how long the instance has been up since the last restart, along with other instance information:

```
select instance_name, host_name, version,
    startup_time, round(sysdate-startup_time) "Days Up",
    status from v$instance;

INSTANCE_NAME  HOST_NAME VERSION    STARTUP_T   Days Up STATUS
-------------- --------- ---------- --------- ---------- ------
rac0           dev       10.1.0.2.0 02-JUN-04        12 OPEN

1 row selected.
```

Creating Sequences and Synonyms

Various other database objects are needed to support the main objects in the database (such as tables). Two such objects are sequences and synonyms.

Sequences

An Oracle *sequence* is a named sequential number generator. A sequence is often used to generate a unique key for the primary key of a table. A sequence object is owned by a single schema, but it can be used by other database users if the proper permissions are granted to the users.

Sequences can begin and end with any value, can be ascending or descending, and can skip (increment) a specified number between each value in the sequence. The basic syntax for CREATE SEQUENCE is as follows:

```
CREATE SEQUENCE sequence_name
    [START WITH starting_value]
    [INCREMENT BY increment_value];
```

sequence

A database structure that generates a series of numbers typically used to assign primary key values to database tables.

If all optional parameters are omitted, the sequence starts with one and increases by increments of one, with no upper boundary.

Sequences are referenced in DML statements by using the syntax *sequence_name*.`currval` or *sequence_name*.`nextval`. The qualifier `nextval` retrieves the next value. The qualifier `currval` retrieves the most recent number generated without incrementing the counter. For example, here are some sample SELECT statements that access the sequence used for employee numbers, EMPLOYEES_SEQ:

```
select employees_seq.nextval from dual;

NEXTVAL
----------
       211

1 row selected.

select employees_seq.nextval from dual;

NEXTVAL
----------
       212

1 row selected.

select employees_seq.currval from dual;

CURRVAL
----------
       212

1 row selected.
```

The HR department has asked the DBA, Janice, to re-create the sequence for the EMPLOYEES table to start at 501 and increment by 10. Janice drops the old sequence and re-creates it:

```
drop sequence hr.employees_seq;

Sequence dropped.

create sequence hr.employees_seq
   start with 501
```

```
    increment by 10;

    Sequence created.
```

After the sequence has been created, the user HR inserts a record into the EMPLOYEES table as follows:

```
insert into employees
    (employee_id, last_name, first_name, email,
     hire_date, job_id)
values
    (employees_seq.nextval, 'JUDD', 'DAWN', 'DRJUDD',
     '25-may-04','QA_MAN');

1 row created.

select employee_id from employees
where last_name = 'JUDD';

EMPLOYEE_ID
-----------
        501

1 row selected.
```

The next time the employees_seq sequence is used, the value returned will be 511.

Synonyms

A *synonym* is an alias for another database object, such as a table, sequence, or view. Synonyms provide easier access to database objects outside the user's schema.

synonym
An alias assigned to a table, view, or other database structure. Synonyms can be either available to all users (public) or available only to one schema owner (private).

There are two kinds of synonyms: public and private. Public synonyms are available to all database users. A private synonym is available only in the session of the schema owner who created it.

Synonyms are useful in providing a common name to a database object, regardless of which username is logged in to the database. The temporary table created by Janice the DBA, called TRAVEL_DEST, must be qualified with the schema name if anyone other than Janice wants to access it. For example, if the user HR is connected to the database and no synonym has been specified, the table must be fully qualified:

```
insert into janice.travel_dest
    values(101, 1201, 320.50, 988.00);
```

The syntax for creating a synonym is as follows:

```
CREATE [PUBLIC] SYNONYM synonym_name
   FOR [schema.]object_name;
```

To facilitate easy access to the table TRAVEL_DEST, Janice creates a public synonym for the table:

```
create public synonym travel_dest for travel_dest;


Synonym created.
```

What happens if a user has a private synonym called TRAVEL_DEST, or worse yet, his or her own table is called TRAVEL_DEST? Unqualified object references (object references that aren't prefixed with a schema name) are resolved in the following order:

1. A real object with the specified name

2. A private synonym owned by the current user

3. A public synonym

Private synonyms can be useful in a development environment when you have a copy of a table with a different name. A private synonym can be created to refer to the copy of the production table with the same name as the production table. During testing, the developer's private synonym points to the copy and does not impact the production table. When development is complete, the developer can remove the private synonym and move the new SQL code into a production environment, without changing any table names in the SQL code.

Terms to Know

composite index	index
CTAS	relational table
data dictionary views	sequence
directory	synonym
dynamic performance views	temporary table
external table	view

Review Questions

1. The data dictionary view IND has the same definition as what other data dictionary view?

2. The most common form of a table in the Oracle database is a(n) _____ table.

3. What clause do you add to the CREATE TABLE statement to create a temporary table?

4. What tables are displayed if a user accesses the ALL_TABLES data dictionary view?

5. Name two ways in which external tables are different from relational tables.

6. True or false: Oracle resolves object references by checking for private synonyms first.

7. What are two reasons for creating a view against one or more tables?

8. What database object type can be used to generate a series of sequential numbers?

9. True or false: Data dictionary tables retain their contents even after the database has been shut down and restarted.

10. An index created on more than one column is known as what kind of index?

Chapter 11

Users and Security

If a company has more than one employee who needs access to the Oracle database, then the security of the database is a prime concern for the DBA. The data integrity of the database and the level of security in the database are maintained, in part, by preventing unauthorized or unintentional actions in the database.

Database security can be divided into roughly two areas: data security and system security. Data security includes monitoring and assigning users permissions to the various objects in the database. System security covers the user login process, how much disk space is assigned to each user, and what kinds of actions each user can perform.

Creating User Accounts

username
An Oracle database account identifier that, along with a password, allows a user to connect to the database.

To connect to the Oracle database, a user must have an Oracle database account, also known as a *username*. When you create the username, you can specify various other characteristics of the account, including a password, a profile, default tablespaces, and disk space quotas.

The basic syntax to create a username is as follows:

```
CREATE USER user <other options>;
```

At a minimum, you should assign a password to the account. Passwords and the other user account options are discussed in the following sections.

Assigning Passwords

The password for the user account is typically assigned at the time the account is created and then changed after the user logs in for the first time. Janice, the DBA, creates an account for one of the new stocking managers with an initial password of DUCTTAPE6:

```
create user scrawford identified by ducttape6;

User created.
```

Passwords are not case sensitive; for example, DucTTape6 or ductTAPE6 would both be stored as DUCTTAPE6 in the database. To ensure that the password won't be easy to guess, it's important to use a mixture of letters, numbers, and punctuation characters in the password. The DBA can define additional rules for allowable passwords by the use of a special stored function owned by the SYS schema. For example, the DBA may require that certain sensitive accounts such as HR have a password that is longer than the password for any other accounts.

The DBA or user can use the ALTER USER command to change the password:

```
alter user scrawford identified by circuitt40;

User altered.
```

To change a password from an iSQL*Plus session, the user can use the Preferences link in the upper-right area of the browser. From within SQL*Plus, the user can change the password using the SQL*Plus PASSWORD command. The advantage to these last two methods is that the old and new passwords are not echoed to the screen:

```
SQL> password
Changing password for SCRAWFORD
```

```
Old password: *********
New password: ********
Retype new password: ********
Password changed
SQL>
```

Creating and Assigning Profiles

Each username in the database has a profile associated with it. A *profile* is a set of predefined resource parameters that can be used to monitor and control various database resources. The following are some examples of resources that can be controlled in a profile:

profile
A set of predefined resource parameters that can be used to monitor and control various database resources, such as CPU time and number of disk reads against the database.

- ◆ Concurrent connections to the database
- ◆ Maximum failed login attempts before the account is locked
- ◆ Elapsed time connected
- ◆ Continuous idle time connected
- ◆ CPU time used
- ◆ Disk reads performed
- ◆ How often a password needs to be changed

When an account is created, a profile can be specified; otherwise, Oracle assigns a default profile. Not surprisingly, this profile is called DEFAULT. The initial values of the DEFAULT profile allow for unlimited use of all resources.

At Scott's widget company, the users in the stocking department are notorious for leaving their sessions connected to the database and forgetting to log off when they are finished. This consumes valuable memory resources, so Janice, the DBA, decides to create a new profile in the database to make sure that users are disconnected from the database after 15 minutes of idle time:

```
create profile st_user limit
   idle_time 15;


Profile created.
```

In the new ST_USER profile just created, all resources are set to UNLIMITED except for the IDLE_TIME resource, which has been set to 15 minutes. The DBA modifies the recently created user to use the newly created profile:

```
alter user scrawford profile st_user;


User altered.
```

For SCRAWFORD's subsequent sessions, the session will be disconnected if the session remains idle for 15 minutes.

Assigning Default Tablespaces and Quotas

When a user creates some type of object—a table, an index, a sequence, or another object—that object uses space in one of the database's tablespaces. In addition, a user may need temporary space for sorting and other operations. Each user has a default tablespace for permanent objects and a default tablespace for temporary objects, although a user may explicitly create objects in a different tablespace if the user has the proper permissions.

If a default permanent tablespace is not specified when the user account is created, or a database-wide default permanent tablespace is not specified when the database is created, the SYSTEM tablespace is used. It is generally not a good idea to leave SYSTEM as the default tablespace. Since the SYSTEM tablespace contains all of the data dictionary objects, there is a high level of contention in the SYSTEM tablespace already, so any new user objects in the SYSTEM tablespace might have a negative impact on overall system performance.

Janice, the DBA, remedies this situation with the new user account and changes the default tablespace:

```
alter user scrawford default tablespace users;

User altered.
```

Janice double-checks her work by querying the DBA_USERS data dictionary view:

```
select username, default_tablespace,
   temporary_tablespace from dba_users
where username = 'SCRAWFORD';


USERNAME      DEFAULT_TABLESPACE    TEMPORARY_TABLESPACE
------------  --------------------  --------------------
SCRAWFORD     USERS                 TEMP


1 row selected.
```

Janice makes a mental note to use the GUI-based Oracle Enterprise Manager (OEM) tool or the web-based EM Database Control interface next time. The OEM tool's Create User facility, shown below, is not only easier to use, but it also automatically specifies the USERS tablespace as the default tablespace for new users, among other defaults.

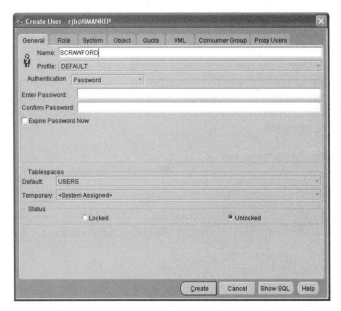

The web-based EM Database Control interface provides similar functionality when creating users.

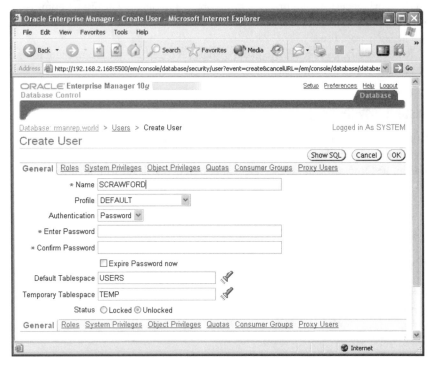

quota

A numeric limit on the amount of disk space that a user can allocate within a tablespace. The quota can also be specified as UNLIMITED.

Although disk space gets cheaper every day, you may also want to limit how much disk space each user can allocate in each tablespace. The limit on the amount of disk space in a tablespace is called a *quota*. Even though each user-name is assigned a default tablespace when the username is created, the quota defaults to zero. Therefore, you must assign a quota to the user before that user can create objects in the tablespace.

Since the new user, SCRAWFORD, is expected to create tables for other people in the stocking department, Janice allocates 15MB of disk space in the USERS tablespace for SCRAWFORD:

```
alter user scrawford quota 15M on users;

User altered.
```

If Janice had specified UNLIMITED instead of 15M, SCRAWFORD would not have any limits on how much space she can use in the USERS tablespace for database objects.

Granting and Revoking Privileges

privileges
The right to perform a specific action in the database, granted by the DBA or other database users.

Privileges are rights to execute specific SQL statements. The DBA grants privileges to user accounts to control what users can do in the database. There are two kinds of privileges: system privileges and object privileges. The GRANT command allocates system and object privileges to a user. The REVOKE command removes privileges from a user.

Roles provide an easy way to group privileges together and assign them to one or more users in the database.

System Privileges

system privileges
Privileges that allow users to perform a specific action on one or more database objects or users in the database.

System privileges allow users to perform a specific action on one or more database objects or users in the database. There are more than 160 system privileges available in the Oracle 10g database. Typically, system privileges will fall into two general categories: DBA privileges and user privileges. There is no distinction at the database level between these two types of system privileges.

In general, system privileges that can affect the database as a whole are considered to be DBA privileges. The following are typical DBA privileges:

Privilege	Description
CREATE USER	Create a new database user
DROP USER	Remove a database user
CREATE ANY TABLE	Create a new table in any schema

Privilege	Description
CREATE TABLESPACE	Create a new tablespace
AUDIT ANY	Turn on or off database auditing
DROP ANY INDEX	Drop an index in any schema

System privileges that allow users to perform specific tasks within a single schema are considered to be user privileges. The typical user privileges are generally a bit more innocuous than the DBA privileges, as you can see by the following examples:

Privilege	Description
CREATE SESSION	Establish a connection to the database
CREATE TABLE	Create a table in the user's schema
CREATE PROCEDURE	Create a stored function or procedure

System privileges are granted with the GRANT command, which has the following syntax:

```
GRANT sys_privilege [, sys_privilege ...]
      TO user [, user, role, PUBLIC ...];
```

Notice that the syntax makes it easy to grant a group of privileges all at once to one user or to many users. Also, a privilege may be granted to a special class of users called PUBLIC. When a privilege is granted to PUBLIC, all current and future users will have that privilege.

The CREATE SESSION privilege is important because a user cannot log in to the database without this privilege. Janice, the DBA, realizes that the new user account she created did not have this privilege. In addition, the new user will be creating new tables, so she needs the CREATE TABLE privilege. Janice applies both of these privileges to SCRAWFORD using the GRANT command.

```
grant create session,
      create table to scrawford;
```

```
Grant succeeded.
```

The user SCRAWFORD can now log in and create tables in the database within the SCRAWFORD schema.

The questions you may be asking are, "Why isn't the CREATE SESSION privilege automatic? Don't we want everyone to be able to log in? Why would we create a user who couldn't log in?"

In some database application environments, it is beneficial to keep all of the tables within a single schema for ease of maintenance, quota, and backups. You might not, however, allow the schema owner to log in. In this way, the application users can be tracked to know who used what table in the application's schema. If only the application's username were used, you would not know which user performed what action against the database. The DBA can set up the proper permissions and synonyms for other users to access this new schema, without the need for the application schema's owner to ever log in to the database.

Object Privileges

object privileges
Privileges that allow users to manipulate the contents of database objects in other schemas.

Object privileges allow users to manipulate the contents of database objects in other schemas. Object privileges are granted on schema objects such as tables, directories, and stored procedures. They are granted to a username in a different schema. In other words, the owner of an object in a schema has all privileges on the object and can grant privileges on the object to another user.

Typical object privileges include the following:

Privilege	Description
SELECT	Read (query) access on a table
UPDATE	Update (change) rows in a table or view
DELETE	Delete rows from a table or view
INSERT	Add rows to a table or view
EXECUTE	Run (execute) a stored procedure or function
INDEX	Create an index on a table

In addition to the ability of the user to grant privileges on objects to other users, a user can grant the privilege for the grantee to subsequently grant the same privilege to yet another user.

Object privileges are granted with a GRANT statement similar to that for granting system privileges:

```
GRANT obj_privilege [(column_list)]
    [, obj_privilege ...] ON object
    TO user [, user, role, PUBLIC ...]
    [WITH GRANT OPTION];
```

The *column_list* parameter is used if the object is a table and only certain columns of the table are made available for updating by other users. The WITH GRANT OPTION clause allows the grantee to pass the privilege on to yet another user.

The HR department at Scott's widget company frequently receives requests to update the EMPLOYEES table. The department asks Janice, the DBA, to make some of the columns of the table available to all employees, so that they can make changes to their phone numbers and e-mail addresses. The GRANT statement is as follows:

```
grant update (email, phone_number) on employees to public;
```

Now employees can update their records if they know their employee IDs. One of the new employees uses the following SQL command to change her e-mail address:

```
update hr.employees set email='KSIMMONS'
where employee_id = 502;


1 row updated.
```

However, trying to update a different column in the table is not permitted:

```
update hr.employees set salary=25000
where employee_id = 502;


update hr.employees set salary=25000
           *
ERROR at line 1:
ORA-01031: insufficient privileges
```

In fact, even selecting rows from the table is disallowed:

```
select * from hr.employees
where employee_id = 502;


select * from hr.employees
                 *
ERROR at line 1:
ORA-01031: insufficient privileges
```

Any user other than HR has only the object privilege on EMPLOYEES to update the EMAIL and PHONE_NUMBER columns.

After a month or so, the HR department has decided that granting the privileges on the two columns in the EMPLOYEES table was not a very good idea. Employees were using the wrong employee number to update the EMPLOYEES table, and they inadvertently updated the wrong e-mail and phone number information. To solve the problem, Janice revokes the privileges on the EMPLOYEES table, as follows:

```
revoke update on employees from public;


Revoke succeeded.
```

Notice that the REVOKE statement did not specify any columns in the EMPLOYEES table. When revoking UPDATE privileges on a table, columns cannot be specified. If the HR department wanted to continue to allow access to one of the columns, a new GRANT statement specifying the desired column would be issued after the REVOKE statement.

Creating and Assigning Roles

role
A named group of privileges created to ease the administration of system and object privileges.

A *role* is a named group of privileges. Using roles makes it easy for the DBA to grant groups of privileges to users. Granting a role takes a lot fewer steps than granting individual privileges. For example, if several users all require the same 15 privileges, it's a lot easier to assign those 15 privileges to a role first and then assign the role to each user who needs it.

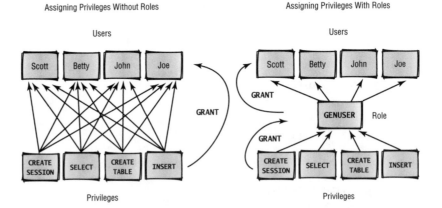

The privileges granted to the role can be a combination of system and object privileges. A user may be granted more than one role in addition to any system or object privileges granted directly. Roles are created with the CREATE ROLE statement. The basic syntax for CREATE ROLE is as follows:

```
CREATE ROLE <rolename> [IDENTIFIED BY <role_password>];
```

As the syntax indicates, a role may have a password. If a role requires a password, a user granted this role must use the SET ROLE command to use the privileges granted to the role.

The Order Entry department at Scott's widget company wants to give employees in certain departments an additional discount on orders placed. To identify a customer as an employee, the Order Entry department will need access to the EMPLOYEES and DEPARTMENTS tables in the HR schema. Janice, the DBA, decides that using a role might be the best way to provide this access, since other departments may be asking for this same functionality in the future.

The first step is to create a role to hold the privileges. Janice creates the role as follows:

```
create role hr_emp_dept;

Role created.
```

Next, the privileges on the tables must be added to the roles:

```
grant select on hr.employees to hr_emp_dept;

Grant succeeded.

grant select on hr.departments to hr_emp_dept;

Grant succeeded.
```

Finally, the role itself is granted to the user OE:

```
grant hr_emp_dept to oe;

Grant succeeded.
```

Now the user OE can read the contents of the EMPLOYEES and DEPARTMENTS tables in the HR schema. In the future, to provide the same access to the HR tables to other departments, only the last GRANT statement needs to be executed.

To check the roles granted to the OE user, Janice runs the following query against the DBA_ROLE_PRIVS data dictionary view:

```
select grantee, granted_role from dba_role_privs
where grantee = 'OE';

GRANTEE                      GRANTED_ROLE
------------------------     ------------
OE                           CONNECT
OE                           RESOURCE
OE                           HR_EMP_DEPT

3 rows selected.
```

To find out which privileges are assigned to the role HR_EMP_DEPT, Janice runs another query against the ROLE_TAB_PRIVS data dictionary view:

```
select role, owner, table_name, privilege from
    role_tab_privs where role='HR_EMP_DEPT';
```

```
ROLE              OWNER     TABLE_NAME            PRIVILEGE
----------------  --------  --------------------  ---------
HR_EMP_DEPT       HR        EMPLOYEES             SELECT
HR_EMP_DEPT       HR        DEPARTMENTS           SELECT

2 rows selected.
```

The role HR_EMP_DEPT has SELECT privileges against two tables in the HR schema: EMPLOYEES and DEPARTMENTS.

Auditing

auditing

Storing information about activities in the database in the SYS.AUD$ table. Auditing is controlled by the DBA.

Auditing in the Oracle database stores information about database activities. The activities to be audited are specified by the DBA. Once enabled, auditing records the activity in the AUD$ table, owned by SYS.

Auditing can be fine-tuned in a number of ways. It can be restricted to particular objects or to specific users or based on whether the action is successful or unsuccessful. In other words, you might not care if users who are granted rights to a table access the table, but you might want to know when users without rights to a table try to access that table.

The types of auditing can be divided into two broad categories: statement auditing and object auditing. The general syntax for AUDIT is as follows:

```
AUDIT {statement_clause | object_clause}
    [BY SESSION | BY ACCESS]
    [WHENEVER [NOT] SUCCESSFUL];
```

The *statement_clause* allows you to specify not only the SQL statement to audit but also, optionally, the username that will be running the SQL statement. The *object_clause* allows you to specify a particular object to audit.

The BY SESSION clause means that an audit record is written to SYS.AUD$ only once in the session that triggered the audit, regardless of how many times the action was performed. BY ACCESS will record all occurrences of the specified action.

The NOAUDIT command turns off auditing and has the same syntax as AUDIT, except that BY SESSION or BY ACCESS is not specified when using NOAUDIT.

Statement Auditing

Statement auditing allows the DBA to trigger audit records in SYS.AUD$ when a given SQL statement is executed, either for all users or a particular group of users.

Recently, Janice, the DBA, created a new user SCRAWFORD and granted the CREATE TABLE privilege to SCRAWFORD. Janice is concerned that the new user is having trouble creating tables, so she decides to turn on auditing to see how often the new user's CREATE TABLE statements are failing:

```
audit create table by scrawford
   whenever not successful;
```

```
Audit succeeded.
```

In the next few days, the user SCRAWFORD runs a variety of CREATE TABLE statements, such as the following:

```
create table temp_emp
   (employee_id number(6),
    email       varchar2(25));
```

```
Table created.
```

```
create table temp_emp
   (employee_id number(6),
    email       varchar2(25));
```

```
ERROR at line 1:
ORA-00955: name is already used by an existing object
```

The user's second attempt failed because the table already exists.

Janice could review the SYS.AUD$ table, but she knows that the data dictionary view called DBA_AUDIT_TRAIL formats the records from SYS.AUD$ into a more readable format. She checks that view:

```
select username, obj_name, timestamp, action_name from
dba_audit_trail;
```

```
USERNAME      OBJ_NAME     TIMESTAMP ACTION_NAME
------------- ------------ --------- ------------
SCRAWFORD     TEMP_EMP     26-OCT-02 CREATE TABLE
```

```
1 row selected.
```

The OBJ_NAME column contains the name of the object affected by the statement, and the ACTION_NAME column contains the type of statement executed. Because Janice is auditing only unsuccessful uses of the CREATE TABLE statement, there is only one row inserted into SYS.AUD$, even though two CREATE TABLE statements were executed.

The following week, Janice turns off the CREATE TABLE auditing with the following command:

```
noaudit create table by scrawford;

Noaudit succeeded.
```

Rows in the SYS.AUD$ table (and as a result, the DBA_AUDIT_TRAIL view) remain there until they are removed by the DBA.

Object Auditing

Object auditing allows the DBA to monitor access to specific objects in the database, along with the operations performed on those objects. For example, the DBA may want to see how often SELECT statements occur on a particular table in a certain period of time versus how many UPDATE statements occur against that same table. As with statement auditing, object auditing can also be further refined to audit only successful or only unsuccessful statements against the object.

Janice, the DBA, wants to find out how often the EMPLOYEES table in the HR schema is being accessed by SELECT, INSERT, UPDATE, and DELETE statements and by whom. She decides that auditing the table for a few hours one day would give her the information that she needs. The AUDIT statement she runs looks like this:

```
audit select, insert, update, delete
    on hr.employees;

Audit succeeded.
```

After a few hours, she reviews the data dictionary view DBA_AUDIT_TRAIL to see what kind of activity has been performed against the EMPLOYEES table:

```
select username, obj_name,
to_char(timestamp,'dd-mon-yy hh:miPM') "Date/Time" from
dba_audit_trail where obj_name = 'EMPLOYEES';

USERNAME          OBJ_NAME           Date/Time
---------------   ----------------   ------------------
HR                EMPLOYEES          27-oct-02 08:53AM
HR                EMPLOYEES          27-oct-02 08:59AM
HR                EMPLOYEES          27-oct-02 10:23AM
HR                EMPLOYEES          27-oct-02 10:56AM
OE                EMPLOYEES          27-oct-02 11:59AM

5 rows selected.
```

From this query, she sees that the activity so far has been very light, with four accesses by HR and one by OE, all in the morning. Janice turns off the EMPLOYEE table auditing using the NOAUDIT command:

```
noaudit select, insert, update, delete
    on hr.employees;

Noaudit succeeded.
```

As with statement auditing, the records in SYS.AUD$ remain there until they are removed by the DBA.

Terms to Know

auditing	quota
object privileges	role
privileges	system privileges
profile	username

Review Questions

1. Privileges can be grouped and assigned as a unit by using what database object?

2. When granting privileges with the GRANT statement, what does the clause WITH GRANT OPTION do?

3. DROP USER and CREATE SESSION are examples of what kind of privileges?

4. What is the name of the table, owned by the user SYS, that contains all audit records?

5. Write a SQL statement that will create audit records when UPDATE statements fail against the HR.EMPLOYEES table.

6. Which system privilege allows a user to make a connection to the database?

7. In addition to assigning a default tablespace to a user, what else must be assigned to a user before that user can create objects in the tablespace?

8. Which tablespace is assigned to a user for the user's permanent objects if one is not explicitly assigned in the CREATE USER statement?

9. DELETE, INSERT, and EXECUTE are examples of what kind of privileges?

10. A profile controls which kinds of database resources?

11. Which keyword can be used in a GRANT command to assign one or more privileges to every user in the database?

Chapter 12

Making Things Run Fast (Enough)

Tuning a database is an ongoing job for the busy DBA. Users never seem to stop complaining about queries running slowly. And once you think that everything is at peak performance, a new application is added to the mix, a new server is added to the server pool, the volume of orders for widgets doubles mysteriously, or a data warehouse is using up more and more of the server's resources.

In this chapter, we'll talk about several ways to optimize the performance of the database, beginning with Oracle's Tuning Methodology. Then we'll cover indexes, data design tuning, application tuning, and memory tuning.

Oracle's Tuning Methodology

When tuning a newly developed database system or a system that has experienced major changes, you can follow *Oracle's Tuning Methodology*. This methodology prioritizes the steps to take when optimizing a database system:

Priority	Tuning Focus
1	Data design
2	Application design
3	Memory allocation
4	I/O and physical structures
5	Resource contention
6	Underlying platform

Oracle's Tuning Methodology
A tuning method recommended by Oracle Corporation that prioritizes areas in tuning database performance. The six areas, in order of priority, are data design, application design, memory allocation, I/O and physical structures, resource contention, and underlying platform.

The tuning focus areas are as follows:

Data design   This step focuses on what kinds of indexes to create and on which tables, using views and other variations on the basic table to achieve better performance, and similar considerations.

Application design   This area is somewhat intertwined with data design, especially when analyzing the SQL statements that run against the tables and indexes. Application design focuses on how to use Oracle tools to write effective and efficient SQL SELECT and other DDL statements against the database tables.

Memory allocation   This step is concerned with making sure that you not only have enough system memory overall but also are dividing that memory judiciously among the main Oracle memory structures. It is possible to allocate too much memory for one Oracle memory structure and potentially have an adverse performance impact on another Oracle memory structure.

I/O and physical structures   This step tunes the communication between the memory structures and disk structures to reduce the amount of time it takes to retrieve data blocks from disk or to avoid disk I/O completely.

Resource contention   This area analyzes the Oracle structures that control concurrent access to the various Oracle structures directly and indirectly accessible by the user. At the table level, this means locking rows versus locking the entire table, for example. At the block level, this means allowing more than one user to insert or update row data concurrently.

Underlying platform   This step deals primarily with placing Oracle file objects on the appropriate physical disk devices, as well as taking advantage of multiple CPUs on a server for improving the overall throughput of queries and data loads.

Ninety percent or more of all tuning issues fall within the first three areas—data design, application design, and memory allocation—and they are the focus of this chapter.

Indexes

Indexes are used to significantly boost the performance of queries by reducing the amount of time needed to retrieve rows from a table. However, too many indexes on a table can be just as bad as not enough indexes.

Once you decide to create an index, you need to choose which type of index will work best. After you've created an index, you may need to change or drop it. Before dropping an index, you may want to monitor it to see how often it is used over a given time span. Finally, you can use data dictionary views to see the structure of the indexes in the database.

When to Create Indexes

In an environment where there are frequent insert, update, and delete operations on a table, it's wise to minimize the number of indexes on that table. For each row that is inserted, updated, or deleted, all indexes on that table must be updated also, which can increase the response time for the user and raise the load on the Oracle server.

An index on a table column makes sense when the column is frequently referenced in a WHERE clause of a SELECT statement or in a join condition. If the table is large and the query is expected to return a small percentage of the rows, an index makes sense there, too. Although there is some overhead when traversing an index looking for a column value, the overhead is far less than the time it would take to search the table itself for the value in question. Oracle's general guideline is that an index on a column makes sense if most queries on the table are expected to retrieve less than about 4 percent of the rows.

NULL values are not included in an index, so an index is recommended if the table is large and a column contains a lot of NULL values. Any queries on non-NULL column values will likely use the index, while queries on NULL values in the column will not.

Index Types

Indexes can be divided into two general categories: b-tree and bitmap. They both serve the same purpose: to reduce the amount of time a query takes to retrieve rows from a table. However, they are constructed completely differently and are chosen based on the expected type and distribution of the data in the column to be indexed.

b-tree index
A type of index structure that resembles an inverted tree. The branches of a b-tree index are balanced. Traversing the tree for any index value reads the same number of blocks.

B-tree Indexes

branch blocks

Index blocks in the traversal path of a b-tree index that either point to branch blocks at the next level or point to leaf blocks.

A *b-tree index* looks like an inverted tree with *branch blocks* and *leaf blocks*. B-tree stands for balanced-tree, because the search of the tree for a given table column's key value always traverses the same number of levels in the tree to find the leaf block containing the address of the desired row. B-tree indexes are the most common type of index and are created by default. The following illustrates how a b-tree index works.

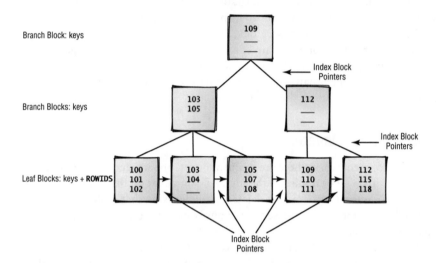

leaf blocks

Index blocks at the bottom of a b-tree index that contain ROWIDs to the rows in the table containing the desired index value.

In this example, the EMPLOYEE_ID column of the EMPLOYEES table is indexed. The b-tree has a depth of three, and each block has up to three entries. Each of the branch blocks at levels one and two contains entries that further subdivide the search and point to successive branch blocks, until the search reaches a leaf block. If the value is in a leaf block, the entry in that leaf block contains the address of the row in the table; this is called a *ROWID* and is unique across the entire database.

The Pseudo-column *ROWID*

The pseudo-column ROWID exists for every row of every table in the database and is unique across the entire database. It is represented externally by an 18-character string of uppercase and lowercase letters and numbers.

```
select dummy, rowid from dual;

D ROWID

- ------------------

X AAAADeAABAAAAZSAAA


1 row selected.
```

Notice that the leaf blocks are also linked horizontally. Sometimes, examining only the leaf blocks for a match, rather than starting at the root of the tree, is a more efficient way to conduct the index search.

B-tree indexes are good for columns with high *cardinality*, which are columns that have many distinct values. For example, a column containing last names and a column containing zip codes have high cardinality; a column containing a gender code has low cardinality.

A b-tree index can be created with a few different options:

Unique or nonunique   In a *unique index*, there are no duplicate values. An error is returned if you try to insert two rows into a table with the same index column values. By default, an index is nonunique.

Keys stored in reverse order   A *reverse key index* stores the key values in reverse order. For example, if an indexed column contains the value 40589, the value would be stored as 98504 in a reverse key index. In applications that insert rows in the ascending order of the indexed column, a reverse key index may improve the performance of applications by reducing the contention (concurrent access by several users) on a particular leaf block.

Function-based   An index created on some kind of transformation of one or more columns in the table is known as a *function-based index*. This type of index is created on an expression, instead of on a column of the database. For example, if the database users frequently search on the fourth and successive characters of the JOB_ID column, an index based solely on the JOB_ID column would not be useful to locate a row in the table. However, a function-based index on the expression SUBSTR(JOB_ID,4) would help speed queries searching on the fourth and successive characters of the JOB_ID column.

Index-organized table   An *index-organized table (IOT)* is a specialized form of a b-tree index that stores both the data and the index in the same database segment. An IOT has advantages for tables that are primarily lookup tables. For example, a state code table, where the access of the table is primarily via the primary key, would be a good IOT candidate. When a state code lookup occurs (for example, WI), the state name (Wisconsin) resides in the index block itself, saving an extra disk I/O of a block in a standard table.

Bitmap Indexes

Bitmap indexes are the other major type of index. As the name implies, a *bitmap index* uses a string of binary ones and zeros to represent the existence or nonexistence of a particular column value. For each distinct value of a column, a string of binary digits with a length equal to the number of rows in the table is stored. Therefore, bitmap indexes are recommended for indexing low-cardinality columns. Using bitmap indexes makes multiple AND and OR operations against several table columns very efficient in a query. The following illustrates how a bitmap index works.

---

cardinality
The number of distinct values in a column of a table.

ROWID
A unique identifier for a row in a table, maintained automatically in the table by the Oracle server. ROWIDs are unique throughout the database.

unique index
A b-tree index whose keys are not duplicated.

reverse key index
A b-tree index whose keys have their byte order reversed to improve the performance of an application by spreading out the key values for adjacent index values to different leaf blocks.

function-based index
A b-tree index that is created based on an expression involving the columns of a table, instead of on a single column or columns in the table.

index-organized table (IOT)
A b-tree index that stores both the data and the index in the same segment.

bitmap index
An index that maintains a binary string of ones and zeros for each distinct value of a column within the index.

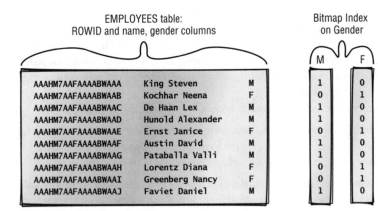

EMPLOYEES table:
ROWID and name, gender columns

Bitmap Index on Gender

			M	F
AAAHM7AAFAAAABWAAA	King Steven	M	1	0
AAAHM7AAFAAAABWAAB	Kochhar Neena	F	0	1
AAAHM7AAFAAAABWAAC	De Haan Lex	M	1	0
AAAHM7AAFAAAABWAAD	Hunold Alexander	M	1	0
AAAHM7AAFAAAABWAAE	Ernst Janice	F	0	1
AAAHM7AAFAAAABWAAF	Austin David	M	1	0
AAAHM7AAFAAAABWAAG	Pataballa Valli	M	1	0
AAAHM7AAFAAAABWAAH	Lorentz Diana	F	0	1
AAAHM7AAFAAAABWAAI	Greenberg Nancy	F	0	1
AAAHM7AAFAAAABWAAJ	Faviet Daniel	M	1	0

In the example, the GENDER column has a cardinality of two, and therefore it is a good candidate for a bitmap index. Two bitmaps are maintained in the bitmap index, each with a length equal to the number of rows in the table.

Creating bitmap indexes on high-cardinality columns makes the index significantly more expensive to maintain during row insertions and deletions. Bitmap indexes for high-cardinality columns are not recommended.

TIP

There are exceptions to every rule. If you suspect a bitmap index might work better than a b-tree index, even on a high-cardinality column, create both types of indexes on the column in question (but not at the same time!). Using the tools discussed later in this chapter, measure the resource consumption for a typical query using the indexed column in the WHERE clause, and see which type of index provides the lowest resource usage and response time.

Bitmap indexes are common in data warehouse environments, where many low-cardinality columns exist, DML is done in bulk, and query conditions against combinations of these columns are used frequently.

Creating, Dropping, and Maintaining Indexes

The CREATE INDEX command is used to create a b-tree or bitmap index. The basic syntax for CREATE INDEX is as follows:

```
CREATE [BITMAP | UNIQUE] INDEX indexname
    ON tablename (column1, column2, ...) [REVERSE];
```

If BITMAP is not specified, a b-tree index is assumed. The UNIQUE keyword ensures that the indexed column or columns are unique within the table; the REVERSE keyword creates a reverse key index. The name of the index must be

unique within the schema that owns the index. Indexes can be dropped with the
DROP INDEX command:

```
DROP INDEX indexname;
```

At Scott's widget company, Janice, the DBA and senior developer, has been
asked to add a GENDER column to the EMPLOYEES table. She modifies the table
and adds the new column using the following ALTER TABLE statement:

```
alter table employees
add (gender  char(1));
```

```
Table altered.
```

Over the next week or two, the HR department populates the new GENDER
column with either an M or an F. As other departments start running queries
against the EMPLOYEES table using the new GENDER column, they start complaining that the queries are running slower than when they run queries against an
indexed column, such as EMPLOYEE_ID or DEPARTMENT_ID. Janice also knows
that a copy of the EMPLOYEES table will be used in a data warehouse environment, so she decides that a bitmap index might be appropriate in this situation.
She uses the BITMAP option of the CREATE INDEX statement, as follows:

```
create bitmap index
bm_employees_gender on employees(gender);
```

```
Index created.
```

The users also tell Janice that they don't use the index on the employee's
name, so she drops the index on the last and first name columns:

```
drop index emp_name_ix;
```

```
Index dropped.
```

Two days later, she gets a call from the HR department, requesting that the
employee name index be re-created:

```
create index emp_name_ix on
  employees(last_name, first_name);
```

```
Index created.
```

In the next section, you'll learn how to monitor the usage of an index to get
an indication of how often an index is actually being used.

As her last task for the day, Janice thinks that the primary key of the EMPLOYEES table might work better as a reverse key index, so she rebuilds the index to re-create it:

```
alter index emp_emp_id_pk rebuild reverse;
```

```
Index altered.
```

In addition to converting the index type, the ALTER INDEX statement can also allow the table to remain available during the rebuild operation by using the ONLINE option. Note that more space is required in the database's temporary tablespace for this operation.

Monitoring Indexes

As Janice just discovered, she can't always rely on the user community to portray an accurate picture of what indexes are actually being used. Starting with Oracle9i, Oracle has a feature that can monitor an index and set a flag in the dynamic performance view V$OBJECT_USAGE. To turn on the monitoring process, you use the MONITORING USAGE clause of the ALTER INDEX statement.

Janice wants to see if the EMP_NAME_IX index is going to be used in the next eight hours. At 9 a.m., she turns on the monitoring process with this statement:

```
alter index hr.emp_name_ix monitoring usage;
```

```
Index altered.
```

She immediately checks V$OBJECT_USAGE to make sure the index is being monitored:

```
select index_name, table_name, monitoring, used, start_
monitoring
from v$object_usage where index_name = 'EMP_NAME_IX';

INDEX_NAME     TABLE_NAME        MON USE START_MONITORING
-------------- ----------------- --- --- --------------------
EMP_NAME_IX    EMPLOYEES         YES NO  06/02/2004 08:57:44

1 row selected.
```

During the day, one of the HR employees runs this query:

```
select employee_id from employees
where last_name = 'King';
```

```
EMPLOYEE_ID
-----------
        100
        156
```

2 rows selected.

At around 5 p.m., Janice checks V$OBJECT_USAGE again to see if the index was used:

```
select index_name, table_name, monitoring, used, start_
monitoring
from v$object_usage where index_name = 'EMP_NAME_IX';

INDEX_NAME    TABLE_NAME       MON USE START_MONITORING
------------  ---------------- --- --- -------------------
EMP_NAME_IX   EMPLOYEES        YES YES 06/02/2004 08:57:44
```

1 row selected.

Janice has decided that the index should stay, since it was used at least once during the day. She turns off monitoring with the NOMONITORING USAGE clause and checks the V$OBJECT_USAGE view one more time to verify this:

```
alter index hr.emp_name_ix nomonitoring usage;

Index altered.

select index_name, table_name, monitoring, used, end_
monitoring
from v$object_usage where index_name = 'EMP_NAME_IX';

INDEX_NAME    TABLE_NAME       MON USE END_MONITORING
------------  ---------------- --- --- -------------------
EMP_NAME_IX   EMPLOYEES        NO  YES 06/02/2004 17:00:40
```

1 row selected.

Because V$OBJECT_USAGE **is a dynamic performance view, the contents will not be retained in the view once the database is shut down and restarted.**

NOTE

Data Dictionary Index Information

As you've learned, data dictionary views can provide you with information about all database objects. The two key data dictionary views relating to indexes that every DBA should know about are DBA_INDEXES and DBA_ IND_COLUMNS, which contain the names of the indexes and the names of the indexed columns, respectively.

DBA_INDEXES

To find out the owners, tablespace names, and index type for all indexes on the EMPLOYEES table, Janice constructs a query against the DBA_INDEXES data dictionary view, as follows:

```
select owner, index_name, index_type, tablespace_name from
dba_indexes where table_name = 'EMPLOYEES';
```

```
OWNER    INDEX_NAME              INDEX_TYPE      TABLESPACE_NAME
-------  --------------------    -------------   ---------------
HR       EMP_EMAIL_UK            NORMAL          EXAMPLE
HR       EMP_EMP_ID_PK           NORMAL/REV      EXAMPLE
HR       EMP_DEPARTMENT_IX       NORMAL          EXAMPLE
HR       EMP_JOB_IX              NORMAL          EXAMPLE
HR       EMP_MANAGER_IX          NORMAL          EXAMPLE
HR       UK1_EMPLOYEES           NORMAL          EXAMPLE
HR       BM_EMPLOYEES_GENDER     BITMAP          EXAMPLE
HR       EMP_NAME_IX             NORMAL          EXAMPLE
```

```
8 rows selected.
```

All of the indexes on the EMPLOYEES table are normal b-tree indexes, except that the primary key index EMP_EMP_ID_PK is a reverse key b-tree index and the new BM_EMPLOYEES_GENDER index is a bitmap index.

DBA_IND_COLUMNS

To further drill down into the details of the indexes on the EMPLOYEES table, Janice queries the DBA_IND_COLUMNS table to find out which columns are in the EMP_NAME_IX index:

```
select index_name, table_name,
       column_name, column_position from
dba_ind_columns where index_name = 'EMP_NAME_IX';
```

```
INDEX_NAME      TABLE_NAME     COLUMN_NAME    COLUMN_POSITION
-------------   ------------   -------------  ----------------
EMP_NAME_IX     EMPLOYEES      LAST_NAME                    1
EMP_NAME_IX     EMPLOYEES      FIRST_NAME                   2
```

2 rows selected.

From this output, Janice can determine that EMP_NAME_IX is a composite index consisting of two columns: LAST_NAME and FIRST_NAME.

Data Design Tuning

Oracle has a number of solutions to improve performance from a data design perspective. We will cover two techniques in this section: partitioned tables and materialized views.

Partitioned Tables

When tables grow very large, it becomes advantageous to use *partitioned tables* to divide the rows of a table into more manageable pieces based on the values of one or more columns. Because the data is subdivided into smaller pieces, it makes the DBA's job easier when doing backups; each partition of a partitioned table may be backed up or restored separately. One partition of a table can be in the process of being repaired, while the rest of the partitions are available to the database users, increasing the overall availability of the table.

> **partitioned table**
> A table that stores its rows in smaller and more manageable pieces based on the values of one or more columns of the table.

Partitioned tables can have a performance benefit for database users. In many cases, a query may need to retrieve rows from only a subset of the partitions of a partitioned table. As a result, either index accesses or direct table accesses are reduced because the partition key automatically limits the partitions that need to be searched for the rows requested by the query.

There are four different ways to partition a table:

Range partitioning   With this type, the partition keys are in a range. For example, each partition can hold sales data by quarter or for a given month date range.

Hash partitioning   When the sizes of each partition may vary widely or you do not know how much data will end up in a partition, hash partitioning is useful. This type of partitioning uses an algorithm on the partition key column to automatically balance the number of rows that end up in each partition.

List partitioning   If you know the values that will divide the data into partitions, but they are not necessarily sequential either numerically or alphabetically, list partitioning is useful. For example, it may be desirable to store all rows with state codes by region into separate partitions. Rows with state codes of WI, IL, IA, IN, and MN would reside in the MIDWEST partition.

Composite partitioning   This is a hybrid method that uses the range partition method for partitions and the hash method for subpartitions.

Creating a partitioned table is very similar to creating a nonpartitioned table, with the addition of the PARTITION BY clause:

```
CREATE TABLE ...
PARTITION BY {RANGE | LIST | HASH} (column1, column2, ...)
    [SUBPARTITION BY {HASH | LIST} (column1, column2, ...)
    SUBPARTITIONS n]
```

Note that the SUBPARTITION BY HASH or LIST clause is valid only if the primary partitioning is BY RANGE. Also, specifying multiple columns in the PARTITION BY clause is valid only for HASH and RANGE partitioning, since LIST partitioning assigns rows to a partition based on the value of a single column.

The Order Entry department has asked Janice, the DBA, to look into improving the performance of the OE.ORDERS table. Response time against this table has been increasing, and the customer service representatives have reported that the web customers are waiting too long for their orders to be confirmed after clicking the Place My Order button on the checkout page.

Janice decides that since the ORDERS table now has hundreds of thousands of rows, she will partition the table by month. Partitioning by a date range makes sense, since rows from the ORDERS table are rarely accessed across more than one month. Janice retrieves the DDL for the original CREATE TABLE statement:

```
create table orders (
  order_id       number (12)   not null,
  order_date     date
        constraint order_date_nn not null,
  order_mode     varchar2 (8),
  customer_id    number (6)
        constraint order_customer_id_nn not null,
  order_status   number (2),
  order_total    number (8,2),
  sales_rep_id   number (6),
  promotion_id   number (6),
  constraint order_mode_lov
        check (order_mode in ('direct','online')) ,
  constraint order_total_min
        check (order_total >= 0),
  constraint order_pk primary key ( order_id ) ) ;
```

Janice creates a new version of the table for testing on the development server by adding partition-related options to the CREATE TABLE statement:

```
create table new_orders (
   order_id       number (12)    not null,
   order_date     date
          constraint new_order_date_nn not null,
   order_mode     varchar2 (8),
   customer_id    number (6)
          constraint new_order_customer_id_nn not null,
   order_status   number (2),
   order_total    number (8,2),
   sales_rep_id   number (6),
   promotion_id   number (6),
    constraint new_order_mode_lov
          check (order_mode in ('direct','online')) ,
    constraint new_order_total_min
          check (order_total >= 0),
    constraint new_order_pk primary key ( order_id ) )
    partition by range (order_date)
     (partition FY2004_07 values less than
       (to_date('08012004','MMDDYYYY')),
      partition FY2004_08 values less than
       (to_date('09012004','MMDDYYYY')),
      partition FY2004_09 values less than
       (to_date('10012004','MMDDYYYY')),
      partition FY2004_10 values less than
       (to_date('11012004','MMDDYYYY')),
      partition FY2004_11 values less than
       (to_date('12012004','MMDDYYYY')),
      partition FY2004_12 values less than
       (to_date('01012005','MMDDYYYY')),
      partition FY9999 values less than (maxvalue)
     );
```

In the new table NEW_ORDERS, all orders before August 1, 2004, will end up in the first partition, FY2004_07. At the other end are partitions defined for the rest of 2004. It is assumed that for 2005, the DBA will create additional partitions on this table to accommodate orders placed in 2005. In the meantime, any orders with a date mistakenly keyed in as 2005 or later will be stored in the partition FY9999. If this partition were not created, any INSERT statement containing a date value outside the range of any partition would return an error.

Materialized Views

materialized view
A view that stores the results of the query the view is based on, in addition to the SQL join statement of the view itself. Materialized views may be refreshed manually (on demand), on a regular basis, or when there is a change in the underlying tables on which that view is based.

A *materialized view* can help speed queries by storing data in a previously joined or summarized format. Unlike a traditional view, which stores only the query and runs that query every time the view is accessed, a materialized view stores the results of the query in addition to the SQL statements of the view itself. Because the materialized view already contains the results of the view's underlying query, using a materialized view can be as fast as accessing a single table.

But what if the underlying tables of the materialized view change? A materialized view can be refreshed either manually or automatically. If the refresh is automatic, it can occur as a scheduled event, such as every day at 2 a.m., or the materialized view can be refreshed automatically whenever the underlying tables of the view change. Materialized views can be refreshed manually by using the REFRESH procedure in the system package DBMS_MVIEW.

To further enhance the performance of a materialized view, it can be indexed and partitioned in the same way as any standard table.

Another key performance enhancement related to materialized views is the QUERY REWRITE feature. If a materialized view is created with the QUERY REWRITE option, any user SQL statements that use tables and columns similar to those found in the materialized view's query are automatically rewritten to use the materialized view directly. In other words, the database user does not need to know about the existence of the materialized view to take advantage of the pre-joined result of the materialized view.

The syntax for creating a materialized view is similar to that of the CREATE VIEW command from Chapter 10, "Creating and Maintaining Database Objects":

```
CREATE MATERIALIZED VIEW materialized_view_name
    [ENABLE QUERY REWRITE] AS subquery;
```

At Scott's widget company, Janice has been helping some of the users in the HR department with their queries. She notices that they often use the view she created for them earlier with this statement:

```
create view
    emp_dept(emp_id, lname, fname, dept_id, dname) as
select employee_id, last_name, first_name,
    department_id, department_name
from employees join departments using(department_id);
```

In its present form, this view must perform the join every time it is accessed. Janice thinks that rewriting this view as a materialized view will not only improve the performance of the view but may also improve the performance of other queries that join the EMPLOYEES and DEPARTMENTS table using Oracle's QUERY REWRITE feature. Janice creates the materialized view as follows:

```
create materialized view emp_dept
    enable query rewrite
as select employee_id, last_name, first_name,
        department_id, department_name
from employees join departments using(department_id);

Materialized view created.
```

The new materialized view looks like any table or regular view:

```
describe emp_dept
```

Name	Null?	Type
EMP_ID	NOT NULL	NUMBER(6)
LNAME	NOT NULL	VARCHAR2(25)
FNAME		VARCHAR2(20)
DEPT_ID	NOT NULL	NUMBER(4)
DNAME	NOT NULL	VARCHAR2(30)

The ENABLE QUERY REWRITE clause directs Oracle to use the materialized view instead of the EMPLOYEES and DEPARTMENTS table when a user writes a query similar to the one used to create the materialized view.

To manually refresh the view, Janice uses the DBMS_MVIEW package:

```
exec dbms_mview.refresh('emp_dept');

PL/SQL procedure successfully completed.
```

SQL Application Tuning

After you've created the optimal tables, indexes, and other database objects, the next step in your quest to improve the performance of the database is to review the users' SQL commands. You can use some of Oracle's GUI-based and web-based tools, such as Top SQL and Explain Plan, to identify and analyze the SQL commands that are not only frequently executed but also use the most resources. Also, you can help the Oracle optimizer do its job of deciding the best way to run a specific query.

Top SQL Tool

Top SQL tool

A GUI-based Oracle tool that can identify SQL statements that may be consuming too many system resources and therefore may be good candidates for tuning.

The *Top SQL tool* can identify SQL statements that may be causing performance problems in the database, such as by using too much CPU or reading blocks from disk instead of from the cache. Even if the SQL command itself does not use many resources, it may still be a candidate for tuning if it is executed hundreds of times an hour!

The Top SQL tool is available in Oracle9*i* through the Oracle Enterprise Manager (OEM) console, via the Diagnostics Pack pull-out, as shown below.

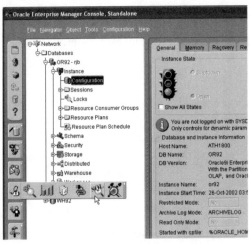

The Top SQL tool shows a number of statistics for each SQL command executed, such as disk reads, buffer reads (data is already available in the buffer cache and does not need a read from disk), CPU time used, and the number of executions. The following illustration shows an example of a Top SQL window.

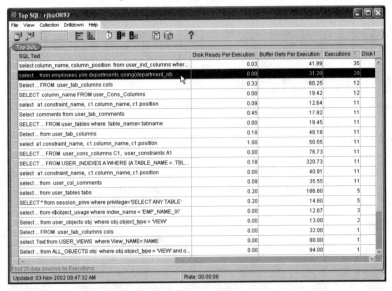

In this example, the SQL statement that joins the EMPLOYEES and DEPARTMENTS table has a high number of executions relative to the other user and system SQL statements. It may be a good candidate for analysis, even though all of the data the query needed was already in memory, as indicated by the Disk Reads Per Execution statistic.

As of Oracle 10g, you can use the web-based EM Database Control to identify SQL statements that may be using an excessive amount of system resources. The Top SQL link is available from multiple places within the EM Database Control environment.

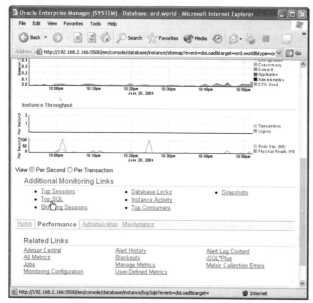

Clicking the Top SQL link displays the top SQL statements in terms of CPU usage within the selected time period.

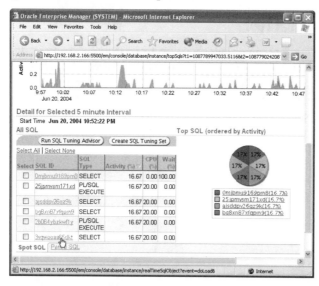

Clicking one of the top SQL statements in the list displays the SQL statement itself along with various statistics and a greater wealth of other information about the SQL statement, including execution history and whether this SQL statement has been tuned.

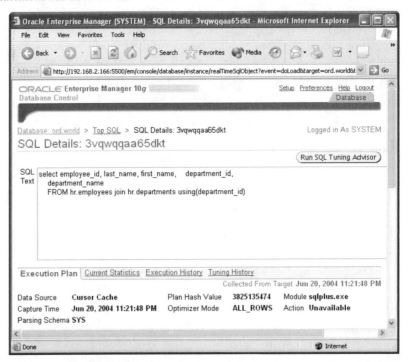

More information about the Oracle optimizer and how you can tune these SQL statements is presented later in this chapter.

Explain Plan Graphical Tool

Explain Plan tool

A GUI-based Oracle tool that details the steps in which a SQL statement is executed, as well as what method Oracle used to access the tables in the query.

Oracle9*i*'s *Explain Plan tool* can be launched directly or from the Top SQL tool. It shows in a step-by-step fashion how a SQL statement is processed and how each of the tables in the query is accessed—for example, by an index or by reading the entire table. With the statement in question highlighted in the Top SQL window, select Drilldown ➤ Explain Plan to bring up the Explain Plan analysis window, as shown below.

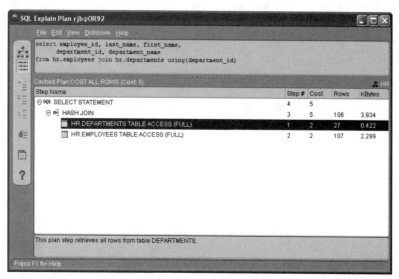

The Explain Plan window is divided into three horizontal sections. The SQL statement itself is displayed in the top section of the window. The steps that Oracle uses to execute the statement are in the middle section of the window. As each step is selected, a brief explanation of what occurs in that step is detailed in the bottom section of the window.

In the case of the join between the EMPLOYEES and DEPARTMENTS tables in this example, both tables are accessed with a full table scan instead of an index. This makes sense because the query retrieves most, if not all, of the rows in both tables. If there were a limiting condition in a WHERE clause, and the tables were still accessed by a full table scan, then it might indicate that you are missing an index on one or both of the tables.

You may see the terms Explain Plan and Execution Plan used interchangeably; they mean the same thing. The SQL command EXPLAIN PLAN generates an execution plan.

TIP

Oracle 10*g*'s EM Database Control provides similar Explain Plan functionality, as you can see on the Execution Plan tab on the following web page.

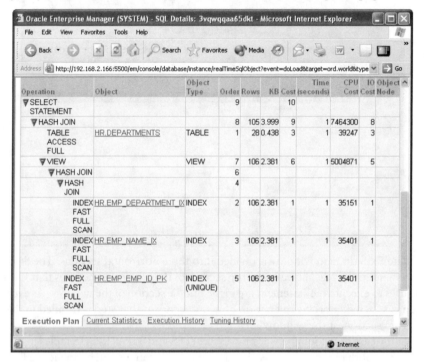

The Oracle Optimizer

As the old saying goes, "All roads lead to Rome." In the case of a SQL query, there are many different ways that a query—even a query on a single table—can be processed. It's the job of the Oracle optimizer to choose the best way to run a query.

Oracle has two optimizer modes: rule-based and cost-based. While the rule-based optimizer is essentially obsolete in Oracle 10*g*, you can expect to find many database shops that still use Oracle9*i*, and therefore you will be expected to understand how the rule-based optimizer works. We'll talk about the differences between those two modes, as well as two different ways to assist the optimizer in finding the best way to run a query.

Rule-Based Optimization

The older *rule-based optimizer* mode uses a fairly simple set of guidelines to decide how a query is run. It will use an index, regardless of the size of the table. Also, it ignores the cardinality of the columns being accessed, even if the cardinality would otherwise indicate that most of the table will be scanned for the results anyway.

Why would you use the rule-based optimizer? Some older Oracle applications might run better since they were written to specifically exploit some of the behaviors of the rule-based optimizer. Otherwise, Oracle strongly recommends that cost-based optimization be used in all new development environments.

For Oracle9*i*, you can set the optimizer mode to rule-based for the session with the ALTER SESSION command:

```
alter session set optimizer_mode=rule;


Session altered.
```

rule-based optimizer
An Oracle optimizer methodology, obsolete as of Oracle 10*g*, that relies on a fixed set of rules to determine the method used to run a query, ignoring the cardinality and distribution of data in the column being queried.

Cost-Based Optimization

The *cost-based optimizer* is much more sophisticated than the rule-based optimizer. It takes into consideration the cardinality of the columns being searched, the potential I/O cost, estimated CPU cost, and sorting cost. The cost-based optimizer will ultimately use the method that has the lowest overall cost, even if it means not using an index on one or more of the columns being searched.

For Oracle9*i*, you can tell Oracle to pick which optimizer mode to use for the session with the ALTER SESSION command:

```
alter session set optimizer_mode=choose;


Session altered.
```

The CHOOSE keyword means that Oracle will decide whether to use the rule-based optimizer or the cost-based optimizer. When analyzing a SQL statement, the optimizer may use a rule-based approach for calculating the CPU cost but may use the cost-based approach for all other calculations. Notice that you cannot specify OPTIMIZER_MODE=COST: The optimizer will always use cost-based optimization if at least one of the tables in the query has *statistics* and the optimizer mode is set to choose. The optimizer will estimate statistics on the fly for any tables in the query that don't already have them. A table's statistics are a set of predetermined characteristics stored in the data dictionary, such as those mentioned above: the cardinality of the indexed columns in the table, the number of rows in the table, the distribution of values in an indexed column, and so forth. Calculating statistics for some or all of the tables in the query will have the same effect as forcing cost-based optimization.

cost-based optimizer
An Oracle optimizer methodology that relies on the characteristics of the tables being queried to determine the method used to run the query. A cost is calculated for estimated CPU, I/O, and sorting for the possible execution paths. The path with the lowest overall cost is used to perform the query.

statistics
Information about tables and indexes stored in the data dictionary used to assist the cost-based optimizer when deciding how to run a given query.

For Oracle 10g, CHOOSE and RULE are no longer valid values for the OPTIMIZER_MODE parameter. The two most common values for OPTIMIZER_MODE in Oracle 10g are FIRST_ROWS and ALL_ROWS. FIRST_ROWS optimizes SQL statements to bring back the first few rows of the query more quickly, whereas ALL_ROWS optimizes the SQL statements to reduce the overall CPU and I/O time to retrieve all of the rows of the query.

Therefore, whether you're using Oracle9i or Oracle 10g, if you want to effectively use the cost-based optimizer it is important to have statistics calculated on the tables present in the SQL statement. We will talk about statistics gathering in the next section.

Gathering Statistics

The cost-based optimizer relies on the cardinality of columns in the table, the size of the table, the number of rows in the table, the length of each row in the table, and other statistics. By default, these statistics are not stored anywhere in the database. You can use the ANALYZE command to store these statistics in the data dictionary for use by the cost-based optimizer.

In general, it is recommended that you analyze all rows of a table and its indexes, but if the table is very large, you might analyze the indexes separately. Alternatively, you can calculate statistics on a subset of the rows in the table by using the ESTIMATE STATISTICS option of the ANALYZE command. ESTIMATE STATISTICS will use about 1,000 rows to calculate its statistics, and in many cases, it is nearly as accurate as scanning the entire table.

TIP   **The Oracle 10g infrastructure includes a number of tools to automate statistics collection.**

To gather the statistics for the EMPLOYEES table and all of its indexes using a sample of all rows, use the following command:

```
analyze table employees estimate statistics;
```

```
Table analyzed.
```

Statistics are not automatically refreshed when rows are inserted or updated; however, unless the table dramatically changes in size or in the cardinality of the indexed columns, the statistics are still useful to the cost-based optimizer. However, statistics gathering should be scheduled to run on a regular basis in order to provide the cost-based optimizer with the best information available.

Optimizer Hints

As good as the Oracle optimizer is, it is not perfect. For example, even with the best statistics, the optimizer may not choose an index; however, your experience tells you that the types of queries users have been running recently may use a very narrow range in the index, so using the index has an advantage over a full table scan. In this case, it is prudent to override the optimizer and provide a *hint* as part of the query.

Insert the hint after the SELECT keyword, between the character strings /*+ and */. There are more than 40 hints available in Oracle. Common hints include the INDEX hint to specify that a particular index is used in a query and the REWRITE hint to force a materialized view to be used to resolve the join condition in the query instead of using the base tables.

hint
A directive placed between /*+ and */ in a query that overrides an execution method that the Oracle optimizer would normally choose.

If the hint is misspelled or otherwise incorrect, it is ignored. Therefore, it is important to double-check the syntax of any hint you provide in a SQL statement.

WARNING

To force the optimizer to use the index EMP_NAME_IX on the EMPLOYEES table, use the INDEX hint, as follows:

```
select /*+ index(employees emp_name_ix) */ employee_id from
employees
where last_name = 'King';
```

Memory Tuning

Some of the memory structures used by Oracle include the database buffer cache, the shared pool, and the redo log buffer cache, as shown below. (These memory structures were discussed in Chapter 8, "Installing Oracle and Creating a Database.") While increasing the memory allocated for any of these structures will usually help, how much is enough? How much is too much?

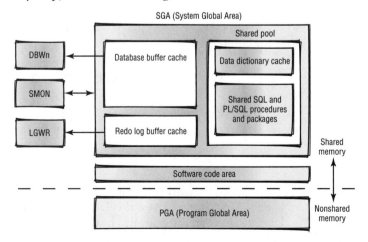

PFILE

A text file containing the parameters and their values for configuring the database and instance at startup.

SPFILE

A parameter file stored in a binary format that gives the DBA more flexibility when changing parameters. Parameters can be changed for the current instance only, can take effect only after the next restart of the instance, or both.

buffer cache advisory

A feature of the Oracle9i and Oracle 10g database that can assist the DBA in determining how large to make the buffer cache. This feature collects statistics on how often a requested database block is found in the buffer cache. The system initialization parameter DB_CACHE_ ADVICE controls whether these statistics are collected, and the data dictionary view V$DB_CACHE_ ADVICE contains the estimated number of physical reads that would occur given a number of different cache sizes.

You can adjust the amount of memory allocated to each of these areas by changing the value of a parameter in the parameter file used by Oracle, called a *PFILE*. A PFILE is a text file containing the parameters and their values for configuring the database and instance.

Oracle9i and Oracle 10g support a more flexible version of a PFILE called an *SPFILE*. An SPFILE is stored in a binary format. A change to a parameter in an SPFILE can be for the current running instance only, can take effect only after the next restart of the instance, or both.

The sizing of the database buffer cache is usually the most problematic, since blocks from all tables read from and written to reside in this cache. A buffer cache that is too small will hurt performance by obtaining blocks from disk instead of from the buffer cache. A buffer cache that is too big will waste memory that can otherwise be used for other memory areas.

Both Oracle9i and Oracle 10g have a feature called the *buffer cache advisory*, which can help the DBA decide how big to make the buffer cache. The first step in monitoring the size of the buffer cache is to turn on the buffer cache advisory feature by setting the DB_CACHE_ADVICE parameter. You can do this either by editing the PFILE and restarting the database or by using an SPFILE and changing the value using the ALTER SYSTEM command.

Janice, the DBA at Scott's widget company, is determined to put off asking for a memory upgrade on the server until she makes the best use of what's already there. First, she will find out if the buffer cache needs to be larger. She changes the value of DB_CACHE_ADVICE, as follows:

```
alter system set db_cache_advice=ON;

System altered.
```

To verify that the parameter is set correctly, she checks the value of that parameter in the V$PARAMETER dynamic performance view, along with the current value for the buffer cache size:

```
select name, value, isdefault, ismodified from v$parameter
where name ='db_cache_advice' or name ='db_cache_size';

NAME                            VALUE       ISDEFAULT ISMODIFIED
------------------------------  ----------  --------- ----------
db_cache_size                   25165824    FALSE     FALSE
db_cache_advice                 ON          TRUE      SYSTEM_MOD

2 rows selected.
```

The value is set correctly, but Janice notices that ON is the default value for this parameter. After this tuning exercise is completed, Janice will remember to change this value back to OFF to eliminate any overhead generated by the monitoring process. It also looks like the value for DB_CACHE_SIZE is currently about 25MB.

After the system has been running for a day or two with the DB_CACHE_
ADVICE parameter turned on, Janice reviews the dynamic performance view
V$DB_CACHE_ADVICE:

```
select size_for_estimate, estd_physical_reads
from v$db_cache_advice;

SIZE_FOR_ESTIMATE ESTD_PHYSICAL_READS
----------------- -------------------
                4             1158418
                8              213691
               12              100625
               16               44844
               20               37598
               24               35000
               28               34727
               32               34590
               36               34590
               40               34590
               44               34590
               48               34590
               52               34590
               56               34590
               60               34590
               64               34590
               68               34590
               72               34590
               76               34590
               80               34590
```

```
20 rows selected.
```

The first column, SIZE_FOR_ESTIMATE, is the proposed size for the buffer
pool in megabytes. The second column, ESTD_PHYSICAL_READS, is the number
of reads from disk that would occur with the corresponding buffer cache size,
given the recent activity level. From this report, Janice sees that her buffer cache
of 25MB is sized optimally. Increasing the buffer cache size to 28MB, for example, would reduce the physical I/O only slightly, and it probably would not jus-
tify a memory upgrade at this time. At 32MB and higher, the additional memory
allocated to the buffer cache would not reduce the reads from disk at all. It
appears that Janice will not need a memory upgrade on the server for the fore-
seeable future.

Terms to Know

bitmap index	materialized view
branch blocks	Oracle's Tuning Methodology
b-tree index	partitioned table
buffer cache advisory	PFILE
cardinality	reverse key index
cost-based optimizer	ROWID
Explain Plan tool	rule-based optimizer
function-based index	SPFILE
hint	statistics
index-organized table (IOT)	Top SQL tool
leaf blocks	unique index

Review Questions

1. What GUI tool analyzes a SQL statement and identifies the steps used to process the query?

2. The two general categories of indexes are _____ indexes and _____ indexes.

3. Which type of index is best for columns with a low cardinality?

4. Which dynamic performance view can assist the DBA in sizing the buffer cache appropriately?

5. Which type of table divides the contents of a very large table into more manageable chunks, both improving the manageability of the table for the DBA and potentially increasing the performance of queries on the table?

6. Which data dictionary views contain information about table indexes and the table columns indexed?

7. Name the six steps in Oracle's Tuning Methodology in order of priority.

8. Which feature associated with materialized views rewrites a query to use the materialized view instead of using the tables that are the source for the materialized view?

9. What is the name of the pseudo-column that exists for every row of every table in the database and is unique across the entire database?

10. Name the two different optimizer modes in Oracle9*i* and identify which one uses statistics from tables and indexes to derive an execution plan; identify two of the most common modes in Oracle 10*g*.

Chapter 13

Saving Your Stuff (Backups)

Sooner or later, you'll lose some data in the database. As a user, you may delete some rows in a table that you really didn't want to delete. As a DBA, you may have a server crash or one of the server's hard disks may fail, resulting in loss of data.

Oracle provides a number of tools for both users and DBAs to minimize data loss in these situations. Some of the tools are primarily for use by the DBA; other tools are primarily used by the database user.

This chapter begins with descriptions of the types of failures possible in the database and then discusses the different ways that you can back up and restore data.

Database Failures

Database failures can be divided into two general categories: media failures and nonmedia failures.

Media failures, the more serious type, occur when a server hardware component fails and the contents of one or more disk files are either unreadable or corrupted. The DBA is solely responsible for recovering from this type of failure by restoring the unreadable or corrupted file from a tape or disk backup. The DBA can perform the recovery process using one of the tools described in this chapter.

Nonmedia failures are all other types of failures, including the following:

Statement failure   The SQL statement being executed has a syntax error or the user executing the statement has the wrong permissions. Recovery from a statement failure is generally simple: Rerun the SQL statement with the right syntax or obtain the proper permissions on the objects in the query, and then rerun the query.

Process failure   The user may be disconnected from the database due to a network problem or because a resource limit was exceeded. One of the Oracle background processes automatically cleans up the terminated process by freeing the memory used by the process.

Instance failure   The entire database instance fails due to a power outage, a server memory problem, or a bug in the Oracle software. When the database instance is restarted, Oracle uses the redo log files to make sure that all committed transactions are recorded properly in the database datafiles.

User error   A user may drop a table or delete rows from a table unintentionally.

In the following sections, we'll cover the processes used by DBAs and users to recover from the two types of errors that Oracle cannot handle automatically: media failures and user errors.

media failure
A type of database failure where a server hardware component fails and the contents of one or more disk files are either unreadable or corrupted.

nonmedia failure
A type of database failure that is not related to a server disk-related hardware component and is one of several types: statement failure, process failure, instance failure, or user error.

User Backup and Recovery Methods

There are a number of methods that database users and developers can use to back up and restore the data in their tables. While a good DBA has a comprehensive database backup and restore plan in place, there are a couple of reasons why database users might make their own backups:

◆ The DBA is typically very busy and may not be able to respond to a user's request to restore data in a timely manner.

◆ The type of backup a DBA typically performs is at an enterprise level— entire tablespaces rather than individual user objects—making it difficult to accommodate requests to restore individual objects.

In this section, we'll talk about two ways that database users can back up and restore the objects they own or objects that are accessible to them in the database: by using the Export and Import utilities and by running flashback queries.

Export and Import for Users

The Export and Import utilities save and retrieve objects stored in an operating system file external to the database. They work with database table objects, along with their associated indexes, constraints, and permissions. These commands are similar in their syntax and are executed outside the database at an operating system prompt.

The Export (EXP) Utility

The *Export utility (EXP)* connects to the database and performs a SELECT statement on the table or tables specified in the EXP command. It places the results of the SELECT statement, along with the DDL statements required to create the tables and their associated indexes, into a single binary dump file. Subsequently, this dump file can be used to restore the tables in case of data loss. In addition, the dump file can be used to copy the table to another database. The format of the EXP command is as follows:

Export utility (EXP)
An Oracle utility that copies the contents of one or more tables to a binary dump file, along with the DDL needed to create the table and its associated indexes, permissions, and constraints.

```
EXP username/password KEYWORD=(value1, value2, ...)
```

If the EXP command is executed without specifying any parameters, Export prompts the user for the parameters in an interactive mode. The username and password belong to the user who owns the objects to be exported. The TABLES keyword specifies the tables that are to be exported to the dump file, which defaults to the filename EXPDAT.DMP. Running EXP -HELP displays all of the Export options. The most common keywords are listed below.

Keyword	Description
FILE	Destination for the dump file; defaults to EXPDAT.DMP
TABLES	List of table names
ROWS	Export rows of the table; defaults to Y
INDEXES	Export indexes; defaults to Y
CONSTRAINTS	Export table constraints; defaults to Y
GRANTS	Export privileges granted on tables; defaults to Y
COMPRESS	Create a single extent for each table in the CREATE TABLE statement generated by EXP; defaults to Y

While the default for the COMPRESS **parameter of Export is** Y**, it should almost always be set to** N **to avoid wasting disk space when new extents are allocated for the imported version of the table.**

At Scott's widget company, one of the developers, Gary, is working on a project to provide customers with customized widgets, made to order. He is working on the order entry part of the system, and he has a copy of the Order Entry department's ORDER and ORDER_ITEM tables in his own schema:

```
select table_name from all_tables
where owner='GARY';


TABLE_NAME
--------------------
ORDERS
ORDER_ITEMS

2 rows selected.
```

Gary decides to use Export to save a copy of these tables to a binary dump file on a local PC's hard drive, just in case one of the tables is inadvertently dropped:

```
E:\TEMP>exp gary/castiron@ord
        tables=(orders, order_items) file=exp_oe.dmp

Export: Release 10.1.0.2.0 -
        Production on Mon Jun 21 22:57:53 2004

Copyright (c) 1982, 2004, Oracle.  All rights reserved.


Connected to: Oracle Database 10g Enterprise Edition
        Release 10.1.0.2.0 - Production
With the Partitioning, OLAP and Data Mining options
Export done in WE8MSWIN1252 character set
        and AL16UTF16 NCHAR character set
server uses WE8ISO8859P1 character set
        (possible charset conversion)

About to export specified tables via Conventional Path ...
. . exporting table        ORDERS        105 rows exported
. . exporting table        ORDER_ITEMS   665 rows exported
```

```
Export terminated successfully without warnings.

E:\TEMP>
```

The operating system file `E:\temp\exp_oe.dmp` contains the definitions of the two tables and their contents, along with any indexes, constraints, and permissions defined on the tables.

As of Oracle 10g, the new utilities EXPDB and IMPDB, the command-line utility interface to Oracle Data Pump, replace most of the functionality of EXP and IMP in Oracle9i and earlier and provide features such as import and export directly between instances. The original Export and Import utilities, however, should still be used in an Oracle 10g database when importing backups from a previous release of Oracle, or you will need to export data to import into a previous release of Oracle.

NOTE

The Import (IMP) Utility

The *Import utility (IMP)* reads a binary dump file produced by the Export utility and restores the tables and any associated indexes, constraints, and permissions saved in the dump file. The format of the IMP command is as follows:

```
IMP username/password KEYWORD=(value1, value2, ...)
```

If the IMP command is executed without specifying any parameters, Import can prompt the user for the parameters in an interactive mode. The username and password belong to the user who owns the objects to be imported. The TABLES keyword lists the tables that are to be imported from the dump file, which defaults to a name of EXPDAT.DMP. Running IMP -HELP lists all of the Import options. The most common keywords are listed below.

Import utility (IMP)
An Oracle utility that takes as input a binary dump file created by the Export utility and restores one or more database tables, along with any associated indexes, permissions, and constraints.

Keyword	Description
FILE	Dump file to restore from; defaults to EXPDAT.DMP
TABLES	List of table names to restore
ROWS	Import rows of the table; defaults to Y
INDEXES	Import indexes; defaults to Y
CONSTRAINTS	Import table constraints; defaults to Y
GRANTS	Import privileges granted on tables; defaults to Y
SHOW	Show just the file contents and do not perform the restore; defaults to N

Later in the week, Gary, the database developer, inadvertently drops the ORDER_ ITEMS table that he was using to test his custom widgets application. He

remembers using Export earlier in the week to create a backup to the file exp_
oe.dmp, but is not sure of its contents. He uses the SHOW option of the IMP command to query the contents of the dump file:

```
E:\TEMP>imp file=exp_oe.dmp show=y


Import: Release 10.1.0.2.0 - Production on Mon Jun 21
23:13:21 2004

Copyright (c) 1982, 2004, Oracle.  All rights reserved.

Username: gary@ord
Password:

Connected to: Oracle Database 10g Enterprise Edition Release
    10.1.0.2.0 - Production
With the Partitioning, OLAP and Data Mining options

Export file created by EXPORT:V10.01.00
    via conventional path
import done in WE8MSWIN1252 character set
    and AL16UTF16 NCHAR character set
import server uses WE8ISO8859P1 character set
    (possible charset conversion)
. importing GARY's objects into GARY

 "CREATE TABLE "ORDERS"
     ("ORDER_ID" NUMBER(12, 0) NOT NULL ENABLE,"ORDER_DAT"
 "E" TIMESTAMP (6) WITH LOCAL TIME ZONE
     CONSTRAINT "ORDER_DATE_NN" NOT NULL E"
 ...
 "CREATE TABLE "ORDER_ITEMS"
     ("ORDER_ID" NUMBER(12, 0) NOT NULL ENABLE, "LINE"
 ...
Import terminated successfully without warnings.

E:\TEMP>
```

Since the SHOW=Y option was specified, the tables were not actually restored to
the database, even though the output from IMP seems to indicate that the restore

took place. Since this file has the table that Gary wants, he performs the import and specifies the file he dropped:

```
E:\TEMP>imp file=exp_oe.dmp tables=order_items

Import: Release 10.1.0.2.0 - Production on Mon Jun 21
23:24:47 2004

Copyright (c) 1982, 2004, Oracle.  All rights reserved.

Username: gary@ord
Password:

Connected to: Oracle Database 10g Enterprise Edition
       Release 10.1.0.2.0 - Production
With the Partitioning, OLAP and Data Mining options

Export file created by EXPORT:V10.01.00
       via conventional path
import done in WE8MSWIN1252 character set
       and AL16UTF16 NCHAR character set
import server uses WE8ISO8859P1 character set
       (possible charset conversion)
. importing GARY's objects into GARY
. . importing table    "ORDER_ITEMS"      665 rows imported
Import terminated successfully without warnings.

E:\TEMP>
```

Gary's ORDER_ITEMS table is now restored. Any changes made to the table since the export was performed are lost. Those changes will need to be manually restored by rerunning the INSERT, DELETE, and UPDATE statements that ran since the last export. To minimize data loss, you should export the table after any major changes are made to the table.

NOTE

As an alternative to importing a dropped table from an export dump file, Oracle 10g supports a recycle bin concept, keeping the contents of the dropped table hidden in a special area on disk and accessible as long as the disk space occupied by the dropped table is not needed for new objects in the tablespace.

Flashback Query

flashback query
A feature of the Oracle database that allows a user to view the contents of a table as of a user-specified point in time in the past. How far in the past a flashback query can retrieve rows depends on the size of the undo tablespace and on the setting of the UNDO_RETENTION system parameter.

One of the features introduced in Oracle9*i* is called *flashback query*. It allows a user to "go back in time" and view the contents of a table as it existed at some point in the recent past. A flashback query looks a lot like a standard SQL SELECT statement, with the addition of the AS OF TIMESTAMP clause.

Before users can take advantage of the flashback query feature, the DBA must perform two tasks:

◆ The DBA must make sure that there is an undo tablespace in the database that is large enough to retain changes made by all users for a specified period of time. This is the same tablespace that is used to support COMMIT and ROLLBACK functionality (discussed in Chapter 7, "Logical Consistency").

◆ The DBA must specify how long the undo information will be retained for use by flashback queries by using the initialization parameter UNDO_RETENTION. This parameter is specified in seconds; therefore, if the DBA specifies UNDO_RETENTION=172800, the undo information for flashback queries will be available for two days.

At Scott's widget company, an error in the Accounting department added $2,000 to two orders placed yesterday:

```
update orders
set order_total = order_total+2000
where order_id in (2367,2361);

2 rows updated.

select order_id, customer_id, order_total
from orders where order_id in (2367,2361);

  ORDER_ID CUSTOMER_ID ORDER_TOTAL
---------- ----------- -----------
      2361         108    122131.3
      2367         148    146054.8

2 rows selected.
```

Today, the customer with customer ID 108 called to complain that his bill from his last order (order number 2361) is $2,000 higher than expected. Sharon, one of the order-entry clerks, retrieves the row from the ORDERS table with the information for order number 2361:

```
select order_id, customer_id, order_total
from orders where order_id = 2361;
```

```
   ORDER_ID CUSTOMER_ID ORDER_TOTAL
---------- ----------- -----------
      2361         108    122131.3
```

1 row selected.

Before calling back the customer, Sharon finds out from the Accounting department that a day ago, two of the orders were incorrectly modified with an additional surcharge. To confirm whether this particular order was affected by the accounting error, she uses a flashback query to see if this order had a different order total two days ago:

```
select order_id, customer_id, order_total from orders
as of timestamp (sysdate - 2)
where order_id = 2361;
```

```
   ORDER_ID CUSTOMER_ID ORDER_TOTAL
---------- ----------- -----------
      2361         108    120131.3
```

1 row selected.

This flashback query confirms that the order total for this order was $2,000 less two days ago. The AS OF TIMESTAMP clause specifies how far back in the past you want to view the contents of this table. In this case, (sysdate - 2) evaluates to today's date minus two days—in other words, two days ago. Sharon concludes that at some point in the past two days, this was one of the orders that were incorrectly modified. To find all of the orders that have the incorrect surcharge, she uses another flashback query as a nested query to compare the order totals:

```
select o.order_id, o.customer_id,
   o.order_total "CURR_TOTAL", oo.order_total "ORIG_TOTAL"
from orders o,
     (select order_id, order_total from orders
      as of timestamp (sysdate - 2)) oo
where o.order_id = oo.order_id and
      o.order_total != oo.order_total;
```

```
   ORDER_ID CUSTOMER_ID ORDER_TOTAL ORIG_TOTAL
---------- ----------- ----------- ----------
      2361         108    122131.3   120131.3
      2367         148    146054.8   144054.8
```

2 rows selected.

In this query, Sharon is comparing the entire contents of the current ORDERS table to the entire contents of the ORDERS table as it was two days ago and selecting records where the order totals don't match. She now knows which records must be updated with the correct order total amount.

DBA Backup and Recovery Methods

The DBA has a number of additional tools for performing backup and recovery, with capabilities for working at a much larger scale than the methods previously discussed. Instead of a couple of tables being dropped by a user, the DBA may need to handle a disk drive failure, resulting in the loss of an entire tablespace.

In addition to using Export and Import to back up database objects, the DBA can perform cold backups or hot backups for an entire tablespace or an entire database. Other tools available to the DBA include Log Miner and RMAN.

Export and Import for DBAs

transportable tablespace

A feature of Oracle's Import and Export utilities that allows a tablespace to be copied to another database. All objects within the tablespace to be copied must be self-contained; in other words, a table in a tablespace to be copied must have its associated indexes in the same tablespace.

Earlier in this chapter, you learned about the Export (EXP) and Import (IMP) utilities that a user can use to save and restore database objects. The DBA can use additional features of these utilities for backing up all user objects in the database or to copy a tablespace to another database. The tablespace copy feature, introduced in Oracle9*i*, is known as *transportable tablespaces*. It is a very convenient way to copy all objects in a tablespace to another database, without needing to specify individual objects in the tablespace.

At Scott's widget company, there are two primary databases:

♦ The OLTP database (ORD), which contains the online widget order system and the HR tables. It has the EMPLOYEES, DEPARTMENTS, and other tables.

♦ The data warehouse database (WH), which contains summaries of orders processed on the online system. Analysts use this summarized information to do "what-if" analyses to predict sales for the upcoming fiscal year.

On a weekly basis, Janice, the DBA, needs to copy the transactions from the online database to the data warehouse database. She decides that using transportable tablespaces is the most convenient and efficient way to move this data, as there are hundreds of tables in several different schemas that need to be merged into the data warehouse.

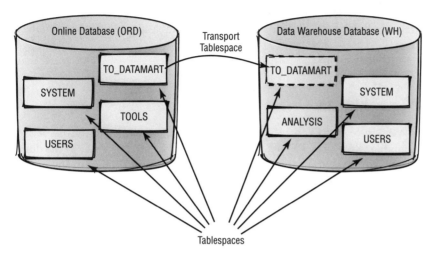

In the online database, Janice reviews the available tablespaces:

```
connect janice/janice@ord;

Connected.

select tablespace_name, status, contents from dba_
tablespaces;

TABLESPACE_NAME                    STATUS     CONTENTS
---------------------------------- ---------- ---------
SYSTEM                             ONLINE     PERMANENT
UNDOTBS1                           ONLINE     UNDO
TEMP                               ONLINE     TEMPORARY
CWMLITE                            ONLINE     PERMANENT
DRSYS                              ONLINE     PERMANENT
EXAMPLE                            ONLINE     PERMANENT
INDX                               ONLINE     PERMANENT
ODM                                ONLINE     PERMANENT
TOOLS                              ONLINE     PERMANENT
USERS                              ONLINE     PERMANENT
XDB                                ONLINE     PERMANENT
TO_DATAMART                        ONLINE     PERMANENT

12 rows selected.
```

The TO_DATAMART tablespace contains the tables that need to go to the data warehouse database. The first step in copying a tablespace to another database is to make it read-only:

```
alter tablespace to_datamart read only;

Tablespace altered.
```

Next, Janice uses Export (EXP) to save the characteristics of the tablespace to a dump file. Note that the contents of the tablespace are not saved to the dump file; only the information about the objects in the tablespace is saved. She will use the datafiles that make up the tablespace to copy the data. In the following EXP command, Janice creates the dump file for the TO_DATAMART tablespace:

```
E:\TEMP>exp transport_tablespace=y
        tablespaces=to_datamart file=exp_mart.dmp


Export: Release 10.1.0.2.0 - Production on
        Mon Jun 21 22:57:53 2004

Copyright (c) 1982, 2004, Oracle.  All rights reserved.



Connected to: Oracle Database 10g Enterprise Edition
        Release 10.1.0.2.0 - Production
With the Partitioning, OLAP and Data Mining options
Export done in WE8MSWIN1252 character set
        and AL16UTF16 NCHAR character set
server uses WE8ISO8859P1 character set
        (possible charset conversion)
Note: table data (rows) will not be exported
About to export transportable tablespace metadata...
For tablespace TO_DATAMART ...
. exporting cluster definitions
. exporting table definitions
. . exporting table                    INVENTORIES
. . exporting table                    SALES001
. . exporting table                    SALES002
...
. . exporting table                    SALES226
. . exporting table                    CUSTOMERS
. exporting referential integrity constraints
```

```
. exporting triggers
. end transportable tablespace metadata export
Export terminated successfully without warnings.
```

```
E:\TEMP>
```

In the next step, Janice copies the datafiles that compose the TO_DATAMART tablespace to the directory location where the rest of the data warehouse datafiles reside. Janice uses the data dictionary views V$TABLESPACE and V$DATAFILE to determine the operating system files that compose the TO_DATAMART tablespace:

```
select d.name "Filenames"
from v$tablespace t, v$datafile d
where t.ts# = d.ts#
and t.name = 'TO_DATAMART';

Filenames
---------------------------------------
D:\ORACLE\ORADATA\ORD\TO_DATAMART.ORA

1 row selected.
```

Janice uses a standard operating system copy command to make a copy of the tablespace in the new database:

```
D:\> copy d:\oracle\oradata\ord\to_datamart.ora
        d:\oracle\oradata\wh

        1 file(s) copied.

D:\>
```

Back in the online database, Janice changes the source tablespace back to read-write:

```
connect janice/janice@ord;

Connected.

alter tablespace to_datamart read write;

Tablespace altered.
```

At this point, the source database is back to its original state, the information about the TO_DATAMART tablespace has been saved to a dump file, and a copy of the TO_DATAMART tablespace datafile is ready to attach to the data warehouse database. Janice will run Import (IMP) to attach the tablespace to the data warehouse database, using many of the same options she used with Export to create the tablespace dump file:

```
E:\TEMP>imp transport_tablespace=y file=exp_mart.dmp
    datafiles=('d:\oracle\oradata\wh\to_datamart.ora')
    tablespaces=to_datamart

Import: Release 10.1.0.2.0 - Production
    on Mon Jun 21 23:16:21 2004

Copyright (c) 1982, 2004, Oracle.
    All rights reserved.

Username: janice as sysdba
Password:

Connected to: Oracle Database 10g Enterprise Edition
        Release 10.1.0.2.0 - Production
With the Partitioning, OLAP and Data
        Mining options

Export file created by EXPORT:V10.01.00
        via conventional path

About to import transportable tablespace(s) metadata...
import done in WE8MSWIN1252 character set
    and AL16UTF16 NCHAR character set
. importing SYS's objects into SYS
. importing RJB's objects into RJB
. . importing table                   "INVENTORIES"
. . importing table                   "SALES001"
. . importing table                   "SALES002"
...
. . importing table                   "SALES226"
. . importing table                   "CUSTOMERS"

Import terminated successfully without warnings.

E:\TEMP>
```

A copy of the TO_DATAMART tablespace is now attached to the data warehouse database and ready for use by the marketing analysts:

```
connect janice/janice@wh;

Connected.

select tablespace_name, status, contents
    from dba_tablespaces
    where tablespace_name = 'TO_DATAMART';

TABLESPACE_NAME                 STATUS    CONTENTS
------------------------------- --------- ---------
TO_DATAMART                     READ ONLY PERMANENT

1 row selected.
```

Before the tablespace can be imported again into the data warehouse database, it must be taken offline and dropped. It is assumed that any objects in the TO_ DATAMART tablespace are copied to other tablespaces shortly after the TO_ DATAMART tablespace is imported.

Cold Backups

A database *cold backup* is most likely the simplest way to make a backup of a database. A cold backup consists of making copies of the datafiles, the control files, and the initialization parameter files, or SPFILEs, while the database is shut down. A cold backup is also known as a *closed backup*.

Cold backups are easy to do, but they have several disadvantages. The database is unavailable to users during a cold backup, so any database that must be available 24 hours a day is not a good candidate for a cold backup. In addition, a database media failure will result in some loss of data—any transactions that are recorded to the database since the last cold backup are lost.

cold backup
A database backup performed while the database is shut down. Also known as a closed backup.

closed backup
See *cold backup.*

Hot Backups

A *hot backup* is similar to a cold backup, except that the backup is performed while the database is open and available to users. A hot backup is also known as an *open backup*.

Hot backups are performed on one tablespace at a time. They are better than cold backups in that the database is always available to users, even while the backup is in progress.

open backup
See *hot backup.*

hot backup
A database backup performed while the database is open and available to users. Also known as an open backup.

To perform a hot backup, you must know the names of the datafiles that belong to the tablespace you are backing up. Janice, the DBA, needs to back up the USERS tablespace while the database is open, so she uses the V$TABLESPACE and V$DATAFILE views to find out the datafile names for the USERS tablespace:

```
select d.name "Filenames"
from v$tablespace t, v$datafile d
where t.ts# = d.ts#
and t.name = 'USERS';

Filenames
-----------------------------------
D:\ORACLE\ORADATA\ORD\USERS01.DBF

1 row selected.
```

Before Janice initiates the backup, she marks the tablespace as being in a backup state:

```
alter tablespace users begin backup;

Tablespace altered.
```

Now any transactions occurring against the tablespace while the backup is in progress will be correctly applied to the objects in the tablespace when the backup is complete.

In the next step, Janice performs a copy operation at the operating system command prompt, similar to the copy she performed when transporting a tablespace:

```
D:\> copy d:\oracle\oradata\ord\users01.dbf d:\backup
        1 file(s) copied.

D:\>
```

To finish the hot backup, Janice takes the tablespace out of backup mode:

```
alter tablespace users end backup;

Tablespace altered.
```

During the time the tablespace was in backup mode, all objects in the tablespace were still available to users.

Log Miner

Oracle Log Miner is another tool the DBA can use to view past activity in the database. The Log Miner tool can help the DBA find changed records in redo log files by using a set of PL/SQL procedures and functions. Log Miner extracts all DDL and DML activity from the redo log files for viewing by a DBA via the dynamic performance view V$LOGMNR_CONTENTS. In addition to extracting the DDL and DML statements used to change the database, the V$LOGMNR_CONTENTS view also contains the DML or DDL statements needed to reverse the change made to the database. This is a good tool for not only pinpointing when changes were made to a table but also for automatically generating the SQL statements needed to reverse those changes.

Log Miner works differently from Oracle's flashback query feature. The flashback query feature allows a user to see the contents of a table at a specified time in the past; Log Miner can search a time period for all DDL against the table. A flashback query uses the undo information stored in the undo tablespace; Log Miner uses redo logs. Both of these tools can be useful for tracking down how and when changes to database objects took place.

Log Miner may be configured and used either from a SQL command line or via a GUI-based interface within Oracle Enterprise Manager (OEM), as shown here, by selecting Tools ➢ Database Applications ➢ Logminer Viewer.

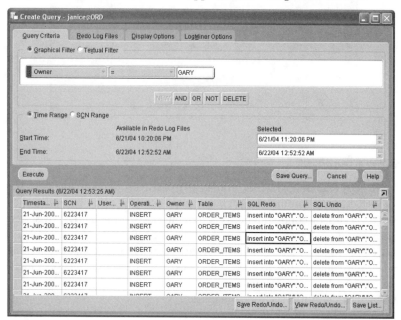

This Log Miner session initiated through OEM shows a sequence of DML statements executed by GARY against the ORDER_ITEMS table. The SQL Redo column shows the DML statement used to change the ORDER_ITEMS table, and the SQL Undo column shows how to reverse the change made by the DML statement in the SQL Redo column. Double-clicking a row in the report brings up a second window that shows the complete text of both the SQL Undo and SQL Redo columns, as shown here.

Recovery Manager

Recovery Manager (RMAN)
A comprehensive set of backup and recovery tools that can streamline the backup and recovery of a database.

The *Recovery Manager (RMAN)* tool is an extensive and comprehensive set of tools that can streamline the backup and recovery of a database. It can be accessed via either a command line or a GUI interface through OEM by selecting Tools ➢ Database Tools ➢ Backup Management ➢ Backup. Using RMAN can reduce errors by automating many of the tasks that a DBA would otherwise need to perform manually, such as checking a backup set for completeness or logging the results of a backup operation.

RMAN can perform the following tasks:

Back up all database objects   RMAN can back up every individual type of database or filesystem object, or the entire database. It can back up tablespaces, datafiles, control files, and log files.

Log all backup operations   RMAN automatically logs the status of the backup as it occurs and when it completes.

Catalog backup information   Information about what database objects were backed up on what days is kept in an Oracle database.

Perform incremental backups   Only the changes to database objects are backed up in an RMAN incremental backup. This saves time and space. A full backup can occur weekly, with incremental backups performed during the week.

Create a duplicate of a database   A copy of an entire database can be made for testing a new release of a software application or testing an upgrade to a new release of the Oracle database software.

Test the recovery process   RMAN can review the contents of backups to validate that the database can be restored successfully in case of a catastrophic failure of the database.

The GUI version of RMAN includes a wizard, as shown below. This interface can help the DBA choose which objects are included in a backup, choose a backup strategy, and automate the backup process through OEM.

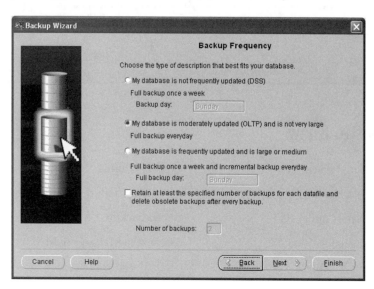

Most of the database features available via the command line or through the OEM application, including RMAN functionality, are available in Oracle 10*g* using a web browser and the Enterprise Manager Database Control application.

Terms to Know

closed backup

cold backup

Export utility (EXP)

flashback query

hot backup

Import utility (IMP)

media failure

nonmedia failure

open backup

Recovery Manager (RMAN)

transportable tablespace

Review Questions

1. A cold database backup occurs when a database is _____, and a hot database backup occurs when a database is _____.

2. The failure of a disk drive containing database datafiles would be considered what kind of a failure?

3. What clause in a SELECT statement specifies the time and date for an Oracle flashback query?

4. The flashback query tool uses which Oracle structure to retrieve information on how a table appeared at some specified point in the past?

5. True or false: A flashback query can retrieve the DDL statement needed to undo a change made to a table in the past.

6. An abnormal termination of the Oracle server software would be considered what type of database failure?

7. Which Oracle utilities can be used by a database user to back up and restore a table and by a DBA to move a tablespace from one database to another?

8. Which Oracle structure allows the automatic recovery of the Oracle database after an instance failure?

9. What option of the Import (IMP) command allows the DBA to view the DDL contained in a dump file without executing those DDL commands?

10. What is the name of the feature of Oracle's Export and Import utilities that allows a DBA to move or copy an entire tablespace from one database to another?

Chapter 14

Troubleshooting

In This Chapter

♦ Reviewing the Oracle alert log file
♦ Monitoring events with OEM
♦ Using system trace files for troubleshooting
♦ Using user trace files for performance tuning

When trouble strikes in your Oracle database, there are many places to turn for clues about what is causing the problem. The approach you take to troubleshooting the database will depend, in part, on whether a few users complain or you get hundreds of phone calls and e-mail messages from irate users.

The alert log file can give you clues about global database errors, and the system trace files can tell you about problems with the background processes. When individual users are having problems with their sessions, and the error messages they are receiving in their SQL*Plus session aren't very descriptive, the user trace files may provide additional clues to the problem.

For Oracle9*i*, you can also use the Event Manager in Oracle Enterprise Manager (OEM) to automatically notify you of problems or potential problems, such as when disk space is close to running out. In Oracle 10*g*, the Advisory infrastructure in conjunction with the web-based Enterprise Manager Database Control provides similar functionality.

The Alert Log File

alert log file

A text file that contains entries about significant database events, such as database startup and shutdown, nondefault initialization parameters, and various errors. The alert log file is stored in the directory specified by the system parameter BACKGROUND_DUMP_DEST.

The *alert log file* is a grab bag of messages about the state of the database instance. It contains entries about significant database events, such as database startup and shutdown, nondefault initialization parameters, ALTER SYSTEM commands, and various errors.

Locating the Alert Log File

At Scott's widget company, Janice, the DBA, doesn't remember when she made the changes to the redo log files. She wanted to increase the redundancy of the redo log files, so she added a second set of redo logs on a different disk. She can find information about the redo logs in the alert log file.

Janice's first step is to locate the alert log file itself; since she recently converted one of the Oracle databases from a Windows server to a Linux server, she hasn't yet memorized the locations of the Oracle-related directories, so she needs to check one of the initialization parameters. This log file is a text file in the directory specified by the initialization parameter BACKGROUND_DUMP_DEST:

```
show parameter background_dump_dest


NAME                TYPE        VALUE
----------------    --------    ------------------------------
background_dump     string      /u01/app/oracle/admin/ord/bdump
_dest
```

From a Linux operating system command-line session, Janice locates the alert log file:

```
[oracle@oltp oracle]$ cd /u01/app/oracle/admin/ord/bdump
[oracle@oltp bdump]$ ls -l alert_*.log
-rw-r--r--    1 oracle    oinstall     4006 Jun 22 22:23
alert_ord.log
[oracle@oltp bdump]$ vi alert_ord.log
```

The alert log file's name on Linux is alert_, followed by the instance's connection identifier and an extension of .log.

Viewing the Alert Log File

Now that Janice knows where to find the alert log file, she opens it using the Linux vi text editor.

It appears that the new redo logs were created on June 22, 2004, at about 10:23 PM You can also see that the control file was automatically backed up by EM Database Control when the new redo log files were created.

Maintaining the Alert Log File

The alert log file grows in size slowly but without limit. After a few weeks, it can become cumbersome to review the file, so it's a good idea to archive or delete the file on a periodic basis.

The alert log file can be safely renamed or deleted, even when the database is up and running. The next time an entry needs to be written to the alert log file and the alert log file is not there, a new one is created.

Janice, the DBA, reviews the alert log file every Friday and renames it with a name containing the date it was renamed:

```
[oracle@oltp oracle]$ cd /u01/app/oracle/admin/ord/bdump
[oracle@oltp bdump]$ ls -l alert_*.log
-rw-r--r-- 1 oracle oinstall 4006 Jun 22 22:23 alert_ord.log
```

```
[oracle@oltp bdump]$ mv alert_ord.log
alert_ord_2004-06-21.log
[oracle@oltp bdump]$ ls -l alert_*.log
-rw-r--r-- 1 oracle oinstall 4006 Jun 22 22:23
alert_ord_2004-06-21.log

[oracle@oltp bdump]$ sqlplus / as sysdba

SQL*Plus: Release 10.1.0.2.0 - Production on Tue Jun 22
23:13:49 2004

Copyright (c) 1982, 2004, Oracle.  All rights reserved.

Connected to:
Oracle Database 10g Enterprise Edition Release 10.1.0.2.0 -
Production
With the Partitioning, OLAP and Data Mining options

SQL> alter system switch logfile;
System altered.

SQL> quit
Disconnected from Oracle Database 10g Enterprise Edition
Release 10.1.0.2.0 - Production
With the Partitioning, OLAP and Data Mining options

[oracle@oltp bdump]$ ls -l alert_*.log
-rw-r--r-- 1 oracle oinstall 4006 Jun 22 22:23
alert_ord_2004-06-21.log
-rw-r--r-- 1 oracle oinstall 1163 Jun 22 23:14
alert_ord.log
[oracle@oltp bdump]$
```

Notice in the example that as soon as a system event occurred, in this case a forced log switch, the new alert log file was created automatically.

Event Notification

Whether your shop is using Oracle9*i* or Oracle 10*g*, it's easy to set up automatic notifications for various types of error or warning conditions. Oracle9*i* uses the

OEM Event Manager, and Oracle 10*g* uses the web-based EM Database Control to set up and proactively monitor database health. In the following sections we'll take a look at both of these.

Oracle9*i* OEM Event Manager

OEM can automatically alert the DBA, through an e-mail message or page, to error conditions or conditions that may signal an impending error. Using OEM's Event Manager, accessible as one of the nodes in the OEM Navigator pane, the DBA can monitor a variety of error conditions, such as an abnormal termination of the Oracle instance or a tablespace running low on space. Even events that would not technically be considered an error condition can be monitored. For example, you could tell Event Manager to notify you when users are performing too many table scans within a certain period of time, as shown here.

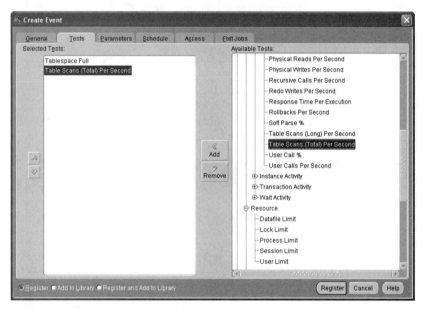

Creating a new event is straightforward. From OEM's toolbar at the top, select Event ➢ Create Event. On the Tests tab in the Create Event window, you can select from a long list of available tests. In this example, the DBA will be notified when any tablespace's used space exceeds a specified threshold percentage or the number of full table scans performed each second exceeds a specified threshold amount. The Parameters tab in the Create Event window is used to specify these thresholds. For the Tablespace Full test, an alert will be sent to the DBA via pager or e-mail whenever any tablespace is 80 percent full or higher, as shown below.

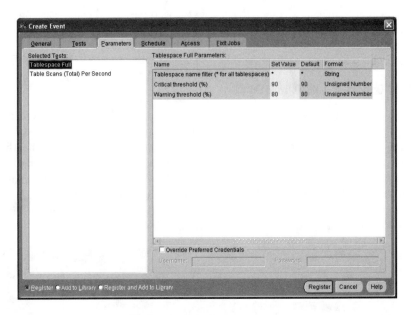

For the Table Scans Per Second test, the DBA will be notified with a warning message if the number of full table scans exceeds 10 per second at least three times, or with a critical error if the number of full table scans exceeds 25 per second at least three times, as shown below.

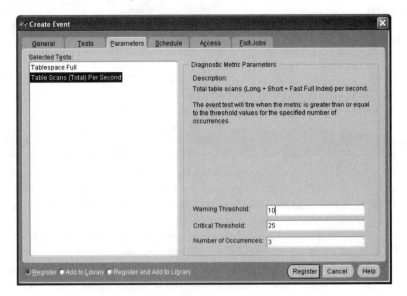

These tests can be performed on the database automatically on a regular schedule, specified on the Schedule tab of the Create Event window:

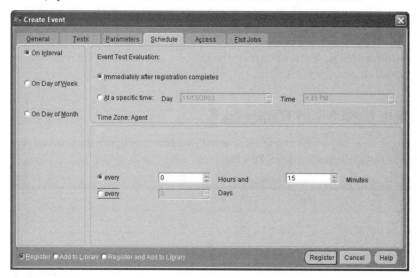

In this example, when the event is saved, the tests in the event will run immediately and then every 15 minutes thereafter.

The DBA can also specify a script to run automatically when event conditions are detected. This is helpful when the DBA is on vacation or not able to receive e-mail or pager messages for some other reason. You can select a script through the Fixit Jobs tab of the Create Event window.

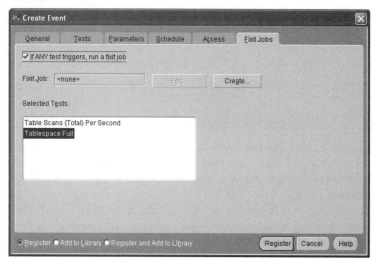

In many cases, a fixit job can repair the problem without any intervention by the DBA at all. The fixit job can, for example, temporarily allocate more disk space on a spare disk volume for the tablespace that is about to run out of space. A fixit job can be a series of predefined actions to be performed when the event occurs, such as shutting down and restarting the database, or a fixit job may call a customized SQL script written by the DBA or any combination of predefined actions and customized scripts.

Oracle 10g Advisory Framework

Using Oracle 10g's EM Database Control, you can configure diagnostics for a number of different potential trouble spots using Advisor Central.

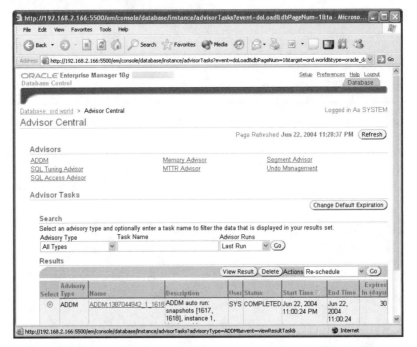

For example, SQL Tuning Advisor can automatically identify and tune SQL statements that have a high CPU and I/O impact on the database; Segment Advisor can identify objects within a schema or tablespace that have a high percentage of unused space.

For each tablespace in a database or across the entire database, you can specify two thresholds at which a notification message is sent if the space threshold is exceeded.

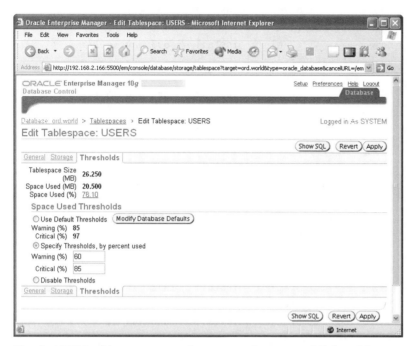

For the USERS tablespace, a warning message is generated if the tablespace exceeds 60 percent full, and a critical message is generated if the tablespace exceeds 85 percent full. For any other tablespace that does not have specific thresholds set, the warning threshold is 85 percent and the critical threshold is 97 percent.

System Trace Files

An Oracle instance's *system trace files* are stored in the same directory as the alert log file, in the directory specified by the system parameter BACKGROUND_ DUMP_DEST. The system trace files contain debugging, status, and error messages for each of the background processes, such as SMON, PMON, DBWx, LGWR, and so forth.

Janice, the DBA, notices that there are quite a few system trace files in the BACKGROUND_DUMP_DEST directory:

```
[oracle@oltp bdump]$ ls -l
total 44888
-rw-r--r--  1 oracle   oinstall   4006 Jun 22 22:23
alert_ord_2004-06-21.log
-rw-r--r--  1 oracle   oinstall  26010 Jun 23 19:40
alert_ord.log
```

system trace file

A text file that pertains to a single background process and contains status, debugging, or error information about that background process. System trace files are stored in the directory specified by the system parameter BACKGROUND_ DUMP_DEST.

```
-rw-r-----  1 oracle    oinstall     691 May 18 07:00
ord_arc0_10663.trc
-rw-r-----  1 oracle    oinstall     693 Mar 14 12:53
ord_arc0_11830.trc
. . .
-rw-r-----  1 oracle    oinstall     688 May 30 11:23
ord_arc1_3306.trc
-rw-r-----  1 oracle    oinstall     772 Mar 28 13:02
ord_arc1_3369.trc
-rw-r-----  1 oracle    oinstall     690 Mar 19 07:51
ord_arc1_3505.trc
. . .
-rw-r-----  1 oracle    oinstall     685 Mar 20 09:54
ord_dbw0_6181.trc
-rw-r-----  1 oracle    oinstall    3820 Mar 14 12:17
ord_dbw0_6399.trc
-rw-r-----  1 oracle    oinstall    1352 Mar 14 12:29
ord_dbw0_9796.trc
-rw-r-----  1 oracle    oinstall     850 Mar 14 12:55
ord_j000_11844.trc
-rw-r-----  1 oracle    oinstall     852 Mar 14 13:15
ord_j000_14335.trc
-rw-r-----  1 oracle    oinstall     859 Mar 14 13:15
ord_lgwr_12043.trc
[oracle@oltp bdump]$
```

She sees quite a few files for the DBW0 (database writer) background process, so she is concerned that there might be a problem with DBW0. She opens one of the DBW0 trace files, `ord_dbw0_6181.trc`, to see what the problem might be.

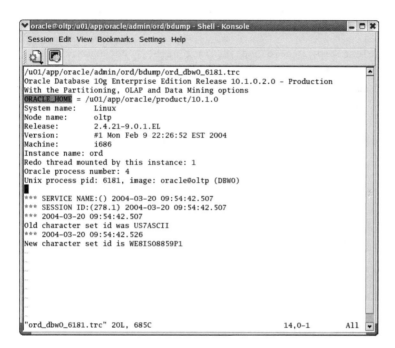

She looks at the contents of the file and realizes that most processes, including DBW0, generate a trace file at database startup. As a result, the trace file is merely informational in this case, and there appears to be nothing wrong with DBW0.

User Trace Files

User trace files, as the name implies, contain information pertaining to any error conditions triggered by a command in an individual user's session. User trace files can also help the DBA to optimize the performance of SQL statements by producing statistics for each SQL statement in a user session. The location for user trace files is specified by the system parameter USER_DUMP_DEST.

Enabling Tracing

The users in the HR department want to optimize some of their queries, so they decide to use user trace files to save the statistics in the USER_DUMP_DEST directory. The first step is to turn on tracing:

```
alter session set sql_trace = true;

Session altered.
```

user trace file
A text file that contains information pertaining to any error conditions triggered by a command in an individual user's session or SQL statement information for the purposes of tuning and optimization. User trace files are stored in the directory specified by the system parameter USER_DUMP_ DEST.

One of the users in the HR department runs a typical query joining the EMPLOYEES and the DEPARTMENTS table and then immediately turns off the tracing:

```
select employee_id emp_id, last_name, first_name,
    department_id dept_id, department_name
from hr.employees join hr.departments
    using(department_id);

  EMP_ID LAST_NAME    FIRST_NAME   DEPT_ID DEPARTMENT_NAME
-------- -----------  -----------  ------- ---------------
     100 King         Steven            90 Executive
     101 Kochhar      Neena             90 Executive
     102 De Haan      Lex               90 Executive
...
     205 Higgins      Shelley          110 Accounting
     206 Gietz        William          110 Accounting

106 rows selected.

alter session set sql_trace = false;

Session altered.
```

Locating the User Trace Files

Janice, the DBA, has agreed to help out the HR department by analyzing the user trace file. First, she needs to find out where the user trace file is stored:

```
show parameter user_dump_dest

NAME              TYPE        VALUE
----------------  ----------  ---------------------------------
user_dump_dest    string      /u01/app/oracle/admin/ord/udump
```

From a Linux operating system command-line session, Janice attempts to locate the trace file:

```
[oracle@oltp udump]$ ls -l ord_ora*.trc
-rw-r----- 1 oracle  oinstall    748 May 30 10:43
ord_ora_11141.trc
```

```
-rw-r-----  1 oracle  oinstall      748 May 18 20:37
ord_ora_11325.trc
-rw-r-----  1 oracle  oinstall      751 May 12 12:08
ord_ora_12283.trc
-rw-r-----  1 oracle  oinstall    97787 Jun 22 00:23
ord_ora_12299.trc
-rw-r-----  1 oracle  oinstall     7611 Jun 20 22:57
ord_ora_13863.trc
-rw-r-----  1 oracle  oinstall  1609855 Jun 22 00:58
ord_ora_13991.trc
-rw-r-----  1 oracle  oinstall     1426 Mar 14 13:15
ord_ora_14115.trc
-rw-r-----  1 oracle  oinstall      798 Jun 22 01:25
ord_ora_15082.trc
-rw-r-----  1 oracle  oinstall     1666 Jun 20 17:50
ord_ora_1531.trc
-rw-r-----  1 oracle  oinstall     1382 Mar 14 13:33
ord_ora_15338.trc
-rw-r-----  1 oracle  oinstall      630 Jun 22 01:25
ord_ora_15763.trc
-rw-r-----  1 oracle  oinstall     1031 Jun 22 01:26
ord_ora_15814.trc
-rw-r-----  1 oracle  oinstall     1665 Jun 22 01:30
ord_ora_16099.trc
-rw-r-----  1 oracle  oinstall      632 Mar 21 15:47
ord_ora_22552.trc
-rw-r-----  1 oracle  oinstall      750 Mar 13 20:54
ord_ora_23172.trc
-rw-r-----  1 oracle  oinstall    63729 Jun 23 20:21
ord_ora_23342.trc
-rw-r-----  1 oracle  oinstall     1668 Mar 10 21:34
ord_ora_31113.trc
-rw-r-----  1 oracle  oinstall      628 Jun 16 20:40
ord_ora_3113.trc
-rw-r-----  1 oracle  oinstall     1177 Mar 29 00:36
ord_ora_3325.trc
-rw-r-----  1 oracle  oinstall      628 Jun 19 19:33
ord_ora_3345.trc
```

```
-rw-r-----  1 oracle  oinstall     976 Mar 21 21:36
ord_ora_4463.trc
-rw-r-----  1 oracle  oinstall     958 Jun 21 22:08
ord_ora_4474.trc
-rw-r-----  1 oracle  oinstall    1665 Mar 22 20:08
ord_ora_4529.trc
-rw-r-----  1 oracle  oinstall    1048 Mar 14 12:29
ord_ora_9813.trc
-rw-r-----  1 oracle  oinstall   39563 Jun 22 23:34
ord_ora_982.trc
-rw-r-----  1 oracle  oinstall    1407 Mar 14 12:51
ord_ora_9843.trc
[oracle@oltp udump]$
```

Which trace file is the right one? The datestamp of each file helps to narrow down the search, but there could be multiple users creating trace files at the same time. Janice must join the V$PROCESS and V$SESSION dynamic performance views to retrieve the operating system process number, which Oracle uses in the trace filename:

```
select spid from v$process v, v$session s
  where v.addr = s.paddr and s.username = 'HR';

SPID
------------
23342
1 row selected.
```

Given the operating system process number of 23342, Janice knows that she needs to analyze the user trace file ord_ora_ 23342.trc. However, when she opens this trace file in Notepad, it is not very readable:

Converting the Trace File

To convert the trace file into something more readable, Janice uses the Oracle utility *TKPROF*:

```
[oracle@oltp udump]$ tkprof ord_ora_23342.trc
ord_ora_23342.txt
```

PE: OK to rebreak here too?

```
TKPROF: Release 10.1.0.2.0 - Production on Wed Jun 23
21:04:24 2004

Copyright (c) 1982, 2004, Oracle.  All rights reserved.

[oracle@oltp udump]$
```

TKPROF

An Oracle utility that reformats a user trace file containing SQL statement statistics into a readable format.

Janice reviews the file `ord_ora_23342.txt` and finds that the output is much easier to interpret. A sample of the output is shown below.

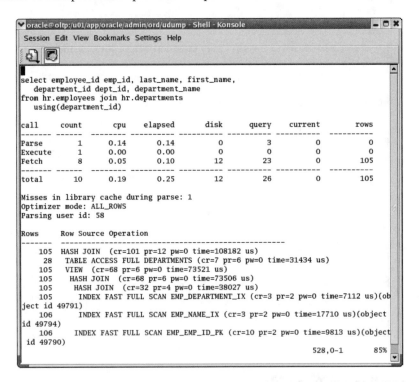

Using statistics from the trace file such as CPU time and elapsed time can help Janice focus on which of the HR department's SQL statements need tuning.

TIP

Oracle provides two websites that can assist the DBA when trouble strikes. MetaLink, Oracle's trouble reporting site at `http://metalink.oracle.com`, is a subscription service that allows DBAs to submit problem reports (either online or by phone) and search the knowledge base of all other problems submitted to Oracle support staff. Oracle's technology network, `http://technet.oracle.com`, is a free service, although user registration is required to access the site. Technet contains searchable product documentation, trial versions of most of Oracle's software, discussion forums, sample code, white papers, and more.

Terms to Know

alert log file	TKPROF
system trace file	user trace file

Review Questions

1. System trace files can be found in the directory identified by which initialization parameter?

2. What Oracle tool can the DBA use to monitor the size of a tablespace and notify the DBA when the tablespace is running out of space?

3. True or false: The alert log file records both successful and unsuccessful logins to the database.

4. The alert log file can be found in the directory identified by which initialization parameter?

5. What does the Oracle utility TKPROF do?

6. User trace files can be found in the directory identified by which initialization parameter?

7. User trace files provide which two benefits for the DBA and database users?

8. True or false: The alert log file is cleared every time the database is started.

9. Which two dynamic performance views contain information about sessions in the database?

10. Oracle Database 10*g*'s EM Database Control can trigger an alert for out of space conditions at how many different threshold levels?

Appendix A

Answers to Review Questions

Chapter 1

1. Name the most important element of a relational database and its components.

    Answer: The table is the most important element of a relational database and it consists of rows and columns. A field exists at the intersection of a row and a column.

2. Which type of table relationship associates more than one record in a given table with more than one record in another table?

    Answer: A many-to-many relationship associates more than one record in a table with more than one record in another table.

3. What type of key can be used to enforce referential integrity between two tables in a database?

    Answer: A foreign key can be used to enforce referential integrity between two tables.

4. What are some reasons why using a spreadsheet is not a good alternative to using a large-scale database?

    Answer: Some reasons why a spreadsheet is not a good alternative to a large-scale database are that it's difficult to use for multiple users, it does not offer transaction control, the cells in a spreadsheet can contain any type of data, and referential integrity controls between spreadsheets are difficult to implement efficiently.

5. What are some of the benefits of abstraction in an object-relational database management system?

    Answer: In an object-relational database management system, new datatypes can be created as aggregates of existing datatypes and other new datatypes, enhancing adherence to standards and reusability.

6. What object-relational feature of Oracle eases the transition between relational and object-relational applications?

    Answer: Object views allow the developer to define an object-oriented structure over an existing relational database table, thus easing the transition between relational and object-relational applications.

7. What are the three steps in the ERA process for database design?

    Answer: The three steps in the ERA (entities, relationships, attributes) design process are to define the entities, then define the relationships between the entities, and then define the attributes of the entities. After one pass through all three steps, one or more iterations may be necessary.

8. Name the three Oracle-compliant ANSI SQL standards.

    Answer: Oracle9*i* is compliant with SQL:1992 and SQL:1999, whereas Oracle 10*g* is compliant with SQL:2003.

9. What is the difference between a relation and a relationship?

    Answer: The difference between a relation and a relationship is that a relation is another name for a table, whereas a relationship is a way to correlate, or join, two or more tables.

10. Which type of relationship associates one row in a given table with one or no rows in another table?

    Answer: A one-to-one relationship associates one row in a given table with one or no rows in another table.

Chapter 2

1. What are the three types of DML (Data Manipulation Language) statements?

    Answer: The three types of DML statements are INSERT, UPDATE, and DELETE.

2. If the user SCOTT is granted the privilege to insert records on the OE.WAREHOUSES table using the command GRANT INSERT ON OE.WAREHOUSES WITH GRANT OPTION, what does the WITH GRANT OPTION clause allow SCOTT to do?

    Answer: It allows SCOTT to grant another user, such as HR, the same INSERT privilege on the OE.WAREHOUSES table.

3. Under which tiers of a three-tier Oracle environment does iSQL*Plus run?

    Answer: iSQL*Plus runs on only the middleware tier where the Apache web server is running. However, Apache can run on the client with the user who is executing the SQL statements, on its own dedicated server, or on the same server as the Oracle database.

4. What two methods are used to rename a column in the report output of a SQL SELECT statement?

    Answer: You can rename a column in the report output by using the SQL*Plus or iSQL*Plus COLUMN command or by specifying the alias name next to the column name in the SQL SELECT statement.

5. ODBC provides what capability to client applications?

    Answer: ODBC (Open Database Connectivity) provides a client application that supports SQL commands and the capability to connect to a variety of different database servers without knowing the specific details as to how to connect and interact directly with the database.

6. Which SELECT statement keyword removes duplicate rows from the result of the query?

    Answer: The DISTINCT keyword removes duplicate rows. If there is only one column in the result of a SQL query, there will be no duplicates of that column returned in the query result. If there are two columns in the result of the query, there will be one row returned for each unique combination of values in the first and the second column.

7. What is the name of the set of library routines that allows a developer to send SQL statements from a C program?

    Answer: The library routines for sending SQL statements from a C program are called the OCI (Oracle Call Interface).

8. What are some of the differences between a DELETE and a TRUNCATE statement?

    Answer: A DELETE statement may be rolled back, whereas a TRUNCATE statement is implicitly committed. A DELETE statement can conditionally specify which rows to delete, but a TRUNCATE statement removes the contents of the entire table. A DELETE statement retains the disk space in the table for future inserts or updates, but a TRUNCATE statement frees the disk space for other tables or database objects.

9. The new MERGE statement combines the functionality of which two other DML statements?

   Answer: MERGE combines the functionality of INSERT and UPDATE.

10. What function does the DESCRIBE command perform in SQL*Plus or iSQL*Plus?

   Answer: The DESCRIBE command displays the structure of a table, including the column name, datatype, and whether the column is a required field.

Chapter 3

1. What is another way to write the following SQL statement by using another function?
```
select empno || lpad(initcap(ename),
40-length(empno),'.')
"Employee Directory" from emp;
```

   Answer: You can rewrite the statement using the CONCAT function:
```
select concat(empno, lpad(initcap(ename),
40-length(empno),'.') "Employee Directory" from emp;
```

2. Which function would you use to perform an explicit conversion from a number to a string?

   Answer: You can use the TO_CHAR function to convert a number to a string.

3. How can you rewrite the function call NUMTOYMINTERVAL(17, 'year') using the function TO_YMINTERVAL?

   Answer: You can rewrite the function call as TO_YMINTERVAL('17-00').

4. What is the result of a number added to a NULL value?

   Answer: The result of a number added to a NULL is NULL.

5. What is the result of formatting the number -232.6 using the format mask '9999.99S'?

   Answer: The resulting format is 232.60-.

6. Rank the following operators or conditionals based on priority, from highest to lowest: *, OR, ||, >=

   Answer: *, ||, >=, OR

7. The DUAL table has how many rows and how many columns?

   Answer: The DUAL table has one row and one column. The column is named DUMMY and has a value of 'X'.

8. True or false: Strings and numbers can be concatenated.

   Answer: True, before the number is concatenated with the string, it is implicitly converted to a string.

9. Write a SELECT statement with a built-in function or functions that will format the string 'Queen' with the '!' character padded for a total of 20 characters on the left side and with the '?' character padded for a total of 30 characters on the right. (Hint: Use nested functions.)

    Answer: SELECT statement:

    ```
    select rpad(lpad('Queen',20,'!'),30,'?') from dual;


    RPAD(LPAD('QUEEN',20,'!'),30,'
    ------------------------------
    !!!!!!!!!!!!!!!Queen??????????
    ```

10. What functionality does the Oracle TIMESTAMP datatype have over the DATE datatype?

    Answer: The TIMESTAMP datatype stores the time in seconds to up to nine digits of precision.

Chapter 4

1. Rewrite the following expression using the CONCAT function.

    ```
    last_name || ', ' || first_name
    ```

    Answer: The expression is rewritten as:

    ```
    concat(concat(last_name, ', '),first_name)
    ```

2. What are two ways that you can indicate a comment in a SQL command?

    Answer: You can indicate a comment in a SQL command by using /* and */ or by using --.

3. The SQL engine converts the IN operator to a series of _____.

    Answer: The SQL engine converts the IN operator to a series of OR operations.

4. Rewrite the following WHERE clause to be case insensitive.

    ```
    where job_title like '%Manager%';
    ```

    Answer: Use the UPPER function to convert the job title to uppercase:

    ```
    where UPPER(job_title) like '%MANAGER%';
    ```

5. What is the only group function that counts NULL values in its calculation without using NVL or other special processing?

    Answer: The COUNT group function using the syntax COUNT(*) counts NULL values without using NVL.

6. The query results from using aggregate functions with a GROUP BY clause can be filtered or restricted by using what clause?

    Answer: The HAVING clause filters or restricts the query results of the GROUP BY clause.

7. Identify the two special characters used with the LIKE operator and describe what they do.

    Answer: The % character matches zero or more characters, and the _ character matches exactly one character.

8. Name two aggregate functions that work only on numeric columns or expressions and two other aggregate functions that work on numeric, character, and date columns.

    Answer: AVG and SUM work only on numeric columns; MIN and MAX work on all datatypes.

9. Put the clauses of a SQL SELECT statement in the order in which they are processed.

    Answer: The proper order is SELECT, WHERE, GROUP BY, HAVING, ORDER BY.

10. Which operator can do valid comparisons to columns with NULL values?

    Answer: The operator is IS NULL.

11. The SQL engine converts the BETWEEN operator to _____.

    Answer: The SQL engine converts the BETWEEN operator to two logical comparisons using >= and <=, connected by an AND operation.

12. Where do NULL values end up in a sort operation?

    Answer: For ascending sorts, the NULL values are at the end; for descending sorts, the NULL values are at the beginning.

Chapter 5

1. Add a clause to the WHERE condition to make the following query return only the department names without employees:

    ```
    select employee_id "Emp ID", last_name || ', ' ||
      first_name "Name", department_name "Dept"
    from employees e,departments d
    where e.department_id(+) = d.department_id;
    ```

    Answer: The following clause added to the WHERE condition makes the query return only department names without employees:

    ```
    and employee_id is null
    ```

2. A type of query that has either too few or no join conditions is known as a _____ query.

    Answer: Cartesian product

3. Name three kinds of equijoins.

    Answer: Inner joins, self-joins, left outer joins, right outer joins, and full outer joins are all examples of equijoins.

4. A natural join makes what assumption between the columns of two or more tables to be joined?

    Answer: A natural join assumes that the tables are to be joined on the columns that have the same names and datatypes.

5. The Oracle9i syntax moves the join conditions from the _____ clause to the _____ clause in a SELECT statement.

    Answer: WHERE, FROM

6. To avoid a Cartesian product, a query with four tables must have at least how many join conditions between tables?

    Answer: A query with four tables must have at least three join conditions to avoid a Cartesian product.

7. To return all the rows in one table regardless of whether any rows in another table match on the join condition, you would use what kind of a join?

    Answer: An outer join returns all rows in one table regardless of whether any rows in another table match on the join condition.

8. What is the symbol used to signify an outer join in a pre-Oracle9*i* query?

    Answer: A (+) is used to signify an outer join in a pre-Oracle9*i* query.

9. A full outer join uses what SQL set operator in a pre-Oracle9*i* database query?

    Answer: A full outer join uses the UNION set operator in a pre-Oracle9*i* query.

10. A primary key in one table would frequently be joined to what in a second table?

    Answer: A primary key in one table would frequently be joined to a foreign key in a second table.

Chapter 6

1. A subquery is allowed in which parts of a SQL SELECT statement?

    Answer: A subquery is allowed in the SELECT clause, the FROM clause, and the WHERE clause.

2. True or false: A correlated subquery references a table in the SELECT clause.

    Answer: False, the correlated subquery references a column in the main query.

3. Which set operator will not remove duplicate rows from the result of a compound query?

    Answer: UNION ALL will not remove duplicate rows from the result of a compound query.

4. What characteristics of the columns in a compound query using INTERSECT must match?

    Answer: The number of columns and their datatypes must match in a compound query using INTERSECT. The lengths of the columns and the names do not need to match.

5. How are NULL values handled using set operators in a compound UNION query?

    Answer: NULL values in one query are considered equal to NULL values in the other query, for the purposes of eliminating duplicates in a UNION.

6. Why are ROLLUP and CUBE the preferred methods for generating subtotals and grand totals for an aggregate query?

    Answer: ROLLUP and CUBE need to make only one pass over the source table(s). Other methods, such as using a UNION between two similar queries, will make more than one pass.

7. Which operators can be used to compare a column to a single-row subquery?

    Answer: The following operators can be used to compare a column to a single-row subquery: =, !=, >, <, >=, and <=.

8. A compound query that needs to find only the rows that are the same between the two queries should use the _____ set operator.

    Answer: `INTERSECT`

9. True or false: The `IN` operator cannot be used with a single-row subquery.

    Answer: False, using `IN` with a single-row subquery would be equivalent to using =.

10. Put the set operators `UNION`, `UNION ALL`, `INTERSECT`, and `MINUS` in order of precedence.

    Answer: All of those operators have equal precedence and are evaluated left to right in a compound query.

11. What can be used to change the precedence of a pair of queries in a compound query with more than two queries?

    Answer: As with any other part of a SQL query, parentheses may be used to change the evaluation order of the set operators.

Chapter 7

1. A `COMMIT` occurs under which three conditions within a transaction?

    Answer: A `COMMIT` occurs from an explicit `COMMIT` command, after a DDL or DCL command is executed, or when a SQL*Plus or iSQL*Plus session is exited normally.

2. Under what circumstances can a foreign key column not match the defined primary key value in the parent table?

    Answer: A foreign key column may not match the defined primary key value in the parent table when the foreign key column allows `NULL` values and is `NULL`.

3. True or false: A `CHECK` constraint cannot check for `NULL` values.

    Answer: False, a `CHECK` constraint can use `IS NULL` and `IS NOT NULL` to check for the existence of `NULL` values in one or more columns of the table.

4. How are `PRIMARY KEY` constraints and `UNIQUE` constraints different? List two ways.

    Answer: `PRIMARY KEY` constraints do not allow `NULL` values, and there can be only one primary key per table.

5. What are the three conditions that may be specified, either implicitly or explicitly, on a foreign key column when the primary key column in the parent table is deleted?

    Answer: By default, the row in the parent table will not be deleted if rows exist in the child table that have a foreign key referencing the parent table's primary or unique key. Alternatively, the child table's foreign key may be set to `NULL` (SET NULL), or the entire row in the child table may be deleted if a parent row is deleted (CASCADE).

6. Write a `CHECK` constraint that ensures `MAX_SALARY` is at least 10,000 more than `MIN_SALARY`.

    Answer: This constraint ensures `MAX_SALARY` is at least 10,000 more than `MIN_SALARY`: check (max_salary - 10000 > min_salary)

7. What statement will allow a partial rollback of certain DML statements within a transaction?

    Answer: The `ROLLBACK TO SAVEPOINT <savepoint>;` statement will allow a partial rollback of certain DML statements.

8. True or false: A NOT NULL constraint can be defined at the table level or at the column level.

    Answer: False, a NOT NULL constraint can be defined only at the column level.

9. What kind of constraint establishes a parent-child relationship between two tables via one or more common columns?

    Answer: A foreign key constraint establishes a parent-child relationship between two tables via one or more common columns.

10. If the database crashes while a user session is active, what type of transaction processing is automatically performed when the database is restarted?

    Answer: If the database crashes, an automatic ROLLBACK of any pending transactions is performed when the database is restarted.

Chapter 8

1. What are the four functions of the Database Creation Assistant (DBCA)?

    Answer: DBCA can create, delete, and modify databases. It can also create a template that can be used to create a database.

2. What is the Oracle background process that writes modified data blocks to disk?

    Answer: The DBWn process writes modified data blocks to disk.

3. What is the difference between a database and an instance?

    Answer: A database is a set of files on disk that is managed by an instance, which is a collection of processes and memory structures that operate against the datafiles on disk.

4. An extent is composed of one or more _____.

    Answer: Database blocks

5. True or false: The control file contains important system tables.

    Answer: False, the control file contains information about the physical structure of the entire database.

6. What is the GUI-based Oracle tool that can manage and monitor one or more Oracle instances?

    Answer: The Oracle Enterprise Manager (OEM) can manage and monitor one or more Oracle instances.

7. DBCA can save the specified database parameters in what kind of file?

    Answer: DBCA can save the database parameters as an HTML file.

8. Which Oracle background process will apply the data in the redo log files to the datafiles in the event of a system crash?

    Answer: The SMON process will apply the data in the redo log files to the datafiles in the event of a system crash.

9. A database schema is closely associated with which other database object?

    Answer: A schema is associated 1:1 with a user account in the database.

10. A segment consists of one or more _____.

    Answer: Extents

Chapter 9

1. An iSQL*Plus substitution variable is preceded by what character(s) in a script?

   Answer: An iSQL*Plus substitution variable is preceded by either one or two ampersands (& or &&).

2. Identify the two iSQL*Plus commands that define the header and footer for a report.

   Answer: The TTITLE and BTITLE commands define the header and footer for an iSQL*Plus report.

3. On which iSQL*Plus web page can you adjust the size of the iSQL*Plus window where you enter your iSQL*Plus commands or SQL statements?

   Answer: The size of the iSQL*Plus Workspace window can be adjusted on the Interface Configuration page.

4. Write an iSQL*Plus footer command to display the text *Page 22*, right-justified on the line.

   Answer: This iSQL*Plus command will display the text *Page 22*, right-justified on the footer line of the report:

   ```
   btitle right 'Page 22'
   ```

5. Sums and averages can be displayed on an iSQL*Plus report using which iSQL*Plus command?

   Answer: Sums and averages can be displayed on an iSQL*Plus report by using the COMPUTE iSQL*Plus command.

6. Write a single iSQL*Plus COLUMN command to format the Salary column with a total of six digits, four to the left of the decimal point and two to the right. In the same COLUMN command, define the header to be Monthly Salary, with the words appearing on different lines in the column header.

   Answer: The following iSQL*Plus command will format the Salary column with six digits, four to the left of the decimal point and two to the right. In addition, the header will be defined as Monthly Salary, with the words appearing on different lines in the column header:

   ```
   column Salary format 9999.99 heading 'Monthly|Salary'
   ```

7. Which iSQL*Plus command controls the row count display after a SELECT statement is executed?

   Answer: The FEEDBACK command controls the row count display after a SELECT statement is executed. By default, the row count from a query is displayed if there are six or more rows in the query output.

8. Which iSQL*Plus command controls how duplicate column values are displayed on a report?

   Answer: The BREAK command will suppress duplicate values in a report for a specified column.

9. The iSQL*Plus BREAK command is almost always specified in conjunction with what SQL SELECT statement clause?

   Answer: The BREAK command is almost always specified on a column that is in the ORDER BY clause of a SQL SELECT statement.

10. In both the TTITLE and BTITLE commands, what option must be used to specify more than one line in the header or footer?

   Answer: The SKIP option must be used in a BTITLE or TTITLE command to specify more than one line in the header or footer.

Chapter 10

1. The data dictionary view IND has the same definition as what other data dictionary view?

   Answer: The data dictionary view IND is equivalent to the data dictionary view USER_INDEXES.

2. The most common form of a table in the Oracle database is a(n) _____ table.

   Answer: Relational

3. What clause do you add to the CREATE TABLE statement to create a temporary table?

   Answer: You add the clause GLOBAL TEMPORARY to the CREATE TABLE statement to create a temporary table.

4. What tables are displayed if a user accesses the ALL_TABLES data dictionary view?

   Answer: The ALL_TABLES data dictionary view contains a row for each table in the user's schema plus a row for each table that the user has access to in other schemas of the database.

5. Name two ways in which external tables are different from relational tables.

   Answer: External tables cannot be updated, and external tables cannot have indexes created on them.

6. True or false: Oracle resolves object references by checking for private synonyms first.

   Answer: False, Oracle resolves object references by checking for a real object owned by the user, then checks for a private synonym, and then checks for a public synonym.

7. What are two reasons for creating a view against one or more tables?

   Answer: A view can be created to hide the complexity of a table join from the user. A view can also be created to restrict the rows or columns seen by users of the view.

8. What database object type can be used to generate a series of sequential numbers?

   Answer: A sequence can be used to generate a series of sequential numbers.

9. True or false: Data dictionary tables retain their contents even after the database has been shut down and restarted.

   Answer: True, data dictionary tables retain their contents even after the database has been restarted. Dynamic performance views, however, lose their contents when the database is shut down and restarted.

10. An index created on more than one column is known as what kind of index?

   Answer: An index based on more than one column is known as a composite index.

Chapter 11

1. Privileges can be grouped and assigned as a unit by using what database object?

   Answer: A role can be used to group system and object privileges and assign them as a unit to database users.

2. When granting privileges with the GRANT statement, what does the clause WITH GRANT OPTION do?

   Answer: The WITH GRANT OPTION clause allows the grantee to pass on the privilege to another database user.

3. DROP USER and CREATE SESSION are examples of what kind of privileges?

   Answer: DROP USER and CREATE SESSION are examples of system privileges.

4. What is the name of the table, owned by the user SYS, that contains all audit records?

   Answer: The table SYS.AUD$ contains all audit records.

5. Write a SQL statement that will create audit records when UPDATE statements fail against the HR.EMPLOYEES table.

   Answer: The following SQL statement will create audit records when UPDATE statements fail against the HR.EMPLOYEES table:

   ```
   audit update on hr.employees whenever not successful;
   ```

6. Which system privilege allows a user to make a connection to the database?

   Answer: The CREATE SESSION system privilege allows a user to make a connection to the database.

7. In addition to assigning a default tablespace to a user, what else must be assigned to a user before that user can create objects in the tablespace?

   Answer: A quota must be assigned to a user before that user can create objects in the tablespace.

8. Which tablespace is assigned to a user for the user's permanent objects if one is not explicitly assigned in the CREATE USER statement?

   Answer: The SYSTEM tablespace is assigned to a user for permanent objects if no tablespace is explicitly assigned in the CREATE USER statement.

9. DELETE, INSERT, and EXECUTE are examples of what kind of privileges?

   Answer: DELETE, INSERT, and EXECUTE are examples of object privileges.

10. A profile controls which kinds of database resources?

    Answer: A profile controls things such as concurrent connections to the database, CPU time used, continuous idle time, disk reads performed, failed login attempts, how often a password needs to be changed, and elapsed time connected.

11. Which keyword can be used in a GRANT command to assign one or more privileges to every user in the database?

    Answer: The PUBLIC keyword can be used instead of an individual username or role in a GRANT command to assign one or more privileges to every user in the database.

Chapter 12

1. What GUI tool analyzes a SQL statement and identifies the steps used to process the query?

    Answer: The Explain Plan GUI tool analyzes a SQL statement and identifies the steps used to process the query.

2. The two general categories of indexes are _____ indexes and _____ indexes.

    Answer: B-tree, bitmap

3. Which type of index is best for columns with a low cardinality?

    Answer: A bitmap index is best for columns with a low cardinality.

4. Which dynamic performance view can assist the DBA in sizing the buffer cache appropriately?

    Answer: The dynamic performance view V$DB_CACHE_ADVICE can assist the DBA in sizing the buffer cache appropriately.

5. Which type of table divides the contents of a very large table into more manageable chunks, both improving the manageability of the table for the DBA and potentially increasing the performance of queries on the table?

    Answer: A partitioned table divides the contents of a very large table into more manageable chunks.

6. Which data dictionary views contain information about table indexes and the table columns indexed?

    Answer: The data dictionary views DBA_INDEXES and DBA_IND_COLUMNS contain information about table indexes and the table columns indexed.

7. Name the six steps in Oracle's Tuning Methodology in order of priority.

    Answer: The six steps in Oracle's Tuning Methodology are data design, application design, memory allocation, I/O and physical structures, resource contention, and underlying platform.

8. Which feature associated with materialized views rewrites a query to use the materialized view instead of using the tables that are the source for the materialized view?

    Answer: The QUERY REWRITE feature rewrites a query to use the materialized view instead of using the tables that are the source for the materialized view.

9. What is the name of the pseudo-column that exists for every row of every table in the database and is unique across the entire database?

    Answer: The pseudo-column ROWID exists for every row of every table in the database and is unique across the entire database.

10. Name the two different optimizer modes in Oracle9*i* and identify which one uses statistics from tables and indexes to derive an execution plan; identify two of the most common modes in Oracle 10*g*.

    Answer: The two different optimizer modes for Oracle9*i* are rule-based and cost-based. The cost-based method uses statistics from tables and indexes to derive an execution plan. For Oracle 10*g*, the two most common optimizer modes are ALL_ROWS and FIRST_ROWS.

Chapter 13

1. A cold database backup occurs when a database is _____, and a hot database backup occurs when a database is _____.

    Answer: Closed and unavailable to users, open and available to users

2. The failure of a disk drive containing database datafiles would be considered what kind of a failure?

    Answer: The failure of a disk drive containing database datafiles would be considered a media failure.

3. What clause in a SELECT statement specifies the time and date for an Oracle flashback query?

    Answer: The AS OF TIMESTAMP clause in a SELECT statement specifies the time and date for an Oracle flashback query.

4. The flashback query tool uses which Oracle structure to retrieve information on how a table appeared at some specified point in the past?

    Answer: The undo tablespace contains information that is used to reconstruct how a table appeared at some specified point in the past.

5. True or false: A flashback query can retrieve the DDL statement needed to undo a change made to a table in the past.

    Answer: False, the flashback query feature does not provide the DDL for undoing changes. Log Miner is the tool that can retrieve the DDL statement needed to undo a change made to a table in the past.

6. An abnormal termination of the Oracle server software would be considered what type of database failure?

    Answer: An abnormal termination of the Oracle server software would be considered an instance failure and therefore a nonmedia failure.

7. Which Oracle utilities can be used by a database user to back up and restore a table and by a DBA to move a tablespace from one database to another?

    Answer: The Import (IMP) and Export (EXP) utilities can be used by a database user to back up and restore a table and by a DBA to move a tablespace from one database to another.

8. Which Oracle structure allows the automatic recovery of the Oracle database after an instance failure?

    Answer: The redo log files ensure that all committed transactions are applied to the database in the event of an instance failure.

9. What option of the Import (IMP) command allows the DBA to view the DDL contained in a dump file without executing those DDL commands?

    Answer: The SHOW=Y option of the Import (IMP) command allows the DBA to view the DDL contained in a dump file without executing those DDL commands.

10. What is the name of the feature of Oracle's Export and Import utilities that allows a DBA to move or copy an entire tablespace from one database to another?

    Answer: The transportable tablespace feature of Oracle's Export and Import utilities allows a DBA to move or copy an entire tablespace from one database to another.

Chapter 14

1. System trace files can be found in the directory identified by which initialization parameter?

   Answer: System trace files can be found in the directory identified by the BACKGROUND_DUMP_DEST parameter.

2. What Oracle tool can the DBA use to monitor the size of a tablespace and notify the DBA when the tablespace is running out of space?

   Answer: Oracle9*i*'s OEM's Event Manager tool or Oracle 10*g*'s EM Database Control can be used to monitor space conditions in database tablespaces.

3. True or false: The alert log file records both successful and unsuccessful logins to the database.

   Answer: False, the alert log file records database startup and shutdown but not user logins.

4. The alert log file can be found in the directory identified by which initialization parameter?

   Answer: The alert log file can be found in the directory identified by the BACKGROUND_DUMP_DEST parameter.

5. What does the Oracle utility TKPROF do?

   Answer: The Oracle utility TKPROF formats a user trace file containing SQL statement statistics into a readable format.

6. User trace files can be found in the directory identified by which initialization parameter?

   Answer: User trace files can be found in the directory identified by the USER_DUMP_DEST parameter.

7. User trace files provide which two benefits for the DBA and database users?

   Answer: User trace files provide information about error conditions encountered in a user's session in addition to SQL statement execution statistics.

8. True or false: The alert log file is cleared every time the database is started.

   Answer: False, the alert log file grows in size indefinitely until it is renamed or deleted by the DBA.

9. Which two dynamic performance views contain information about sessions in the database?

   Answer: The dynamic performance views V$SESSION and V$PROCESS contain information about user sessions.

10. Oracle Database 10*g*'s EM Database Control can trigger an alert for out of space conditions at how many different threshold levels?

    Answer: Oracle Database 10*g* triggers alerts for all database error conditions, including out of space conditions, at two threshold levels: warning and critical.

Appendix B

Common Database Platforms

This appendix offers an overview of some common database platforms for enterprise and "personal" use. Most popular databases today can be considered relational or object-relational in nature, and they support SQL. When choosing a database platform, price, market sector, interoperability, and scalability are sometimes the deciding factors over features.

Enterprise Databases

There are a few heavy-hitters in the database world, including the key players in the enterprise relational database management system (RDBMS) market listed here. The following list of vendors is not intended to be comprehensive but to give an overview of the various approaches to solving the problems of a large, distributed enterprise.

Oracle

Historically, Oracle is the granddaddy of them all. In 1979, Oracle Corporation released the first commercially viable RDBMS, based on the work of Dr. E. F. Codd. In 1983, however, the true power and cross-platform capabilities of Oracle were evident when the source code for Oracle was rewritten in the C language, making Oracle extremely portable across any hardware and software platform that has a C compiler.

As a database, Oracle 10g has become "unbreakable." All market hype aside, so much redundancy and failover capability has been built into the product that Oracle has a written guarantee that your database won't go down!

What really distinguishes Oracle from many of its competitors is its availability on so many operating systems and hardware platforms. Products such as Microsoft SQL Server run strictly on Windows operating systems with Intel hardware, and many of the other potential contenders run on only Windows or Linux or a combination of the two.

Many independent benchmark tests of Oracle versus its competitors, such as the March 26, 2002, *PC Magazine* review of SQL databases, show Oracle to be one of the key market leaders.

More information about Oracle 10g can be found at `http://www.oracle.com/database/`.

IBM DB2/UDB

IBM DB2/UDB had its humble beginnings as a mainframe database but has now grown to be implemented on almost as many hardware and software platforms as Oracle. The strengths of DB2 lie in its strong text-search capabilities, on par with the Oracle interMedia product. The integration with its WebSphere middleware product also makes it a good all-in-one enterprise solution, although the WebSphere product can be used with an Oracle database as the back end.

More information about DB2/UDB can be found at `http://www-306.ibm.com/software/data/db2/udb/`.

Sybase

Sybase's Adaptive Server Enterprise finds its strengths in its financial application suites, but it is also on par, feature for feature, with similar products from IBM and Oracle. The SQLAnywhere product suite is crafted for small workgroups as well as embedded and mobile applications.

More information on Sybase products can be found at `http://www.sybase.com/products/databaseservers`.

Microsoft SQL Server

Microsoft SQL Server picked up where Sybase left off at version 6, when Microsoft and Sybase broke their development ties, although SQL Server has diverged quite a bit from Sybase's products. SQL Server's dependence on the Windows operating system and Intel hardware as a host rule it out as a choice for enterprises that rely on Unix and non-Intel hardware for their base infrastructure.

More information about Microsoft SQL Server can be found at `http://www.microsoft.com/sql/`.

Personal and Freeware Databases

The term *personal* may be interpreted two ways: by cost and by the size of the target end-user audience. What further muddies the water are vendors from the "big list" in the previous section who have designed their products to run on anything from a cell phone up to large network clusters. When you get down to the cell phone level, however, it's a sure bet that there is some powerful middleware in the mix and a very thin client on the cell phone!

Two examples of personal database platforms are presented here. This list is not intended to be comprehensive but to give an overview of various approaches to solving the problems of an individual or a small workgroup that needs more than a spreadsheet to manage corporate data.

Microsoft Access

Microsoft Access is not an easy product to categorize. It is part of the Microsoft Office suite for data management. This self-contained database has powerful query facilities yet lacks the recovery and robust multiple-user support that Oracle and SQL Server have. It can link to any external database that has an ODBC-compliant driver under Windows, which makes it a good cross-platform choice for the individual analyst or small workgroups that don't need 24 × 7 availability or highly flexible recovery options.

More information on Microsoft Access can be found at `http://office.microsoft.com/home/office.aspx?assetid=FX01085791`.

MySQL

MySQL is billed as "the world's most popular open source database." This product is free under the GNU General Public License (GPL), with technical support being an added cost option. It runs under almost any operating system, including all flavors of Unix and Windows. It is somewhat lacking in some of the features common to commercial databases; however, it is highly extensible and customizable. Its lack of features is offset by its high performance and reliability.

More information about MySQL can be found at `http://www.mysql.com/products/mysql/`.

Glossary

abstract datatypes New datatypes, usually user-created, that are based on one or more built-in datatypes and can be treated as a unit.

aggregate A type of function in Oracle SQL that performs a calculation or transformation across multiple rows in a table, rather than just on a single row.

alert log file A text file that contains entries about significant database events, such as database startup and shutdown, nondefault initialization parameters, and various errors. The alert log file is stored in the directory specified by the system parameter BACKGROUND_DUMP_DEST.

alias An alternate name for a column, specified right after the column name in a SELECT statement, seen in the results of the query.

associative table A database table that stores the valid combinations of rows from two other tables and usually enforces a business rule. An associative table resolves a *many-to-many relationship*.

auditing Storing information about activities in the database in the SYS.AUD$ table. Auditing is controlled by the DBA.

bitmap index An index that maintains a binary string of ones and zeros for each distinct value of a column within the index.

branch blocks Index blocks in the traversal path of a b-tree index that either point to branch blocks at the next level or point to leaf blocks.

b-tree index A type of index structure that resembles an inverted tree. The branches of a b-tree index are balanced. Traversing the tree for any index value reads the same number of blocks.

buffer cache advisory A feature of the Oracle9*i* database that can assist the DBA in determining how large to make the buffer cache. This feature collects statistics on how often a requested database block is found in the buffer cache. The system initialization parameter DB_CACHE_ADVICE controls whether these statistics are collected, and the data dictionary view V$DB_CACHE_ ADVICE contains the estimated number of physical reads that would occur given a number of different cache sizes.

cardinality The number of distinct values in a column of a table.

Cartesian product A join between two tables where no join condition is specified, and as a result, every row in the first table is joined with every row in the second table.

CHECK constraint A constraint that evaluates the condition defined in the constraint and permits the INSERT or UPDATE of the row in the table if the condition is satisfied.

closed backup See *cold backup*.

cold backup A database backup performed while the database is shut down. Also known as a closed backup.

column The component of a database table that contains all of the data of the same name and type across all rows.

comment Documentation for SQL statements. Comments are specified by using the pair /* and */ or by using --.

composite index An index that is created on two or more columns in a table.

concatenation The process of combining two or more data elements into a single element. In Oracle SQL, concatenation can be accomplished by using the concatenation operator (a pair of vertical bars, ||) or the CONCAT function.

connection identifier   See *host string*.

constraint   A condition defined against a column or columns on a table in the database to enforce business rules or relationships between tables in the database.

control file   A file that records the physical structure of a database, the database name, and the names and locations of datafiles and redo log files.

correlated subquery   A subquery that contains a reference to a column in the main, or parent, query.

cost-based optimizer   An Oracle optimizer methodology that relies on the characteristics of the tables being queried to determine the method used to run the query. A cost is calculated for estimated CPU, I/O, and sorting for the possible execution paths. The path with the lowest overall cost is used to perform the query.

CTAS   Also known as Create Table As Select, a method for creating a table in the database by using the results from a subquery to both populate the data and specify the datatypes of the columns in the new table.

data dictionary views   Read-only views owned by the user SYS that are created when the database is created and contain information about users, security, and database structures, as well as other persistent information about the database.

data modeling   A process of defining the entities, attributes, and relationships between the entities in preparation for creating the physical database.

database   The collection of all physical files on disk that are associated with a single Oracle instance.

database block   The smallest unit of allocation in an Oracle database. One or more database blocks compose a database extent.

database buffer cache   The memory structure in the SGA that holds the most recently used or written blocks of data.

Database Configuration Assistant (DBCA)   A multiplatform GUI tool that allows a DBA to easily create, modify, and delete databases, as well as manage database templates.

datafiles   Files that contain all of the database data that the users of the database save and retrieve using SELECT and other DML statements. A tablespace comprises one or more datafiles.

date function   A function that performs some kind of transformation on a date literal, a column containing a date, or an expression consisting of date literals and table columns. Date functions return a date or a string containing a portion of the date as the result of the transformation.

DCL (Data Control Language)   Includes statements such as GRANT and REVOKE to provide or deny users or roles system or object privileges.

DDL (Data Definition Language)   Includes statements such as CREATE, ALTER, and DROP to work with objects such as tables. DDL modifies the structure of the objects in a database instead of the contents of the objects.

directory   A database object that stores a reference to a directory on the host operating system's filesystem.

DML (Data Manipulation Language)   Includes INSERT, UPDATE, DELETE, and MERGE statements that operate specifically on database tables. Occasionally, SELECT statements are included in the SQL DML category.

DUAL   A special table, owned by the Oracle SYS user, that has one row and one column. It is useful for ad hoc queries that don't require rows from a specific table.

dynamic performance views   Data dictionary views owned by the user SYS that are continuously updated while a database is open and in use and whose contents relate primarily to performance. These views have the prefix V$ and their contents are lost when the database is shut down.

encapsulation   An object-oriented technique that may hide, or abstract, the inner workings of an object and expose only the relevant characteristics and operations on the object to other objects.

equijoin   A join between two tables where rows are returned if one or more columns in common between the two tables are equal and not NULL.

Explain Plan tool   A GUI-based Oracle tool that details the steps in which a SQL statement is executed, as well as what method Oracle used to access the tables in the query.

explicit conversion   Conversion of one datatype to another in an expression using function calls such as TO_CHAR instead of relying on automatic conversion rules (See *implicit conversion*).

Export utility (EXP)   An Oracle utility that copies the contents of one or more tables to a binary dump file, along with the DDL needed to create the table and its associated indexes, permissions, and constraints.

extent   A contiguous group of blocks allocated for use as part of a table, index, and so forth.

external table   A table whose definition is stored in the database but whose data is stored externally to the database.

field   The smallest piece of information that can be retrieved by the database query language. A field is found at the intersection of a row and a column in a database table.

flashback query   A feature of the Oracle database that allows a user to view the contents of a table as of a user-specified point in time in the past. How far in the past a flashback query can retrieve rows depends on the size of the undo tablespace and on the setting of the UNDO_RETENTION system parameter.

foreign key   A column (or columns) in a table that draws its values from a primary or unique key column in another table. A foreign key assists in ensuring the data integrity of a table.

FOREIGN KEY constraint   A constraint that establishes a parent-child relationship between two tables via one or more common columns. The foreign key in the child table refers to a primary or unique key in the parent table.

function   A named set of predefined programming language commands that performs a specific task given zero, one, or more arguments and returns a value.

function-based index   A b-tree index that is created based on an expression involving the columns of a table, instead of on a single column or columns in the table.

heading separator   A single character embedded in an iSQL*Plus column alias that indicates where the alias is split to appear on multiple lines in the output. The heading separator itself does not appear in the output.

hierarchical   A table design where one of the foreign keys in the table references the primary key of the same table in a parent-child relationship.

hint   A directive placed between /*+ and */ in a query that overrides an execution method that the Oracle optimizer would normally choose.

host string   A text string that represents a shortcut or reference to a set of parameters that provide the information needed to connect to a database host from the client application.

hot backup   A database backup performed while the database is open and available to users. Also known as an open backup.

implicit conversion   Conversion of one datatype to another that occurs automatically when columns or constants with dissimilar datatypes appear in an expression.

Import utility (IMP)   An Oracle utility that takes as input a binary dump file created by the Export utility and restores one or more database tables, along with any associated indexes, permissions, and constraints.

index   A database object designed to reduce the amount of time it takes to retrieve rows from a table.

An index is created based on one or more columns in the table.

index-organized table (IOT)   A b-tree index that stores both the data and the index in the same segment.

inheritance   Acquiring the properties of the parent, or base object, in a new object.

inner join   See *equijoin*.

instance   The collection of memory structures and Oracle background processes that operates against an Oracle database.

intersection table   See *associative table*.

JDBC (Java Database Connectivity)   A set of library routines specific to the Java language that allows a Java application to easily connect to and process SQL statements against an Oracle database.

join   To combine two or more tables in a query to produce rows as a result of a comparison between columns in the tables.

leaf blocks   Index blocks at the bottom of a b-tree index that contain ROWIDs to the rows in the table containing the desired index value.

logical structures   Structures in an Oracle database that a database user would see, such as a table, as opposed to the underlying physical structures at the datafile level.

LRU (least recently used) algorithm   An algorithm used to determine when to reuse buffers in the database buffer cache that are not dirty or pinned. The less frequently a block is used, the more likely it is to be replaced with a new database block read from disk.

many-to-many relationship   A relationship type between tables in a relational database where one row of a given table may be related to many rows of another table, and vice versa. Many-to-many relationships are often resolved with an intermediate *associative table*.

materialized view   A view that stores the results of the query the view is based on, in addition to the SQL join statement of the view itself. Materialized views may be refreshed manually (on demand), on a regular basis, or when there is a change in the underlying tables on which that view is based.

media failure   A type of database failure where a server hardware component fails and the contents of one or more disk files are either unreadable or corrupted.

methods   Operations on an object that are exposed for use by other objects or applications.

multiple-column subquery   A subquery in which more than one column is selected for comparison to the main query using the same number of columns.

multiple-row subquery   A subquery that can return more than one row for comparison to the main, or parent, query using operators such as IN.

nonmedia failure   A type of database failure that is not related to a server disk-related hardware component and is one of several types: statement failure, process failure, instance failure, or user error.

NOT NULL constraint   A constraint that prevents NULL values from being entered into a column of a table.

NULL   A possible value for any Oracle column that indicates the absence of any known value for that column. A NULL is usually used to represent a value that is unknown, not applicable, or not available.

numeric function   A function that operates on numeric literals, columns containing numbers, or an expression containing numeric literals and table columns, returning a number as the result.

numeric literal   A constant that can consist of numeric digits, plus the characters +, -, ., and E.

object privileges   Privileges that allow users to manipulate the contents of database objects in other schemas.

object view   A database construct that overlays an object-oriented structure over an existing relational database table. As a result, the table can be accessed as a relational table or as an object table and make the transition to a fully object-oriented environment easier.

object-relational database   A relational database that includes additional operations and components to support object-oriented data structures and methods.

OCI (Oracle Call Interface)   A set of library routines that allows a C application on virtually any development platform to easily connect to and process SQL statements against an Oracle database. The OCI routines are called as native C library functions; therefore, no preprocessor is necessary when compiling a C application using OCI.

ODBC (Open Database Connectivity)   A set of standards that allow applications that are not dependent on any one specific database to process SQL statements against any database that supports SQL.

ODBC driver   An interface, usually at the operating-system level, that supports the connection of an ODBC-compliant application to a specific database platform.

one-to-many relationship   A relationship type between tables where one row in a given table is related to many other rows in a child table. The reverse condition, however, is not true. A given row in a child table is related to only one row in the parent table.

one-to-one relationship   A relationship type between tables where one row in a given table is related to only one or zero rows in a second table. This relationship type is often used for subtyping. For example, an EMPLOYEE table may hold the information common to all employees, while the FULLTIME, PARTTIME, and CONTRACTOR tables hold information unique to full-time employees, part-time employees, and contractors, respectively. These entities would be considered subtypes of an EMPLOYEE and maintain a one-to-one relationship with the EMPLOYEE table.

open backup   See *hot backup*.

Oracle block   See *database block*.

Oracle Enterprise Manager (OEM)   A GUI tool that allows access, maintenance, and monitoring of multiple databases or services within a single application.

Oracle Home   A common directory location used to store the associated program files for a specific release of the Oracle database software.

Oracle Universal Installer (OUI)   A GUI-based tool used to install or uninstall Oracle software components and tools.

Oracle's Tuning Methodology   A tuning method recommended by Oracle Corporation that prioritizes areas in tuning database performance. The six areas, in order of priority, are data design, application design, memory allocation, I/O and physical structures, resource contention, and underlying platform.

outer join   A join between two or more tables returning all the rows in one table whether or not the second table contains a match on the join condition.

partitioned table   A table that stores its rows into smaller and more manageable pieces based on the values of one or more columns of the table.

pattern matching   Comparing a string in a database column to a string containing wildcard characters. These wildcard characters can represent zero, one, or more characters in the database column string.

PFILE   A text file containing the parameters and their values for configuring the database and instance at startup.

physical structures   Structures of an Oracle database, such as datafiles on disk, that are not directly manipulated by users of the database. Physical structures exist at the operating system level.

primary key   A column (or columns) in a table that makes the row in the table distinguishable from every other row in the same table.

PRIMARY KEY constraint   A constraint that uniquely defines each row of a table and prevents

NULL values from being specified in the column or combination of columns. Only one PRIMARY KEY constraint may be defined on a table.

privileges   The right to perform a specific action in the database, granted by the DBA or other database users.

process   An executing computer program in memory that performs a specific task.

profile   A set of predefined resource parameters that can be used to monitor and control various database resources, such as CPU time and number of disk reads against the database.

Program Global Area (PGA)   A nonshared area of memory used for storing all connection information, including SQL statement information, in a dedicated server configuration for a user who is connected to the database. In a shared server configuration, a large portion of the memory for each connection is stored in the SGA instead of the PGA.

quota   A numeric limit on the amount of disk space that a user can allocate within a tablespace. The quota can also be specified as UNLIMITED.

read consistency   A feature of the Oracle database that ensures a database reader (in a SELECT statement) will see the same data in a table regardless of changes made to the table by database writers that were initiated after the reader initiated the SELECT statement.

Recovery Manager (RMAN)   A comprehensive set of backup and recovery tools that can streamline the backup and recovery of a database.

redo log buffer   A buffer in the SGA that contains information pertaining to changes in the database.

redo log files   Files that contain a record of all changes made to both the data in tables and indexes, as well as changes to the database structures themselves. These files are used to recover changed data that was in memory at the time of a crash.

referential integrity   A method employed by a relational database system that enforces one-to-many relationships between tables.

relation   A two-dimensional structure used to hold related information, also known as a table.

relational database   A collection of tables that stores data without any assumptions as to how the data is related within the tables or between the tables.

relational table   The most common form of a table in the Oracle database; the default type created with the CREATE TABLE statement. A relational table is permanent and can be partitioned.

reverse key index   A b-tree index whose keys have their byte-order reversed to improve the performance of an application by spreading out the key values for adjacent index values to different leaf blocks.

role   A group of related privileges that is referenced by a single name. Privileges can be assigned to a role, and a role can be assigned to a database user or to another role. Roles ease the maintenance issues with managing privileges for a large number of users who can be grouped into a relatively small number of categories based on job function.

row   A group of one or more data elements in a database table that describes a person, place, or thing.

ROWID   A unique identifier for a row in a table, maintained automatically in the table by the Oracle server. ROWIDs are unique throughout the database.

rule-based optimizer   An Oracle optimizer methodology that relies on a fixed set of rules to determine the method used to run a query, ignoring the cardinality and distribution of data in the column being queried.

schema   A group of related database objects assigned to a database user. A schema contains tables, views, indexes, sequences, and SQL code. The schema name can be used to qualify objects that are not owned by the user referencing the objects.

script   A set of one or more SQL or iSQL*Plus commands that is executed as a group. Scripts may be retrieved from within an iSQL*Plus session or saved to an operating system file and retrieved later in another session.

segment   A set of extents allocated for a single type of object, such as a table.

self-join   A join of a table to itself where a non-primary key column in the table is related to the primary key column of another row in the same table.

sequence   A database structure that generates a series of numbers typically used to assign primary key values to database tables.

shared pool   An area of memory within the total amount of memory allocated for the Oracle database that can hold recently executed SQL statements, PL/SQL procedures and packages, as well as cached information from the system tables.

SID   A system identifier, which is a unique name assigned to an Oracle instance. A user must supply a SID to connect to an Oracle instance.

single-row function   Functions that may have zero, one, or more arguments and will return one result for each row returned in a query.

single-row subquery   A subquery that returns a single row and is compared to a single value in the parent query.

Software Code Area   A location in memory where the Oracle application software resides. The Software Code Area can be shared among several Oracle instances.

SPFILE   A parameter file stored in a binary format that gives the DBA more flexibility when changing parameters. Parameters can be changed for the current instance only, can take effect only after the next restart of the instance, or both.

SQL (Structured Query Language)   The industry-standard database language used to query and manipulate the data, structures, and permissions in a relational database.

statistics   Information about tables and indexes stored in the data dictionary used to assist the cost-based optimizer when deciding how to run a given query.

stored function   A sequence of PL/SQL variable declarations and statements that can be called as a unit, passing zero or more arguments and returning a single value of a specified datatype. Built-in stored functions are created when the database software is installed. Customized or user-defined functions are defined by application developers or DBAs.

string function   A function that operates on string literals, columns containing strings, or an expression containing string literals and table columns, returning a string as the result.

string literal   A constant that can consist of any string of letters, digits, and special characters enclosed in single quotation marks.

subquery   A query that is embedded in a main, or parent, query and used to assist in filtering the result set from a query.

substitution variable   A string literal with no embedded spaces, preceded by & or &&, that will prompt the user for a value when an iSQL*Plus script containing one of these variables is executed. A substitution variable preceded by & will not prompt the user for a value if the same substitution variable, preceded by &&, exists earlier in the script.

synonym   An alias assigned to a table, view, or other database structure. Synonyms can be either available to all users (public) or available only to one schema owner (private).

System Global Area (SGA)   A group of shared memory structures for a single Oracle instance.

system privileges   Privileges that allow users to perform a specific action on one or more database objects or users in the database.

system trace file   A text file that pertains to a single background process and contains status, debugging, or error information about that background process. System trace files are stored in the directory specified by the system parameter BACKGROUND_DUMP_DEST.

system variable A variable maintained in the iSQL*Plus, SQL*Plus, or SQL*Plus Worksheet environment that holds a status or a setting for a particular feature in that environment. PAGESIZE is an example of a system variable in iSQL*Plus.

table The basic construct of a relational database that contains rows and columns of related data.

tablespace A logical grouping of database objects, usually to facilitate security, performance, or the availability of database objects such as tables and indexes. A tablespace is composed of one or more datafiles on disk.

temporary table A table whose definition is persistent and shared by all database users but whose data is local to the session that created the data. When the transaction or session is completed, the data is truncated from the temporary table.

thin client A workstation or CPU with relatively low-powered components that can use a web interface (or other application with a small footprint) to connect to a middleware or back-end database server where most of the processing occurs. iSQL*Plus is an example of a web application that runs on a thin client.

tiers Locations where different components of an enterprise application system reside. In a typical three-tier environment, the client tier runs a thin application such as a web browser, which connects to a middleware server that is running a web server. The web server and its related components typically manage the business rules of the application. The third-tier database platform controls access to the data and manages the data itself. This approach partitions the application so that it is easier to maintain and segregates the tasks into tiers that are best equipped to handle a particular function.

TKPROF An Oracle utility that reformats a user trace file containing SQL statement statistics into a readable format.

Top SQL tool A GUI-based Oracle tool that can identify SQL statements that may be consuming too many system resources and therefore may be good candidates for tuning.

transaction A logical unit of work consisting of one or more SQL statements that must all succeed or all fail to keep the database in a logically consistent state. A transfer of funds from a bank account is a logical transaction, in that both the withdrawal from one account and the deposit to another account must succeed for the transaction to succeed.

transportable tablespace A feature of Oracle's Import and Export utilities that allows a tablespace to be copied to another database. All objects within the tablespace to be copied must be self-contained; in other words, a table in a tablespace to be copied must have its associated indexes in the same tablespace.

UNIQUE constraint A constraint that prevents duplicate values from being specified in a column or combination of columns in a table. NULL values may be specified for columns that have a UNIQUE constraint defined, as long as the column itself does not have a NOT NULL constraint.

unique index A b-tree index whose keys are not duplicated.

user trace file A text file that contains information pertaining to any error conditions triggered by a command in an individual user's session or SQL statement information for the purposes of tuning and optimization. User trace files are stored in the directory specified by the system parameter USER_DUMP_DEST.

user-defined function A function that is written by an analyst, user, or database administrator and does not come as part of the default installation of the Oracle server software.

username An Oracle database account identifier that, along with a password, allows a user to connect to the database.

view A database object that is based on a SELECT statement against one or more tables or other views in the database. A regular view does not store any data in the database; only the definition is stored. Views are also known as stored queries.

Index

Note to the Reader: Throughout this index **boldfaced** page numbers indicate primary discussions of a topic. *Italicized* page numbers indicate illustrations.

O

P

Technology Fundamentals for IT Success
from SYBEX®

Whether you are considering a career in IT or just want a general understanding of the basics, refer to the new Foundations series from Sybex. Concise introductions to core technologies provide the fundamentals for any endeavor in IT. Assuming no prior technical skills, each book is written in simple terms with tangible examples and offers the solid foundation necessary to pursue more advanced IT training.

JAVA FOUNDATIONS
by Todd Greanier
ISBN: 0-7821-4373-3 • US $24.99

NETWORK SECURITY FOUNDATIONS
by Matthew Strebe
ISBN: 0-7821-4374-1 • US $24.99

ORACLE DATABASE FOUNDATIONS
by Bob Bryla
ISBN: 0-7821-4372-5 • US $24.99

NETWORKING FOUNDATIONS
by Patrick Ciccarelli
and Christina Faulkner
ISBN: 0-7821-4371-7 • US $24.99

TCP/IP FOUNDATIONS
by Andrew Blank
ISBN: 0-7821-4370-9 • US $24.99

SYBEX®
www.sybex.com

Celebrating 15 Years!

OVER 1.5 MILLION COPIES SOLD

THE COMPLETE

PC Upgrade & Maintenance Guide FIFTEENTH EDITION

Updated to Cover Latest PC Technologies

Includes Videos of Key Hands-on Tasks

The Most Informative and Entertaining PC Hardware Book on the Market

SYBEX

The Complete PC Upgrade and Maintenance Guide, 15th Edition
by Mark Minasi
ISBN: 0-7821-4310-5 • US $49.99

The 15th edition of *Mark Minasi's Complete PC Upgrade and Maintenance Guide* is another milestone in the evolution of a title recognized as the market leader. With over 1.5 million copies of previous editions sold, this masterwork is completely updated to cover new and emerging PC and networking technologies, and reorganized for easier navigation. Written in Mark Minasi's friendly style and based on his world-renowned seminars, it shows you how to get the best performance from your systems through upgrading and how to prevent disasters and fix them when they occur. The companion CD includes instructional video of critical hands-on PC upgrade and maintenance tasks.

SYBEX®
www.sybex.com

TELL US WHAT YOU THINK!

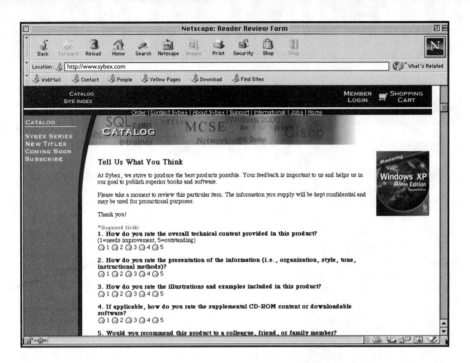

Your feedback is critical to our efforts to provide you with the best books and software on the market. Tell us what you think about the products you've purchased. It's simple:

1. Go to the Sybex website.
2. Find your book by typing the ISBN or title into the Search field.
3. Click on the book title when it appears.
4. Click **Submit a Review.**
5. Fill out the questionnaire and comments.
6. Click **Submit.**

With your feedback, we can continue to publish the highest quality computer books and software products that today's busy IT professionals deserve.

www.sybex.com

SYBEX Inc. • 1151 Marina Village Parkway, Alameda, CA 94501 • 510-523-8233